BEYOND
BOND

BEYOND BOND

Spies in Fiction and Film

WESLEY BRITTON

PRAEGER

Westport, Connecticut
London

Library of Congress Cataloging-in-Publication Data

Britton, Wesley A. (Wesley Alan)
    Beyond Bond : spies in fiction and film / Wesley Britton.
      p. cm.
    Includes bibliographical references and index.
    ISBN 0–275–98556–3 (alk. paper)
    1. Spy films—United States—History and criticism.   2. Spy films—Great
Britain—History and criticism.   3. Spy television programs—United States—
History and criticism.   4. Spy television programs—Great Britain—History and
criticism.   5. Spy stories, American—History and criticism.   6. Spy stories,
English—History and criticism.   I. Title.
PN1995.9.S68B75 2005
791.43'6556—dc22   2005006042

British Library Cataloguing in Publication Data is available.

Library of Congress Catalog Card Number: 2005006042
ISBN: 0–275–98556–3

First published in 2005

Praeger Publishers, 88 Post Road West, Westport, CT 06881
An imprint of Greenwood Publishing Group, Inc.
www.praeger.com

Printed in the United States of America

The paper used in this book complies with the
Permanent Paper Standard issued by the National
Information Standards Organization (Z39.48–1984).

10 9 8 7 6 5 4 3 2 1

Contents

Preface and Acknowledgments

When I began work on *Spy Television* (2004), my first book on fictional espionage for Praeger, two motivations prompted the project. First, I wanted to write about a subject I enjoyed, a genre that had fascinated me since childhood. Second, to my delight and surprise, no one had written such a book before. When I began compiling the first notes for this, my second foray into the world of spies, I discovered I was in the same happy position. As of this writing, I am aware of no other attempt to pull together spy-oriented fiction, film, and fact from over a century into one book-length overview.

Some may find this doubtful, with the wealth of books on espionage available on seemingly every related topic. Such doubts are most appropriate when discussing spy literature. Excellent studies of novels and novelists include books by the likes of Julian Symons, Robin Winks, John G. Cawilti, Bruce Rosenberg, and Frederick Hitz. Among the various encyclopedias on mystery and spy writers, Donald McCormick's *Who's Who in Spy Fiction* (1977) is an invaluable reference source about writers up to the publication date. Likewise, Andy East's quirky *The Cold War File* (1983) also surveys such novelists with an emphasis on pulp paperback writers.

In addition, the important writers in spy fiction, particularly through the 1970s, have all earned in-depth analysis from a variety of perspectives. Studies of Ian Fleming, John Le Carré, and Len Deighton are not rare. Writers like John Buchan and Eric Ambler have been examined in more than one full-length appreciation. Web sites on the Internet contain information about Jack Ryan that Tom

Clancy has likely forgotten. With all this, what can a new author contribute that isn't merely a synthesis of these sources, updating information through the new millennium?

First, I've tried to focus on trends within the genre from the nineteenth century to the present, showing how influential and popular authors were participants in a continuum of shifting social tides. No doubt, many readers will find sins of both omission and emphasis here. I spend most of these pages seeking connections between the generations of writers, relationships between film and literature, and how "reality" was, and was not, woven into hardcover and paperback adventures. In short, I was interested in the contexts of the espionage milieu and seek to look at spy literature as one important thread in our popular thoughts regarding the "world's second-oldest profession."

Exploring films dealing with spies and related projects was a different challenge. For example, there is no lack of studies on Alfred Hitchcock. But the emphasis in such books is more on the director's techniques and canon as a whole than on spy projects per se. I gleaned what I needed from a variety of these sources and think an entire book on the subject has yet to be written. Of course, James Bond is the topic of a bottomless pit of interest. Any new thoughts on 007 can only be compilations of available information pointing to the most important responses to the saga. Beyond Bond and Hitchcock, looks into spy films tend to be found in short overviews of specific decades, notably the 1940s and 1960s. Perhaps the most detailed overview to date is Michael Strada and Harold Troper's 1997 *Friend or Foe: Russians in American Film and Foreign Policy (1933–1991)*. Their emphasis is strictly applied to the cold war duels between the Soviet Union and the Western powers, showing how American and British movies reflected governmental policies during these crucial decades. While a valuable resource, the overview doesn't intend to examine films in the context I've pursued. Other helpful books by J. Fred Macdonald, Michael Barson, and Stephen Heller also deal with cold war themes.

This leads us to the third important theme of this book, the role of real espionage in popular culture. Looking into the history of espionage in film, novels, television shows, radio dramas, and even comic books is tracing cultural changes that often worked in tandem. Still, without question, "realism" in print and in film is far more a reflection of what those outside the intelligence community perceive it to be than much actual unveiling of the covert world. True, many writers for the page and screen brought their experiences from undercover pursuits into their works, from the veterans of British Imperial wars to firsthand reflections on the war on terrorism. So, where fact overlaps with fiction is one motif of this book. But in a wider view, I believe my use of historical contexts helps demonstrate why we have seen our covert protectors the ways we have and how this has changed—or not—over the years. One surprising theme of this book turned out to be that fiction may try to emulate fact, but as often as not, reality often follows both intended and accidental prophecy of the imagination.

However, I fear that since most published looks into the Central Intelligence Agency (CIA) and Federal Bureau of Investigation (FBI), in particular, point to either failures or misdeeds, I'm not certain that I've been as balanced in my portrayals of our secret agencies as I would like. Let me make it clear—I believe we need our covert warriors, but I also despair of the marching orders they are often obliged to obey. True, it is naïve to think intelligence agencies can function usefully without performing both illegal and immoral actions. But I share the commonplace notion that our fears of shadow conspiracies are due, in large part, from presidents who create their own units outside of constitutional oversight to further their own political agendas. The failed Bay of Pigs invasion, Watergate, and Iran-Contra are but a few examples of such thinking. On the other hand, as of this writing, it seems apparent that the war in Iraq launched in 2003 was fueled not only by faulty "Intel," but also by an organizational mind-set within the CIA that saw weapons that weren't there. Law enforcement and intelligence organizations alike are often victims of self-inflicted wounds.

But such policies, as demonstrated in spy fiction, reveal something more widespread in Western culture. In Len Deighton's 1966 *Billion Dollar Brain*, British agent Harry Palmer ironically said the idealistic mad general wanting to instigate World War III was trying to bring "freedom and Coke" to countries behind the Iron Curtain. For many of our global neighbors, our interest in their affairs seems more to do with selling soft drinks than establishing voting rights. For another example, in Adam Hall's 1994 *Quiller: Salamander*, one operative bitterly complained the West was disinterested in the "Killing Fields" in Cambodia because the country held neither oil nor industry. No wonder former Peace Corps volunteers who had served in Peru and Chile told me one of their difficulties was the belief among townspeople that all Americans worked for the CIA. America, in the common wisdom, was more interested in ruthless dictators opposed to Communism than freedom or democracy. Such troubling issues are part of our collective history, and the role of undercover agents in the international theater is but a window into wider concerns.

In addition, I would like to echo Norman Mailer's explanatory notes written as an appendix for his 1991 *Harlot's Ghost*. Describing his attempt to fictionalize history based on extensive research, Mailer said there is no single CIA—even insiders only know or knew aspects of the agency from their often compartmentalized viewpoints. A writer, Mailer claimed, can find much of the tone and fundamentals of spycraft even if he or she is not either a major or minor player in the covert world. Like Mailer, my purpose is to use research to show how culture responded to what we saw and believed our protectors were up to based on fact, propaganda, speculation, and fears in an increasingly cynical climate. Therefore, the contexts I sketch from chapter to chapter focus on how views changed as we learned more and more about the Office of Strategic Services (OSS), FBI, CIA, National Security Agency (NSA), and British agencies, and how both information and disinformation made their way into our collective consciousness. If our perceptions were off the mark, well, they were nonetheless the context from which we drew our views of espionage.

I must admit that many of my choices regarding films and fiction were governed by my own informal study of spies that began in the 1960s when, while in the fifth grade, I recorded in a scrapbook that I wanted to grow up to be a "secret agent." I remember well the day this dream died. In my classroom, I carefully studied career brochures from the FBI and learned they recommended a background in accountancy for anyone interested in joining the bureau. After that mathematical dose of cold water drowned my illusions, I contented myself with reading everything I could find, from novels to nonfiction to *Newsweek* articles to fanzines and books on television series. So when I think of "popular culture," I am reminded of all the headlines and reviews of films and books widely available during my lifetime.

Along the way, I had other interests and earned a Ph.D. in American Literature. I put all my spy interest aside as mere hobby. Did I say "mere"? When I began work on *Spy Television* and this book, I first drew from my files, bookshelves, and boxes of material from my basement to my attic. Then I put all my scholarly skills to work. I must confess, as I looked for insights and ideas about movie projects, in particular, I found myself damning theoretical studies as more dissertations than readable sources, at least for my purposes. I became suspicious of any text that took forty to fifty pages to explain the jargon to be used before the critic got around to telling the reader about the ostensible subject implied in the title. I wasn't interested in post-lesbian Marxist deconstructionaltarianism, shaken, stirred, or on the rocks of abandoned critical trends. While I felt a responsibility to look over such studies, I should tell all readers of this book that this overview is not an exercise in using the spy genre to promote a new critical theory, nor is it an academic treatise designed to impress graduate students or their learned mentors. From beginning to end, I had the general reader in mind, from casual fans to devoted aficionados of the wide, wild world of spies and/or secret agents. I hope experts will find fresh ideas and approaches here, but I trust that all any reader needs to appreciate this book is an interest in at least one aspect of spies in fact and fiction.

Another commonplace—books like this one are framed by pages demonstrating the author's debts. The last pages of this book comprise a bibliography listing print and electronic sources I poured over looking for clues and open secrets uncovered by others; the paragraphs here express my deep gratitude to friends and contacts who took time and effort to help this project become what it is. To begin, I must thank Internet friends Emily Kelley, Tim Naumann, James South, Bill Koenig, James Mcmahon, Bev Wiles, Aloma Pedersen, Thomas Rucki, Eric Whitfield, and Betty Glass, all of whom helped with research and insights. Bond experts Matt Sherman, Robert Short, Jon Heitland, Lee Pfeiffer, and Vic Flick helped with my photo hunt and contributed much to the content of this book. While bribed with extra credit points, even though a few didn't need them, I wish to acknowledge my English students who did online research for me. Thanks to Dale Masters, Rebecca Novac, Sonia Souchet, Amy Weikert, and Matt Windish. Thanks also to Jon Foulk at OTRCAT.com

(Old Time Radio Show Catalog) for very unselfishly providing me a number of rare radio shows, and Philip Nel, who helped me shape my brief discussion on Don DeLillo. I'm also grateful to Matt Cvetic, Jr., who shared his memories as son of the man who inspired *I Was a Communist for the FBI*. I regret I couldn't include more of his observations. In addition, Peter Earnest and Amanda Abrell provided support and information from the International Spy Museum.

Two people I cannot thank enough are Kevin Bochynski, master of my Web site, and my wife, Betty, a longtime sufferer of my interests. Neither of these folks share any of my passions (in terms of spies, that is), but they have contributed immeasurably to all my projects. My parents, Royce and Betty Britton, helped with online research as well. I must also thank Eric Levy, acquisitions editor at Praeger Publishers, who first signed me on to do *Spy Television* and then immediately supported me when I floated the idea of this book. I here thank the various friendly voices that answered the reference desk phone at the East Shore Public Library, and Diane Wiedemann, mistress of interlibrary loans at the McCormick Library at Harrisburg Area Community College.

Before diving into the origins of modern spy fiction, I must make at least a passing explanation of what I mean by "espionage," "spy," "covert action," and related terms in this book. Many studies are very particular about their terms, and histories of actual intelligence operatives and agencies do need to be as specific as possible to clarify distinctions between various job descriptions and responsibilities. In terms of popular culture, however, these concepts are largely what we have perceived them to be, whether based on fact or not. This book begins with a Hollywood producer and an ex-spy discussing two types of secret agents—patriotic and mercenary spies—but the genre quickly widens even in the first decades of the twentieth century. "Espionage" has been very loosely applied to acts of gathering intelligence and counterintelligence performed by anarchists, informants, saboteurs, strike forces, assassins, sleepers, adventurers, moles, couriers, Ninjas, engineers, historians, art restorers, recruiters, handlers, innocents being pulled into nasty business, you name it. In fact and fiction, spies have numbered children, grandmothers, committed terrorists, coerced criminals, sophisticated gentlemen and ladies, brutish terrorists, code-breaking mathematicians, sexy high-heeled "swallows," and Mr. Ed, the talking horse. (Well, perhaps Ed has a valid claim for inclusion. A distant ancestor, the Trojan horse, was an early example of creative spy technology.) Some spies deal in international geopolitics, others in criminal activity. Some agents work for sanctioned agencies, others shadow entities with questionable authority. Others are lone wolves who stumble across conspiracies and nefarious plots. As a result of such multiple approaches, some resources simply avoid any specific labels at all. Covert adventures are largely stacked in "thriller" sections in bookstores. Most secret agent films are labeled merely "action adventure." No wonder critics often disagree on just whom should be included in their studies.

In my view, "espionage" has become a very inclusive concept that gives breadth and depth to the genre, even if some of the depths are very low indeed. This book is therefore peppered with quotes from print and film sources that sometimes are quick tastes of the writers or movies discussed, but many are slices of works from different time periods showing how attitudes and concepts echo and reverberate throughout history. In addition, I think our connections to the covert world are not as removed as some might believe. After learning more and more about the corporate and bureaucratic framework of intelligence agencies, I became convinced that the day-to-day activities of most spies are not much different from those of any worker in a large institution. As discussed in my *Spy Television*, fans of the ruthless Section One in *La Femme Nikita* related to the series because they felt their own workplaces were as cold, amoral, and prone to interoffice spying as those with licenses to kill. In 1965, actor David McCallum observed that his success in *The Man from U.N.C.L.E.* was partly due to his belief that:

[W]e all live in an atmosphere of intrigue. These days there's as much scheming in the dry goods wholesalers or the college classroom as in the UN to the degree that we're daily schemers, we strive to be invisible, since you can't pull any fast ones if you're very much in sight and can be seen through. (Britton 2004, 331)

I suspect these thoughts are truer now than when McCallum first uttered them. Like the "Red Scare" of the 1950s when all citizens were asked to be vigilant about Communists in local neighborhoods, we now live in an era where surveillance includes cameras at city intersections and we have again been asked to become watchers of potential terrorists in the post-9/11 world. According to a report in the November 2004 *Atlantic Monthly*, businesses are now often better at getting international intelligence, as the American government is not considered credible in some quarters. At home, if we choose, we can spy on our own families. Minicams disguised as smoke detectors are easily available. Anyone can stick these to their walls to watch the results from their own personal computer. As I write this, my online server is suggesting I download its "Spy Sweeper" to protect my computer from Spyware programs seeking information about me.

I remember one day at a Dallas airport in December 2003, my arms and legs forced wide apart, as a security officer asked me questions to determine if this blind English teacher might want to blow up the plane on his flight home. "We didn't start this war," he told me as he ran the magic wand from my head to toe. "Neither did I," I replied, remembering Richard Hannay and all the reluctant agents drawn into matters well outside of their normal lives. The following spring during an "Orange Alert," I tried to send videotapes of my talk show appearances promoting *Spy Television* to friends and family. Two of these packages were picked out by postal inspectors and sent for checking in their Atlanta office. For two months, the packages disappeared. When they were finally tracked and sent to their addresses, the postal supervisor said, "We're at war, and these things will happen." In this climate, to one degree or another, we are now all spied on or are potential spies, whether armchair or active. Your mission: to discover your history in these pages.

1

The 39 Steps : Creating a Genre

In principle, I should lay it down that the existence of secret agents should not be tolerated, as tending to augment the positive dangers of the evil against which they are used. That the spy will fabricate its information is a commonplace. But in the sphere of political and revolutionary action, relying partly on violence, the professional spy has every facility to fabricate the very facts themselves, and will spread the double evil of emulation in one direction and of panicked, hasty legislation and unreflecting hate in the other.

Alfred Hitchcock, quoting Joseph Conrad's *Secret Agent*

On December 13, 1937, film director Cecil B. DeMille stepped to his usual place behind the microphone as host for the CBS *Lux Radio Theatre* broadcast from Hollywood.[1] As he did each week, DeMille introduced the evening's program, invariably an audio adaptation of a successful movie. In this case, Robert Montgomery and Ida Lupino starred in their version of Alfred Hitchcock's 1935 film, *The 39 Steps*, the British director's own adaptation of the 1915 book by John Buchan, the story widely held as the first modern spy novel. As it happened, this broadcast was an unintentional watershed in fictional espionage. For one matter, the radio drama and its intermission interview featuring special guest Major C. E. Russell of U.S. Army Intelligence showcased America's views on spycraft between the world wars. In addition, the actors onstage, standing side by side with an actual spy, were unknowingly foreshadowing elements in American popular culture that lasted into the twenty-first century.

That evening, DeMille introduced the drama proclaiming that there are two types of spies—mercenary and patriotic. Of course, the program's hero, Montgomery's Richard Hannay, was cast from the latter mold. Then, after the second act in the hour, DeMille brought Major Russell to the stage, noting his guest had trained spies in World War I, worked with Scotland Yard, and written an espionage manual. Reflecting the spirit of the times, DeMille asked Russell about those who viewed secret agents as "vicious, double-dealing scoundrels who'll stop at nothing to obtain their ends." Prefiguring later propaganda efforts during World War II, the cold war, and beyond, Russell defended his profession, saying, "These people would change their minds if they realized that spies are one of the greatest forces for world peace." Patriotic spies, and not the other kind, he said, keep their country informed and enable it to prepare itself against enemies. A prepared country, he read from his script, is rarely attacked.

With this in mind, DeMille wondered what the qualifications would be for a good spy. Russell replied that the requirements hadn't changed since biblical times. Just like Moses, modern spymasters send out those trained in observation and memory, and gifted with descriptive skills, "the least developed of all human traits." Education, common sense, the ability to take orders, and hopefully knowledge of foreign languages were key assets, in Russell's opinion. DeMille wondered about how women served in this profession of "brains instead of bayonets." Women compared well with men, Russell replied, "up to a point." Stating a view still debated behind closed doors and on the silver screen, Russell said, "A woman's heart will rule her head more quickly than a man's. . . . We've learned that, if you want a man to talk, send in a pretty woman. And when we want a woman to talk, we make her jealous." To underline his point, Russell told of one actual case when a female singer was discovered to be a spy carrying secrets on an undergarment. The unlucky woman was tripped up because she wore a starched petticoat out of season.

After laughing at such anecdotes, a modern listener would likely then raise his or her eyebrows hearing both DeMille and Russell agree that spying has changed little over the centuries except in new technologies. Most twenty-first-century audiences would be amused to hear the two speakers discussing how a map of a country could be etched on a single flake of Lux Soap—the program's sponsor. As would become true for so many espionage projects over the next seventy years, fact, fiction, and commercial interests would become inseparable, as was shown in that 1937 advertisement.

To close their discussion, DeMille and Russell returned to the theme of patriotism in espionage. DeMille recalled the famous phrase by French general Ferdinand Fauch telling his agents, "You will die a thousand deaths before oblivion comes. While the man in the trenches dies but once." Agreeing with this sentiment, Russell concluded the interview by telling the audience the story of Revolutionary War spy John Honeyman. Because Honeyman's services were unknown, he was seen as a scoundrel and outcast before George Washington publicly announced what Honeyman had done behind enemy lines. "His example will always remain a shining light to Americans," Russell read, "who seek to serve in the silent, secret, and sometimes inglorious ways of espionage." After thunderous applause, Russell retired and the play began anew, the story of two bantering and reluctant partners saving their country, running from the enemy and the law alike, and finding love on the battlefield of honor.[2]

On a number of levels, Major Russell's short discussion of a spy's character, the roles of women, and new technologies in spycraft point to ways in which fact, fiction, and cultural perceptions have merged in the many realms of espionage. In addition, the various versions of *The 39 Steps*—from print to screen to radio broadcast—can serve as benchmarks demonstrating how public attitudes about the covert world have changed in the twentieth and twenty-first centuries. For example, Major Russell was called to the microphone not only to describe some history of intelligence gathering, but to defend and seek popular support for his profession. While such an approach might surprise those raised in a culture where spycraft has permeated entertainment and the evening news alike, before the 1930s, there was little mainstream interest in real or fictional spies in America. Overseas, however, the situation was quite different.

THE ORIGINS OF MODERN ESPIONAGE FICTION

In 1981, new CIA director William Casey drove to the agency's Langley, Virginia, headquarters and noticed the standing figure of America's most famous spy, Nathan Hale. The statue of a man bound by his feet and hands with a rope around his neck didn't represent the service Casey hoped for in his agents. He thought a statue of his old boss, General William "Wild Bill" Donovan, would better represent American intelligence. After all, Hale had been caught (Persico 1990, 213).

The new spy master had several reasons to prefer Donovan as a more representative image of espionage. Casey knew that Donovan, the founder of the OSS (Office of Strategic Services) in World War II, believed that Americans wished to exclude espionage from their perceptions of the country's character. He felt Americans refused to embrace the covert world as part of the work of the Founding Fathers. In 1958, Donovan had encouraged Casey to write a book based on Donovan's collection of documents about George Washington's use of secret agents. For Donovan, Washington wasn't only father of his country, but also father of American espionage (Persico 1990, 99). Washington hadn't only emphasized using secret agents, he had been one himself when, in 1753, the then twenty-one-year-old British soldier went behind enemy lines to listen to drunk French officers (Persico 2001, 90). In July 1976, William Casey indeed published a book on the subject, *Where and How the War Was Fought: An Armchair Tour of the American Revolution*. This study dealt with an era that had been long neglected, even in fiction.

Still, the notion of "patriotic spies" championed by Major Russell in *The 39 Steps* broadcast was a central theme in a novel considered among the first books to employ American settings, characters, and situations. The story of Harvey Birch in James Fenimore Cooper's 1821 *The Spy: A Tale of the Neutral Ground* planted several seeds developed in future works. First, Birch's disguise as a traveling merchant, or "peddler spy," was a precursor to later operatives using business covers to give them means and reasons to go behind enemy lines. Living in a secret hideaway, Birch was a master of disguise, able to play both genders and two races, telling one man falsely accused of espionage, "The man who fights and kills and plunders is honored. But he who serves his country as a spy, no matter how faithfully, no matter how honestly, lives to be reviled" (Cooper 1971, 371). Like the history of John Honeyman as recounted by Major Russell, Birch's hardships and sufferings from those he was sworn to aid underlined that espionage is often unrewarded labor undertaken in self-sacrificing patriotism above and beyond battlefield valor.

While being far less fanciful than later writers such as John Buchan and Ian Fleming, Cooper's use of extensive research regarding the history of western New York during the Revolutionary War made *The Spy* an early fusion of literary romance with credible, footnoted realism, an approach that would have much to do with later fictional secret agents. For example, according to James H. Pickering, Cooper was keenly interested in his conversations with former New York governor John Jay, who served on "several highly secret committees organized to detect and defeat conspiracies among the large Loyalist elements in New York" (Cooper 1971, iii). Jay chose his spies from poor, ignorant men who were "cool, shrewd, and fearless by nature." Such agents, like Birch, turned down pay, saying patriotism was its own reward. The "literary nationalism" of *The Spy* was thus an early example of using secret agents to promote cultural values. This would be an important aspect in much twentieth-century espionage fiction.

However, Cooper's *The Spy* was something of an anomaly in the 1800s in English and American literature. In the early part of the century, passing references can be found to "cloak-and-dagger" stories, which were earlier "cloak and sword" French and Spanish romantic dramas characterized by mystery, espionage, intrigue, and melodrama in which the main characters were from the ranks of society that wore cloaks and swords.[3] Two Edgar Allan Poe stories have been proposed as early spy yarns. "The Purloined Letter" (1845) featured C. Auguste Dupin who, in at least one critic's opinion, was more spy than detective. As Donald McCormick notes, the story's ingredients included a top-secret document stolen from a royal apartment. The main culprit was suspected of being a highly placed minister. The secret police first searched the apartment, fearing the influential suspect must be caught with the evidence before prosecution could be considered. Dupine was called in to assist, just as today MI5 (U.K. Security Service) or French Counter-Espionage would be asked to aid authorities (1977, 154). In addition, McCormick suggests, Poe's "The Gold Bug" (1843) can also be considered to be a spy story, as the focus was on the author's interest in ciphers and codes.

In England, a handful of other literary characters such as Sherlock Holmes, who occasionally worked for British and foreign secret services in Sir Arthur Conan Doyle stories, were also clearly important predecessors to twentieth-century detective and espionage fiction. For one matter, Sherlock was the younger brother of Mycroft Holmes, the shadowy head of the British Secret Service. According to English-born Alfred Hitchcock, seeds for his own spy projects, most notably his famous "McGuffins," came from the writings of British novelist Rudyard Kipling, the man who dubbed espionage "The Great Game." "Most of Kipling's stories," Hitchcock said in 1967, "were set in India and they dealt with the fighting between the natives and the British forces on the Afghanistan border. Many of them were spy stories and they were concerned with the efforts to steal the secret plans out of a fortress. The theft of secret documents was the original 'McGuffin' " (Truffaut and Scott 1967, 98). Beginning in the 1930s, Hitchcock made such McGuffins staples in his films, describing them as "the device, the gimmick . . . or the papers the spies are after" (1967, 98).

In Hitchcock's home country, a variety of writers had used espionage in their stories at the beginning of the twentieth century. There was William Le Queux, who wrote fiction impressing the then prime minister Arthur Balfour, although later critics believed Le Queux wasn't especially literary and was questionable in his factual information. But, according to Kingsley Amis, realism wasn't yet the point. In his view, espionage based on imagination rather than actual life began at the beginning of the century "with the almost completely free-lance status of a Bulldog Drummond" and William Le Queux's Duckworth Drew (Amis 1965, 2). Drew's early adventures were precursors to later ones focused on new technology, such as when he encountered an "electronic eye," an Italian device that detonated mines (Amis 1965, 2). In addition, Le Queux's novel *The Great War in England in 1897* (1894) was an early example of literary speculations about an invasion of England. *The Secret Service* (1896) dealt with Jews in Russia, and *England's Pearl* (1899) was an early novel shifting British fears from the French to Germany. This fear continued in *The Invasion of 1910* (1905) in which Germans wormed secrets out of shipyards, arsenals, factories, and individuals (McCormick 1977, 112). Le Queux's later books, *No. 70, Berlin* (1915) and *The Mystery of the Green Ray* (1915), had increasingly preposterous plots. Despite the extremely minor literary contributions of these fanciful adventures, Le Queux can be seen as a logical predecessor to Tom Clancy and the subgenre of "speculative fiction" that became popular in the 1980s and 1990s.

Fellow UK novelist A.E.W. Mason's *The Courtship of Morrice Buckler* (1896) also fared better with contemporary critics than it does in hindsight. One reviewer claimed this book put Mason "in the forefront of cloak and dagger writers" (McCormick 1977, 134). More successful, in terms of output, was E. Phillips Oppenheim, who produced 115 novels and 39 short story collections, many of which were Edwardian spy stories emphasizing gambling and secret diplomacy, as in *The Mysterious Mr. Sapine* (1898). Praised by John Buchan as his "master in fiction," Oppenheim spiced up his tales with local color in major city settings, as in *Mr. Grex of Monte Carlo* (1915). Oppenheim was also later lauded by Eric Ambler as one of the earliest outstanding writers of cloak-and-dagger stereotypes including "the black-velveted seductress, the British Secret Service numbskull hero, the omnipotent spymaster," and the appeal to the snobbery of readers of the era (McCormick 1977, 144). Kingsley Amis saw Oppenheim as a logical forefather to Ian Fleming (1965, 87). Perhaps the best of Oppenheim's output was *Kingdom of the Blind* (1917) featuring raids by submarines and zeppelins.

An anarchist is an artist. The man who throws a bomb is an artist because he prefers a great moment to everything. An artist disregards all governments, abolishes all conventions, the poet delights in disorder.

G. K. Chesterson, *The Man Who Was Thursday*

In the first decade of the twentieth century, British espionage was colorful in both fact and fiction. According to some sources, the actual profession had become so amateurish that the first twentieth-century British spy in Germany was the Hamburg representative of the Courage and Co. Brewers, who pressured their agent to send home reports of harbor traffic and military movements. After two years of non-specific instructions, he began making up his reports and no one noticed. In 1909, the founder of the modern British Secret Service was former sea captain Mansfield George Smith Cumming, a colorful figure known for his peg leg, the fact he'd been retired from the navy because of his propensity for seasickness, and his cheerful boasting that espionage was "a capital sport!" (Richelson 1995, 10). A similar attitude could be seen in novelist G. K. Chesterson's surreal classic, *The Man Who Was Thursday* (1908). While not the first spy novel some have claimed it to be, the fanciful story has more undercover agents

7

than most books of the era. In this case, one agent thinks he's investigating a group of anarchists who are only disguising themselves as anarchists because their leader says that if anyone trumpets their beliefs out loud, no one will take them seriously. Chesterson's spy joins the inner circle of seven scheming bombers, six of whom turn out to be police informants spying on each other. The evil leader is the mysterious Scotland Yard official who'd hired them in the first place. Clearly, this parable used spies as a means to comment on British social conditions, a humorous seed for future writers with similar purposes, from Eric Ambler to John Le Carré. More seriously, FBI double agent Robert Hanssen thought highly of *Thursday*. He gave at least one copy to a fellow agent. Author David Wise thought Hanssen might have named his dog, Sunday, after one character (Wise 2002, 6).

They seek him here, they seek him there,
Those Frenchies seek him everywhere.
Is he in heaven or is he in hell,
That damned elusive Pimpernel?

From the film *The Scarlet Pimpernel*

Other fanciful adventures looked to the past, as in the "Scarlet Pimpernel" series penned by the baroness Orczy (whose full name was Emma Magdalena Rosalina Marie Josepha Barbara Orczy). First appearing in a play in 1903 and then in *The Scarlet Pimpernel* (1905), Percy Blakeney was a brave and efficient English secret agent rescuing kindly, victimized French aristocrats from the guillotine under the noses of French revolutionaries. He was something of a Robin Hood figure in reverse, saving the lives of the rich who were unfairly tormented by a cold-blooded government ostensibly run on behalf of working peasants. While the Pimpernel appeared too early to be a commentary on Soviet totalitarianism, it's difficult not to see comparisons between French revolutionaries calling each other "citizen" in the same fashion as later discussions between Russian leaders and spies calling each other "comrade."

Blakeney was a character masking his heroism behind seeming idleness and frivolity, a master of quick disguises in a series of books including *I Will Repay* (1906), *El Dorado* (1913), and *Sir Percy Hits Back*

(1927). In the first film adaptation of the character, *The Scarlet Pimpernel* (1935), Sir Percy (Leslie Howard) admits to a British admiral that he's partly motivated by his belief his French wife (Merle Oberon) is a collaborator for the government—which he learns is untrue—but he also jokes about his adventures with words similar to those of the actual Mansfield Cumming: "I've got a smack in the eye, and I've become engaged in sport. And what a sport! What a game." This attitude remained popular in England, especially on television. In 1982, *The Scarlet Pimpernel* was a British Television movie starring Anthony Andrews and Jane Seymour. In 1999, the story became a three-part miniseries (rebroadcast on American A&E) starring Richard E. Grant and Elizabeth McGovern.

Not always focused on such costumed derring-do, the baroness Orczy also wrote *The Spy of Napoleon* (1934). Filmed in 1936, the story centered on a French aristocrat married to a daughter of Napoleon III who infiltrates a ring of traitors. In a similar vein, Italian-born Rafael Sabatini's *Scaramouche* (1902) was set during the French Revolution and featured pistol duels and disguises. Like his contemporary Joseph Conrad, Sabatini wrote in a language not his own, but ostensibly based some of his fiction on his wartime experience in intelligence (McCormick 1977, 160).

Then the famous and trusty secret agent, so secret that he was never designated otherwise but by the symbol [triangle] in the late Baron Stott-Wartenheim's official, semi-official, and confidential correspondence; the celebrated agent [triangle], whose warnings had the power to change the schemes and the dates of royal, imperial, grand ducal journeys, and sometimes caused them to be put off altogether!
Joseph Conrad, *The Secret Agent*

Still, in the first decades of the new century, British literature pointed to serious concerns. In the spirit of William Le Queux, English fears about possible invasions from France and Germany led to a series of magazine stories and films about secret German armies infiltrating England. One notable author was Edgar Wallace who wrote a number of serialized stories like *Code No. 2*, which appeared in *The Strand* magazine in

April 1916. The adventure was later published in paperback as *The Little Green Man* and in various anthologies. The plot anticipated technology of the future including a computer-controlled hidden camera and infrared photography (McCormick 1977, 181–84).

Novels with these characteristics included Erskine Childer's 1903 *Riddle of the Sands*, a book based on the author's own yachting adventures in a clear warning against coming militarism. In the view of later critics, the book was a blend of realism, particularly in the author's precise descriptions of settings and commonsense approach to the coming war, along with elements of "pure adventure" (Sauerberg 1984, 9). During this era, spies were often far from champions of patriotic virtues. For example, Joseph Conrad's 1907 *The Secret Agent* is frequently dismissed in discussions of spy literature, but many points in this complex novel are worthy of reexamination. Often mentioned with Conrad's Russian set *Under Western Skies* (1911), which also deals with prerevolutionary anarchists, *Secret Agent* does, in fact, contain motifs and themes characterizing the espionage genre.

Based loosely on an actual bombing, the story focuses on Mr. Verloc, a lazy and vulgar "secret agent" assigned to spy on anarchists while posing as a small business owner. In the opening pages, Verloc's supervisor, Mr. Vladimir, the first secretary of a foreign embassy, pressured him to bomb the Greenwich Observatory so the British people would renew their European responsibilities. While far from a model of a "patriotic spy," Verloc believed such action would be irrational and likely to spark an antianarchist campaign by the London police. As Frederick Hitz noted, Verloc was an early example of literary trade-craft—he sent messages by moving his wares around his store window—but the spy believed such practices were useless and that revolutionary activity would only result in harm to innocents (Hitz 2004, 73). Thus, Verloc preceded many later fictional spies who were characterized by their distrust in their superiors' methods and goals long before the term "collateral damage" became commonplace.

Many character types in spy fiction can be traced to *Secret Agent*. For one, the plodding detective, Chief Inspector Heat, was a methodical man unable to work beyond conventional, standard procedures to solve crimes. Like Sherlock Holmes adventures, this concept was often a staple of espionage and mystery stories when amateurs and maverick operatives accomplished what restricted law enforcement could not. Another character type was a tragic foreshadowing of terrorists in fact and fiction into the twenty-first century. Professor X (a name all too typical in later pulp fiction and similar endeavors) was portrayed as the perfect anarchist. Like later villains in film and literature, he had grand visions of creating the perfect detonator. For protection, he strapped explosives to his own deformed body, and supplied Verloc with the explosives for the bombing. However, Verloc relied on a pawn, the imbecilic brother of his wife, who bungled the attack and blew himself up instead. Such moments evoke later news stories about Palestinian and Chechen terrorists in modern times, as does the speech by "spymaster" Vladimer justifying terrorism:

There could be nothing better. Such an outrage combines the greatest possible regard for humanity with the most alarming display of ferocious imbecility. . . . And there are other advantages. The whole civilised world has heard of Greenwich. The very boot-blacks in the basement of Charing Cross Station know something of it. See? (Conrad 1992, 44)

The Secret Agent warrants continuing consideration beyond its text. In 1923, a four-act play was produced based on the novel; in 1936, Alfred Hitchcock adapted the tale into his film, *Sabotage*. In this version, the Verlocs (Sylvia Sidney, Oscar Homolka) owned a movie theater. John Loder played an immoral police officer, suspicious of the husband while pursuing the affections of the wife. In this adaptation, a child is the innocent victim when the bomb he carries explodes prematurely. In the end, the wife kills her husband in revenge and escapes with her new lover.

Hitchcock expert Donald Spoto believed the director chose the novel because "he shared several of its concerns, the banality of evil, the transference or assumption of guilt . . . the duplicity inherent in the enterprise of espionage, and the enterprise of tracking down the spies" (1983, 172). Richard Porton believed the film showed Hitchcock's mistrust of criminal elements and of law enforcement as well. The police were bland and the agents in the film were "shadowy terrorists" with ambiguous motives. *Sabotage* "immerses the audience in the destructive urges that Conrad kept at arm's length" (Porton 1999, 20). Even in this early project, both sides of the conflict were characterized by flaws. No single participant can be described as heroic. Graham Greene, though not a Hitchcock fan, found much in the film to praise, saying the script retained some of the ruthlessness of the original book with admirable dialogue. He noted that the motif of disturbed domesticity was seen in settings such as the scene where a bomb maker worked on his craft surrounded by children's toys and ordinary laundry. Later, we see the mother learning of her child's death as she passes the theater audience watching a Disney movie in which voices sing the children's song "Who Killed Cock Robin?" (Greene 1980, 122–23).

The film also demonstrated that many espionage-oriented projects took on trappings of topical issues that gave the stories more weight than simple detective mysteries. According to actor Tony Curtis's introduction to the LaserLight DVD edition of *Sabotage*, the movie was produced in London when England was full of espionage fears as no one knew yet what to expect of Adolf Hitler. Curtis related these concerns to Conrad's novel, saying Hitchcock's theme of warning about the Nazis echoed the earlier book's backdrop of worries before World War I. Of course, when current issues are central to a plot, the story can become quickly dated. New interpretations must find other means to keep the source material relevant for new audiences. For example, *Sabotage* wasn't the last attempt to bring Conrad's story to the screen. In 1997, Christopher Hampton directed a more literal adaptation, *The Secret Agent*, focused on a reconstruction of the nineteenth-century London anarchist milieu at a time when the Unabomber was the newest representation of such characters (Porton 1999, 22).

How I loath our new manners in foreign policy! The old English way was to regard all foreigners as slightly childish and rather idiotic, and ourselves the only adults in a kindergarten world. That meant we had a cool, detached view and even-handed, sympathetic justice. But now we have gotten into the nursery ourselves and are bare fighting on the floor.
John Buchan, *The Three Hostages*

But the first important shift in literary, and later film and television adventures, came from the work of novelist John Buchan and his fellow British "Clubland" writers. With tales beginning in World War I, Buchan, Dornford Yates, and Sapper set the stage for many characteristics in all subsequent spy fiction.

Significantly, in 1915, John Buchan worked as head of the Department of Information during World War I, describing his work as "part propaganda, part politics, and part espionage . . . something of a conundrum. I have queer macabre recollections of those years meeting with odd people in odd places, of fantastic duties which a romancer would have rejected as beyond probability" (Bold 1988, 92–96). From this background, Buchan established several important aspects in espionage literature, notably the formulas for plot development and the importance of interesting settings (Osbourne 1953, 92–94).

As Robin Winks observed, one typical plot first seen in Buchan was to transport a code, person, or device from point A to point B, getting past any number of obstacles (1982, 48). In such stories, the adventure often began with someone observing a trivial detail that launched into an investigation involving an evil plot with potential grave consequences to the world, or worse, English-speaking civilization. Buchan's Richard Hannay and later spies were often uncertain about their mission's goals, so the reader learned what was going at the same time as the agent. Hannay and his successors were frequently surrounded by a pyramid of opponents—the villain, unsuspecting policemen, and even the agent's own controllers. Often, like Richard Hannay, the agent couldn't seek help, as this would compromise his cover (Winks 1982, 50). There was usually a time frame with an ominous deadline. Such templates, established during World War I, would be expanded and layered over the next century, but few books, films, or other media endeavors would stray far from the format laid out by John Buchan.

Later that evening, I found myself waiting in the rose garden reflecting that each part of the world seemed to have its own peculiar disadvantage for undercover work. During the past few years, in the practice of my profession, I had sloshed through Arctic bogs full of tangled laurel, fought my way across snow covered mountains, and sweated over deserts full of spiney cacti. Now I had honeysuckle and roses to contend with. Only the people remained the same. And the job.

Donald Hamilton, *Murderer's Row*

In addition to these formulas, according to Robin Winks, location and a sense of place remain of special importance in spy fiction, a motif established by Buchan. Beyond allowing writers to describe both native and exotic places in realistic detail, knowing the terrain was an important influence on any agent's course of action, especially in Buchanesque tales where the hero spent considerable time outdoors running from his hunters and was forced to adapt to the landscape. As James Bond himself put it in *Man with the Golden Gun*, "The first law for a secret agent is to get his geography right. His means of access and exit assure his communications with the outside world" (Fleming 1965, 26). Such was true of other authors, as in Eric Ambler's *Send No More Roses* (1977) in which the hero looked to his role model, Sir Robert Baden-Powell, the actual founder of the Boy Scouts and former spy. "He believes that both spies and Boy Scouts need to blend with their surroundings. They must use landscape rather than allow it to hamper them" (Wolfe 1993, 205).

Beyond giving stories descriptive settings, the need for interesting locations added romance to such tales. According to Lars Sauerberg, Buchan's Scottish landscape was, and is, considered exotic, even among native English islanders (1984, 23). More importantly, the descriptive transitions from normal, everyday life into fantastic situations helped ground readers. As the agents went abroad, they also moved from the real to the unreal (Sauerberg 1984, 29). In addition, taking agents out of their home settings made their actions of more consequence than those of normal detectives limited to crimes of local interest. On a more commercial level, when the spy boom of the 1960s began in earnest, thrillers were designed for an international market. James Bond, in particular, was a globe-trotting tourist with many travel scenes in Fleming's books. Such descriptions appealed to readers who were traveling themselves, after picking up these titles in airports and terminals (Lindner 2003, 65).

Before all that, despite Buchan's emphasis on setting and chase plots, his primary character, Richard Hannay, was an unimportant archetype in spy fiction. Most significantly, he was a gifted amateur able to accomplish remarkable things because of his military background. In the original *39 Steps*, in a plot dropped by Hitchcock, Hannay prevented naval secrets from getting to the Germans before the outbreak of war. While being seen as an innocent in the game of espionage, Hannay had learned from the natives in South Africa how to throw knives and catch them in his teeth, how to wander quietly in the heath, and how to take out an opponent by pressing on the body's pressure points. While being drawn into the secret world by accident in *The 39 Steps*, he became an agent by design in the sequel, *Green Mantle* (1916). In *Green Mantle*, Hannay, a master linguist and disguise expert, helped keep the Near East and Asia from going ablaze and opposed to the allied effort. In the opinion of Christopher Hitchens, *Green Mantle* was Buchan's masterpiece. Reflecting an interest in Islam and jihad, Buchan showed his fascination with German abilities to use their Turkish allies to enlist Muslim sentiment against the British Empire (Hitchens 2004, 104). In his fiction, Buchan wrote, "The Persian Muslims are threatening trouble. There is a dry wind blowing in the East, and the parched grasses wait the spark." In fact, Buchan helped light the spark. From his propaganda office, the novelist suggested that American reporter Lowell Thomas meet with his personal friend, T. E. Lawrence. Directly, Buchan thus helped launch the legend of famous intelligence officer "Lawrence of Arabia" (Hitchens 2004, 105).

Other harbingers of the future also appeared in Buchan's fiction. In *Mr. Standfast* (1919), Hannay posed as a pacifist to uncover a German spy planning to destroy the English army by releasing anthrax germs on its mainline of communications. In Buchan's last Hannay novel, *The Three Hostages* (1924), powerful international demigods manipulated groups like women's suffragettes and trade unions to stir up social discontent with brainwashing and hypnotism. As Richard Osbourne noted, this novel featured important characteristics of books not set during war. In the relatively peaceful decades after World War I, nations and ideology tended to recede in the stories of thrillers, so private villains and criminal cartels came forward. In such adventures, writers had to "pile on the personal devilishness of their foreign villains to make their capture . . . worthwhile" (Osbourne 1953, 212). Without a political background, the more villainous the opponent, the more acceptable the violence used to end their schemes. Heroes like Buchan's Richard Hannay tended to kill in the name of government service without authority or moral questioning. They didn't need them—gentlemen didn't murder in the name of petty quarrels, but they felt little legal constraint when defending their homeland (Osbourne 1953, 6). Of course, such killings in fiction were more for dramatic effect than any moral statement. The justice dealt out to villains was more satisfying in a climactic death scene than the turning over of such prey to legal authorities, as would be expected in radio scripts that were under watchful eyes of various groups of censors (Osbourne 1953, 9).

One aspect that distinguished Buchan from his fellow "Clubland" writers was that he pointed to problems within his own government, a foreshadowing of many books and films exploring this concern in later decades. Disliking Prime Minister Arthur Balfour, Buchan allegedly made him the model for chief villain Andrew Lumley in his 1916 thriller, *Power House*, the book described an "invisible, string-pulling, sinister secret government" (Hitchins 2004, 105). Without question, Buchan had a profound influence on espionage fiction beyond writers in the romantic tradition. "Even when the spy genre itself became a synonym for cynicism, John Le Carré had his George Smiley adopt the nom de guerre 'Mr. Standfast'" (Hitchins 2004, 104).

SPORTING SPIES

Alongside Buchan, writer Dornford Yates, pen name for Major Cecil William Mercer, established many staples of future spy adventures. His thirty-four books featured the idle rich wandering around England, Austria, and France fighting criminals and spies with the help of connections with local police and high-level government contacts. Yates was best known for two interrelated series of ongoing short story collections. The first began with *The Brother of Daphne* (1914), which introduced various members of the eccentric Berry Playdell family. One of the main characters was Jonathan ("Jonah") Manscell, a cousin always disappearing on secret missions. Manscell also appeared in many of the Richard (William) Chandos books such as *Jonah and Co.* (1922).

Yates's purpose was always light entertainment and there was little use of realism in his stories. Still, seeds of future spy elements were in his fantastic yarns. Before Bond had his Q, Chandos's Manscell set out on European adventures in a Rolls-Royce equipped with staff and customized caches of rifles, revolvers, maps, waterproof clothes, medicine chests, grave-digging tools, handcuffs, and passports. Jonah carried torches for flashing messages, ropes for hanging crooks, rubber tubes for gassing criminals, and spare clothes to lend girls whose own attire had been drenched (Osbourne 1953, 68, 80). Young readers were titillated with the witty, beautiful women popping up in such stories accompanied by descriptions of shapely feet, ankles, and patent-leather shoes (Osbourne 1953, 29). Like Richard Hannay, none of these characters ever needed money or work, but rather desired interesting things to do to demonstrate accomplishment between the wars.

Yates was not alone creating such adventures. Sapper (pen name for Lt. Col. Herman Cyril McNeile) also created characters who were largely gentlemen whose lives circled around sports clubs. Most tended to be leaders of teams, or private armies, rather than independent operatives. They enjoyed hunting, fishing, boxing, and fencing, and referred to World War I with Kipling's words, "The Great Game" (Osbourne 1953, 145). In particular, the famous "Bulldog" Drummond short stories emphasized the teamwork of Englishmen in overtly racist terms, with many unkind references to Italians and Jews. "The breed," as Richard Osbourne called such heroes, were curt, able to throw back knives tossed at them, loved beer, and mistrusted the press. While untrained, they knew enough to tear off the next two or three pages of telegraph paper to ensure no copies of their messages were left behind. They defeated foes who kept gorillas, dwarfs, and legless monsters, who used blowpipes, dum-dum bullets, acid baths, and compressed-air rifles. The heroes always preferred hand-to-hand combat, even when the enemy threatened them with spiked boxing gloves. In their attempt to destroy the English way of life, such madmen stooped so low as to kiss married women while these victims were tied to chairs (Osbourne 1953, 153–59).

Despite these colorful characteristics, the novels of Sapper are now largely remembered for their cliché-ridden, crude, and unsophisticated literary style. Beginning with *Bulldog Drummond* (1920), the sometimes secret agent Hugh C. Drummond battled his major foe, Carl Peterson, along with a parade of "other 'Hun,' 'Wog,' 'Dago,' or any other foreigner" (McCormick 1977, 160–61). During his heyday, Drummond was the subject of a series of popular films beginning with the silent *Bulldog Drummond* (1929). Throughout the series, Drummond was portrayed as a suave ex-British officer by the likes of Ronald Coleman, Ralph Richardson, Ray Milland, John Howard, and

Tom Conway. These short features drained off much of the brutality and racial perspectives of the novels in favor of a light, comic approach. In one effort, for example, Drummond seeks bank robbers while a French police chief keeps trying to make sure Drummond marries his fiancée, Phyllis, either in jail or at the crime scene. Some of the spy adventures include *Bulldog Drummond at Bay* (1937), in which the hero looks for foreign agents seeking plans for a secret warplane, and *Bulldog Drummond Escapes* (1937), in which he rescues a beautiful girl from spies.

After Sapper died in 1937, the Drummond books continued under the authorship of Gerald Fairlie, the actual model for the Bulldog Drummond character (Osbourne 1953, 163). Before Sapper's death, the two discussed the originator's last novel, *Bulldog Drummond Hits Out* (1937), and Fairlie agreed to complete the book (McCormick 1977, 70). Fairlie had Drummond battling the new enemies of the Berlin-Rome-Moscow axis before World War II, a change from battles with independent merchants and mercenary spies to duels with political states in books like *Bulldog Drummond at War* (1940) and *Captain Bulldog Drummond* (1945). In these tales, Drummond battled saboteurs, prevented riots, and helped inspire rearmament in England. Drummond, along with intelligence officer Ronald Standish, dealt with ongoing villains, notably old foe Carl Peterson and his new wife, Irma (Osbourne 1953, 189–99).

Fairlie can be considered the last of the "Clubland" authors and credited with his own new characters in the spy canon. His special agent Standish, with many nods to Sherlock Holmes, dominated three books. He was joined by new hero Jim Maitland in twelve short stories. Maitland was the international figure juxtaposed against Drummond's English-based adventures. Harkening back to the global background of Richard Hannay, Maitland described his efforts as "research work in the native populations," England's means to control its far-flung interests (Osbourne 1953, 202). His character inspired W. Somerset Maugham to write in what can serve as a summary of the "Clubland" era:

He toils secretly in remote and inaccessible places of the world. He guards the marshes of the Empire. You will find him at the gates of India, in the lonely wastes of the Great Dominion, and in the tropical forests of darkest

Africa. No one can contemplate him without a thrill of pride. (Osbourne 1953, 193)

Clearly, modern spy literature can trace its beginnings to writers rooted in British Imperialism. But the influence of the "Clubland" group and their direct heirs went beyond establishing plots, settings, and characterizations. For one thing, the long practice of Western involvement in international affairs was strongly connected to first British and then American colonialism. Such activity had much to do with later proxy battles during the cold war. Throughout the twentieth century, defending the realm meant more than protecting the homeland—it included protecting international interests, both political and commercial. But until the rise of Adolf Hitler, for the "Clubland" authors, national defense was more a matter of the imagination and romance and not a reflection of cultural and ideological fears beyond the racism and anti-Semitism that dominated the period.

But literary trends always include waves of romance followed by more realistic, grounded explorations in many genres. Espionage was no exception. In the decades between the world wars, readers continued to enjoy the heroics of characters like Richard Hannay and Jim Maitland, but the next important shift in spy stories was something quite different from what came before. "The Great Game" would quickly be replaced by a deepening interest in the meaning of espionage, the roles of heroes, and more literary uses of a new genre.

2

Maugham, Ambler, and Greene: The Loss of Innocence

"There's just one thing I think you ought to know before you take on this job. And don't forget it. If you do well you'll get no thanks and if you get into trouble, you'll get no help. Does that suit you?" He shook hands with Ashenden and showed him out. Ashenden was well aware that he would never know what happened then. . . . It was as unsatisfactory as those modern novels that give you a number of unrelated episodes and expect you, by piecing them together, to connect in your mind the connected narrative.

W. Somerset Maugham, *Ashenden: Or the British Agent*

In the 1930s, many of the themes of the "Clubland" group dramatically changed when the "thrill of pride" for independent adventurers shifted into a new climate where the British, in particular, had new questions regarding European affairs and international monetary concerns, as well as new literary interests in realism, cynicism, and what the rise of both Nazis and Communists meant in a troubling new world order. One notable trend beyond the themes of Buchan, according to Peter Wolfe, was that the books of Eric Ambler included characters sent overseas where different cultures muddled English moral certainties regarding the impact of free enterprise (1993, 1). According to Wolfe, W. Somerset Maugham and Ambler both moved away from the patriotism of the "Clubland" era, with heroes no longer defending the Empire with smug certainty (1993, 5). Their characters endured a "loss of innocence," especially these "innocents abroad" because people are less secure on foreign soil where they must invent themselves anew, find their inner resources eroding, and expose their frailties.

Without question, the first signs of new directions were seen in the stories of W. Somerset Maugham, a figure linking several generations of spy writers. As Maugham was happy to emphasize, his spy fiction was based on his experience in Russia in 1917. There, he unsuccessfully tried to block the Bolshevik Revolution and keep Russia in World War I (Maugham 1941, ii). He later claimed it was impossible to develop long fiction based too closely on fact, as reality was full of loose ends, dead ends, and unconnected plots. In addition, Maugham observed, "The work of an agent in the intelligence department is on the whole extremely monotonous. A lot of it is uncommonly useless. The material it offers for stories is scrappy and pointless. The author has himself to make it coherent, dramatic, and prevalent" (Maugham 1941, i).

Maugham's 1928 *Ashenden: Or the British Agent* was his attempt to make spycraft both dramatic and prevalent with his agent, Richard Ashenden, frequently referring to what he observed as "grist for his mill," a literary allusion to the fictional spy's cover as a novelist. Often praised as the first realistic spy book, *Ashenden* is sometimes considered a collection of interrelated character sketches and short stories. Other readers see the book as a fully realized novel partly due to the author's sense of cynicism and development of the antiheroic protagonist. In addition, the jumping from incident to incident illustrates Maugham's points that espionage is not a venture where secret agents work on one task at a time with satisfactory endings and explainable conclusions.[1] In the opinion of some later reviewers, the novel also underlines Maugham's belief that espionage is neither glamorous nor high-adventure. Instead, as Frederick Hitz notes, Maugham introduced bureaucracy in fiction based on his war experiences (2004, 37).

These concerns were perhaps best illustrated in one early passage where Ashenden pondered what his chiefs were doing in London. In his notes, Ashenden said, "their hands [were] on the throttle of this great machine," moving their pieces here and there, seeing the patterns woven by disparate threads. They might be enjoying the excitement of espionage, but "the small fry" did not live the adventurous lives the public thought (Maugham 1941, 99). Ashenden's own duties were to "see his spies at stated intervals and paid them their wages." When he could get a hold of a new one, he engaged him, gave him his instructions, and sent him off to Germany. He weighed the information that came through and dispatched it. He went into France once a week to confer with his colleague over the frontier and receive his orders from London" (1941, 99). Ashenden compared his work to that of a clerk and is amused to learn that his supervisor, "R," has someone spying on him to make sure he's working. He understands the wisdom of this, as one of his missions uncovered an informant selling information without ever going over the border.

One of the most successful writers of his generation, Maugham openly admired Joseph Conrad and aspired to emulate his literary status. On the other hand, Ian Fleming later praised Maugham, and himself, saying they were the only two authors "who write about what people are really interested in—cards, money, gold, and things like that" (Allen 2004, 9). Perhaps Fleming thought of Maugham's emphasis on boredom and routine when he wrote passages describing James Bond's malaise between assignments, his talents only needed once or twice a year. One Maugham story, "Behind the Scenes," is a clear model for Fleming's 1959 short story, "A Quantum of Solace," which appeared in *For Your Eyes Only* (1960). In both tales, Ashenden and Bond complete missions and are obligated to spend an evening with a local government official who has to come up with some entertainment for his guest. In both stories, the hosts narrate simple memories of a young civil servant at the beginning of his career before being hardened by bad love affairs. In both stories, the agents are first disinterested before becoming engaged in a slice of life removed from their own worlds. Many of Maugham's stories are similar sad character studies of spies caught up in relationships that force them to betray lovers and colleagues, more so than all the governments conspiring against each other. For example, the book ends with the juxtaposition of the outbreak of the Russian Revolution against the stubbornness of a man refusing to flee until his washing is collected. The final description is of the man clutching his laundry with a bullet in his head.

At the outset of World War II, Maugham offered his services to British intelligence, but was turned down because of his age. In a new introduction for the 1941 reissue of *Ashenden*, Maugham observed that insiders now considered the British Secret Service less efficient than it had been. "The circumstances are different," he admitted, "and I daresay more difficult." For one matter, he said, it wasn't as easy for foreign nationals to move around as had been the case in his day (Maugham 1941, iii). Instead, Maugham bemusedly heard Nazi propaganda chief Dr. Joseph Goebbels denounce *Ashenden* over German radio as an example of British cynicism and brutality (Maugham 1941, ii–iii). Beyond the hypocrisy in this broadcast, Goebbels's choice of literature was odd, as most spy novels up to that point were far more violent than any scene in *Ashenden*. Ironically, because of his espionage work in Russia, Soviet intelligence assigned one unit to study not only Maugham's fiction but all British authors afterward. While gleaning possible tidbits into British spycraft, the unit's primary purpose was to examine the propaganda uses of such books to both study what was being said against the Soviet Union and how Russian intelligence could do likewise (McCormick 1977, 6).

If I were asked to single out one specific group of men, one type, one category as being the most suspicious, unbelieving, unreasonable, petty, inhuman, sadistic, double-crossing set of bastards in any language, I would say without any hesitation the people who run counter-espionage departments.

Eric Ambler, *The Light of Day*

While Maugham wrote only one entry into spy fiction, other authors of the period built their reputations on undercover books. One of the most important and prolific was Eric Ambler, who also helped change direction in the genre. Of course, he owed a debt to those who came before. According to Peter Wolfe, *The Mask of Dimitrios* (1939), in particular, was an overt nod to Sapper's Bulldog Drummond and Dashiell Hammett stories (1993, 67). But the novelist quickly progressed far beyond his inspirations. In 1943, Alfred Hitchcock observed that Ambler's insight into the long-term dangers and corruption inherent in European business and politics lifted Ambler's thrillers above most intrigue fiction of the day (Wolfe 1993, 31–32).

Eric Ambler's early best sellers included *Epitaph for a Spy* (1938) and *Journey into Fear* (1940). Both transformed the genre from heroic stories into more complex and ironic tales of corruption, betrayal, and conspiracy (Cawilti and Rosenberg 1987, 46). As Alfred Hitchcock observed, Ambler's characters were passive—things happen to them instead of their initiating action (Wolfe 1993, 5). *Epitaph for a Spy,* in particular, was a major turning point in spy fiction, as the theme of the innocent being blackmailed into government service was introduced. In this case, a photographer is threatened with deportation back to the Communist bloc if he doesn't perform what turns out to be bungling duties (Wolfe 1993, 49). While the coercion motif became a dominant staple in spy fiction, with the exception of Russian blackmail schemes, agents under such pressures rarely worked well in actual spycraft (Hitz 2004, 14). Thus, Ambler's inept agent was as much a reflection of fact as comic fantasy. Another noted work was *The Mask of Dimitros* (book 1939, film 1944) where Ambler made allusions to the political situation in the Balkans, adding authenticity to his story. In such books, Ambler made such devices as show trials and Balkan intrigues a mainstay of the spy genre (Cawilti and Rosenberg 1987, 105).[2]

Over the years, Eric Ambler's themes and approaches changed dramatically. In his earlier works, Ambler had been noted for his use of the thriller form to examine big business and international politics, stating, "It is not important who pulled the trigger but who paid for the bullets" ("Eric" 2000). For example, in Ambler's first novel, *Dark Frontier* (1936), one character observes, "What else could you expect from a balance of power adjusted in terms of land, of arms, of manpower and of materials: in terms, in other words, of money? . . . Wars were made by those who had the power to upset the balance, to tamper with international money and money's worth" ("Eric" 2000). On this subject, Ambler reflected contemporary concerns both in politics and popular fiction, as well as being prophetic. *Dark Frontier*, an overt parody of Oppenheim, Buchan, and Yates, dealt with fears about an atomic bomb a full decade before one actually existed. But before Ambler conceived his tale, the U.S. Senate had decided America had been drawn into World War I by international bankers, munitions manufacturers, and war profiteers. During that era, this consortium was known as "The Merchants of Death" (Persico 2001, 25). Graham Greene's *This Gun for Hire* (1936) also dealt with such worries, as did Leslie Charteris in his early "Saint" books. As chronicled in the opening pages of *The Saint in New York* (1934), The Saint's first adventures include thwarting political assassinations, fighting arms merchants, and destroying mad scientists who've created diabolical weapons that Simon Templar fears would instigate rather than deter war.[3] One updating of this theme was Jeffrey Archer's 1977 *Shall We Tell the President?*, a novel built around an assassination plot including a U.S. senator beholden to gun manufacturers wanting to block passage of a gun control bill. More typically, future film and television plots would have arms merchants seeking buyers in Third World revolutions or anyone interested in fantastic new weapons that would give world domination to forces more criminal than political. All such stories owed something to the warnings of Ambler, Charteris, and Greene.

But during the 1930s, Ambler's interests in economic concerns weren't limited to arms merchants. Typical of the times, Ambler shared leftist sympathies with many intellectuals. In part, he attacked blindness to threats of fascist ideology and nationalism by using a heroic Soviet agent, Andreas Zaleshoff, in two of his novels, *Uncommon Danger* (1936) and *Cause for Alarm* (1938). The latter book showed signs of influence from Hitchcock films. Like *The 39 Steps*, *Alarm* also has a hero and heroine bound together, who escape by cutting their bonds. As *Foreign Correspondent* used windmills as a signal device for spies, *Alarm*'s characters hide in windmills (Wolfe 1993, 127–28). In the view of some critics, Ambler largely left his socialist leanings behind him after World War II, as he included commentary on totalitarian states, both Nazi and Communist, in books like *Alarm* and *Judgment on Deltchev* (1951) (Wolfe 1993, 61).

But in postwar thrillers, Ambler adopted a seemingly neutral stand to cold war antagonisms in novels like *Passage to Arms* (1959) and collections of shorter works like *To Catch a Spy* (1964) (Wolfe 1993, 90). While some claim his novels in the 1950s broke little new ground, *The Schirmer Inheritance* (1953) and *State of Siege* (1956) brought in new levels of sexuality while pointing to the new worries about truth versus illusion conflicts in the cold war that would dominate spy fiction in subsequent decades. In particular, *Judgment on Deltchev*, about a mock trial of a supposed traitor, included misdirection, tricks, and courtroom diversions, making it impossible to clearly establish guilt either for observers in the book or readers of the text. Ambler's characters included "naïve Western liberals, misled terrorists, corrupt post-colonial politicians, unscrupulous representatives of multinational capitalism, and political refugees. A relatively clear clash between different ideologies, familiar from pre-war novels, has now become a complex web of intrigues" ("Eric" 2000).

During the 1950s, Ambler wrote under the pseudonym of Elliott Reed in books reflecting simpler, more conventional morality. Three of the five Reed books were written by Ambler with cowriter Charles Rada, the final two by Rada himself (Wolfe 1993, 117). These stories included *Charter to Danger* (1954) and *Tender to Danger* (1956). In the passages thought to be Rada's, musical themes were added along with more romance, an aspect Ambler avoided.

Eric Ambler's place in the fictional spy milieu cannot be overstated, both in terms of how he helped shift directions from the "Clubland" writers, and in his sometimes prophetic use of techniques and approaches in later projects. For example, while Ambler's style preceded "the fast-paced, over-heated international thrillers of Robert Ludlum and Tom Clancy," Peter Wolfe noted Ambler was far less violent than his descendents, most killings taking place offstage (1993, 14). Still, Ambler used torture repeatedly in his stories, carrying on the tradition of Kipling and Peter Chaney and setting the stage for the "sadism" of Ian Fleming. The often bisexual or asexual men were often engineers forced to work on machinery for despots and the occasional mad scientist, a precursor to later works pointing to the overemphasis of technology over the human factor (Wolfe 1993, 29). And, as Alfred Hitchcock praised Ambler's depth in his themes, Ambler helped shape the film director's use of his famous "McGuffins." "Just as the secret message in Hitchcock's *The Lady Vanishes* (1938), for which several people risk their lives, turns out to be a scrap of a popular song, so do the plans in *The Dark Frontier* turn out to be in the roll of lint or gauze" (Wolfe 1993, 38).

Among Ambler's novels to be filmed was *Journey Into Fear* (1940), in which an unwitting bystander ends up being hunted across wartime Europe. The book was filmed in 1942, starring Joseph Cotton, produced by Orson Welles's Mercury company. A remake was released in 1976 starring Zero Mostel and Shelley Winters ("Eric" 2000). *Epitaph for a Spy* was filmed under the title *Hotel Reserve* (1944), starring James Mason and Lucie Mannheim. In the story, a teacher on vacation is accused of espionage in France before World War II. *Topkapi* (1964), adapted from *The Light of Day* (1962) was reportedly the film inspiring the first of the "Pink Panther" parodies of the genre ("Eric" 2000). The film starred Peter Ustinov, who was nominated for an Academy Award for his acting. In the story, an inept crook is first blackmailed by a ring of spies into helping them before Turkish police also trap him and force him into spying for them.

> He had no sense of safety walking up and down on this English ship, sliding imperceptibly into Dover. Danger was part of him. It wasn't like an overcoat you sometimes left behind. It was your skin. You died with it. Only corruption stripped it from you. The one person you trusted was yourself . . . and sometimes, you weren't certain whether after all you could trust yourself.
>
> Graham Greene, *The Confidential Agent*

Alongside Eric Ambler, novelist Graham Greene helped elevate the espionage genre into mainstream literature, notably his *The Ministry of Fear* (1943), a book Greene admitted was heavily influenced by John Buchan (McCormick 1977, 92). But, in Greene's own opinion, times had changed much since the days of Buchan's heroic adventures. He wrote, "One could no longer believe in the kind of simple, direct patriotism of Hannay and his creator, nor in many of Buchan's sentiments" (Cawilti and Rosenberg 1987, 121). For critic Donald McCormick, Greene came to write with an anguish and self-consciousness "the Clubland writers never even tried to achieve" as he looked at the malaise in Europe (1977, 91).

During the early years of his career, most comparisons to other writers were best applied to the shared motifs of Greene and Ambler. Before the cold war, Greene's spies, like Ambler's, tended to be non-professionals who succeeded through blind luck or with last minute intervention from government agencies. In Greene's books, and less so in the films made from them, one recurring theme was capitalist corruption in opposition to patriotism where the protagonists happened to be spies. Unlike the "Clubland" group, Greene's secret agents were typically middle-aged, cynical, "more-or-less stateless heroes" described in a semidocumentary style with inconclusive adventures in shabby hotels, slow-moving ships, or on uncomfortable continental trains (McCormick 1977, 89–90). In such stories, espionage was more a setting than the central element of the plots. Still, Greene's first books contained innovations important for the genre as a whole. In particular, *The Confidential Agent* (1939) is often considered one model for modern espionage stories employing humor. It tells the story of an unwilling hero who compromises his principles to secure the safety of a coal delivery.[4] One issue regarding the novel, a carryover from the "Clubland" books, is that the antagonist, the mysterious Forbes/Furstein, was a rich Jew planning to destroy traditional English culture from within ("Graham" 2000).

While Greene's writing career included many projects unrelated to espionage, like Ambler, his books showed how a writer can change significantly from decade to decade. After World War II, in particular, Greene became known for anti-American comments that gave him access to such Communist leaders as Fidel Castro and Ho Chi Minh. But fellow English writer Evelyn Waugh wrote privately that Greene was "a secret agent on our side and all his buttering up of the Russians is 'cover' " ("Graham" 2000). Greene had family connections to support this belief. His uncle, Sir William Graham Greene, helped establish the Naval Intelligence Department; his oldest brother, Herbert, served as a spy for the Imperial Japanese Navy in the 1930s; and his younger sister, Elisabeth, was a member of MI6 (Secret Intelligence) and recruited him into the service ("Graham" 2000). But Greene's criticism of various aspects of Western culture, his connections with Communist leaders, and particularly his friendship with KGB spy Harold "Kim" Philby, made Greene's reputation rather ambiguous in some circles.

In 1937, Kim Philby—who reportedly was given the name "Kim" after the character in Kipling's spy stories—began his long career as a double agent in British intelligence, establishing the groundwork for his infamous "Cambridge Spy Ring." For a time, this circle, the cream of the crop of forty Cambridge Communists, almost took complete control of the British Secret Service before the group was forced to defect. Philby's "Magnificent Five," in Moscow's opinion, included Guy Burgess, Donald Maclean, Sir Anthony Blount, and John Cairncross. New revelations about the group continued up to 1981 when the *London Daily Mail* outed Roosevelt speechwriter Michael Strait as the American end of the ring (Steyn 2004, 46). Along the way, Philby formed a friendship with Graham Greene, with whom he worked in Secret Intelligence Services (SIS) in Sierra Leone during World War II. Later, Greene described his spy work with Philby as "a silly useless job." One mission took Greene to West Africa, which he recalled more for the plague of flies than any government service ("Graham" 2000).

Before and after Philby's escape to Russia in 1963, the close friendship between the novelist and the traitor was never secret. But Greene's relationship with Philby became publicly problematic in the 1960s, especially after rumors began that Philby was an inspiration for the film and radio series, *The Third Man* (1949). According to the 2004 Turner Classic Movies documentary, *Shadowing the Third Man*, Greene and Philby were obviously more than mere acquaintances in espionage circles. Philby was likely thinking of Greene when he wrote that his cover as an SIS agent had no more significance than if he had pretended to be a vacuum cleaner salesman (Bloom 1987, 140). This image clearly referred to Greene's 1958 *Our Man in Havana*, which chronicled the tale of a vacuum cleaner salesman who relocated to Cuba. He became a reluctant government agent (code numbered 529-double-O/5) and passed off vacuum cleaner designs as plans for an enemy installation. In his 1968 memoirs, *My Silent War*, with a sympathetic introduction by Greene, Philby quoted from Greene's *The Confidential Agent* in a scene where the hero is asked if his leaders are better than others. No is the answer. The choice of a spy, Philby said using Greene's words, is to choose their course and stay with it, right or wrong (Hitz 2004, 31). Greene's friendship with Philby lasted into the 1980s. When Greene began work on *The Human Factor* (1978), a story about an agent falling in love with a black woman during an assignment in South Africa, Greene wasn't happy with the manuscript and sent a copy to Philby in Moscow for his comments. Greene ended up denying that his double agent in the book, Maurice Castle, was based on Philby ("Graham" 2000). (A later connection between an actual spy and Greene occurred when an FBI agent gave KGB supervisor Dimitri Lapushkin a copy of Greene's 1973 *The Honorary Consel* in hopes of inspiring the Russian to defect in 1982. The ploy didn't work (Wise 2002, 196).)

The relationship between these two men remains one of the most unusual cross-pollinations between fact and fiction in modern espionage. More importantly, Greene's perspectives regarding the cold war set the stage for John Le Carré making the spy genre synonymous with criticism of British class structures and questionable methods in his duels between George Smiley and Moscow Central. One Greene novel, *The Quiet American*, is perhaps the best example of how the novelist's themes were precursors for what would later be dubbed the "anti-Bond trend" in fiction and film.

Suddenly I was angry. I was tired of the whole pack of them with their private stores of Coca Cola and their portable hospital and their wide cars and their not-quite-latest guns. I said, "Yes, they killed him because he was too innocent to live. He was young and ignorant and silly and he got involved. He had no more of a notion than any of you what the whole affair is all about. And you gave him money and your books on the East and said go ahead. Win the East for democracy. He never saw anything he hadn't heard in a lecture hall and his writers and his lecturers made a fool of him. When he saw a dead body, he couldn't even see the wounds. A Red Menace, a soldier of democracy.

Graham Greene, *The Quiet American*

On the most basic level, the story of *The Quiet American* is a human drama revolving around a love triangle between a journalist, a Vietnamese girl, and a CIA operative, without the comic aspects of earlier Greene books. Again using the backdrop of espionage as prophecy, the book was once seen as a plea for common sense in Vietnam before American involvement could escalate (McCormick 1977, 92). For other readers, the book was considered sympathetic to Communism. A play of the novel was produced in Moscow. In a wider view, the story includes clear themes of how misguided interference can lead to disaster. In particular, the academic and innocent spy, Pyle, was allegedly based on real CIA agent Col. Edward Lansdale, a man portrayed as an idealistic operative who can be potentially more dangerous than any enemy. Like his superiors, Pyle is knowledgeable in books and principles, but out of his depth in the field, where the Vietnamese understand none of his sermons on liberty and democracy. Evoking scenes from Conrad's *Secret Agent*, Pyle sets up a bomb intended to take out a military parade. But, not knowing the parade was cancelled, Pyle's explosion kills a number of innocent civilians.

Instead of showing remorse, Pyle says the casualties were martyrs for democracy and pays for his blunder with his life. This theme of policymakers and analysts making decisions removed from field experience became a mainstay in spy fiction, as in Norman Mailer's 1991 *Harlot's Ghost*, where Lansdale was again a character (with his real name). In Mailer's novel, Lansdale was described in equally unflattering terms as a "maverick" working from a set of ideals more military than covert. In such works, the aspects of the "innocent" in espionage had changed from heroic adventurers to either naïve blunderers—reflecting various writers' perspectives on national interference on the world stage—or as victims in the cold war. When John Le Carré picked up the mantle of realism in the 1960s, even professional agents were but pawns in larger games. Much had indeed changed since the tales of Richard Hannay. (See chapter 3 for a detailed discussion of Greene films and film criticism.)

GOLDEN AGE OF SPY FICTION

Without question, the 1930s was a decade that saw an explosion of espionage literature—some trendsetting, some forgettable artifacts of the times. Nearly as important as Maugham, Ambler, and Greene were the works of John Creasey. His "Department Z" stories included *The Death Miser* (1933), which introduced department leader Gordon Craigie, who led a surprising variety of patriotic and intrepid agents guarding England's interests. This team's adventures were chronicled in novels such as *First Came a Murder* (1934) and the prophetic *Mark of the Crescent* (1935). After the beginning of the war, Creasey's *The Wizard Man* (1940) was told through the eyes of a Nazi Secret Service agent.

In 1938, Creasey took the pen name of Gordon Ashe and created his character Patrick Dawlish in the Bulldog Drummond tradition. A powerful figure in MI5 (Security Service), Dawlish would have been more appropriate in MI6 (Secret Intelligence Service) as he went into occupied Europe to organize resistance. After the war, Dawlish retired, became a private eye, and assisted Scotland Yard in fighting the highly successful Dr. Palfrey, whose followers owed allegiance to corporations and not any country or government. These books reflected Creasey's belief in "one world," a theme he pursued after the war (McCormick

1977, 60). From 1966 to 1967, some of Creasey's stories became the basis for the TV series, *The Baron*, set around John Mannering (Steve Forrest). The title character drew his name from his family's manor in Texas. Filmed in England, the series cast Mannering as an owner of antique shops in London, Paris, and Washington, D.C. British intelligence called on Mannering whenever priceless art exhibits were involved in espionage, blackmail, or murder (Britton 2004, 181).

Equally successful was novelist F. Van Wyck Mason, who cranked out spy novels over four decades including *The Branded Spy Murders* (1932), *Two Tickets to Tangier* (1936), and *Zanzibar Intrigue* (1964). Mason's principal character, Major Hugh North, became the leading figure in the radio series, *The Man from G-2*, also known as *Major North, Army Intelligence (1945–1946)* starring Staats Cotsworth (Britton 2004, 19). Another writer to see his works adapted for popular media was Geoffrey Household, whose *Rogue Male* (1938) was filmed, broadcast as a radio drama, and subject of a praised BBC film in 1976. Cited by Lars Sauerberg as an example of a hero seeking personal vengeance before turning professional, the plot involved an Englishman, Sir Robert Hunter, ultimately given a one-man spy mission to hunt down and kill a dictator who was a thinly disguised Adolf Hitler (1984, 8). Later, the story was rumored to be the basis for an actual attempt to kill the Fuhrer (McCormick 1977, 101). According to Michael Denning, the story's kill-or-be-killed motif, the hunter/hunted narrator progressively shedding all trappings of civilization, continued in books such as Gavin Lyle's *The Most Dangerous Game* (1964) and Desmond Blakley's *Running Blind* (1970) (Lindner 2003, 61). The film version, directed by Fritz Laing, was retitled *Manhunt* starring Walter Pidgeon and John Huston. According to Andrew Lycett, before *The Rogue Male* became something of a sensation, Ian Fleming liked Household's first novel, *The Third Hour* (1937). He sent at least six copies to friends (1995, 86). In the story, Toby Manning, a liberal businessman going to Mexico to sell toys, runs across French and German exiles acting as revolutionaries. The scene that likely most impressed Fleming was when Manning raped the German baroness (Lycett 1995, 86).

One clear trend in fiction was the continuation of real agents using their experiences for literary endeavors. One interesting case was Marthe McKenna, a former British spy who wrote memories of her experiences as a nurse fighting to retain her virtue behind enemy lines. Winston Churchill wrote the introduction for her first nonfiction book, *I Was a Spy* (1933) followed by *Spies I Knew* (1934), in which she described how churches were meeting places for spies in Flanders (McCormick 1977, 126). She published four novels based on these experiences but turned her attention to threats from Nazis in *Hunt the Spy* (1939) and *Spying Blind* (1939) when World War I adventures lost public favor. In 1937, her *Lancer Spy* became a film starring George Sanders, Peter Lorre, and Delores Del Rio as the heroine.

Another female author of note was Phyllis Bottom, who published *The Mortal Storm* (1937) and *The Lifeline* (1946). Bottom and her husband are now best remembered for mentoring Ian Fleming when he composed his first unpublished short story, "Death on Two Occasions."[5] Such influence, according to Andrew Lycett, was profound. Fleming attended a private school in the Austrian Alps run by Bottom and her husband, former British diplomat and spy Ernan Forbs Dennis. There, the nineteen-year-old Fleming was encouraged, for the first time, to pursue his interests in foreign affairs (Lycett 1995, 35–36). Another book with an unusual Fleming connection was diplomat Harold Nickelson's *Public Faces* (1932). After Nickelson met the young reporter who was then working for Reuters, the novelist was so impressed by Fleming he used him as a character in the book. Another indictment of the international arms trade, *Public Faces* raised very early concerns about atomic weapons (Lycett 1995, 51). The story centers on a British agent trying to forestall a French plot by planting stories in newspapers about an atomic experiment going wrong and destroying Charleston, South Carolina (1995, 51).

Another writer of special interest was Compton Mackenzie, who described the machinations of the British Secret Service in Greece in his *Athenian Memories* (1931) and its follow-up, *Greek Memories* (1940), which got him into trouble with the British government. Withdrawn from publication in 1933, the book finally appeared in 1940 because censors didn't want to reveal Mackenzie's meticulous details about plans to blow up a bridge in Constantinople. After being charged with violating the Official Secrets Act, Mackenzie struck back by spoofing MI5 and MI6 in *Water on the Brain* (1933). It featured a henpecked, retired spy recruited into the Secret Service under the cover of a banana importer. Mackenzie said the book must have seemed like a fantastic Marx Brothers affair, "but during the Second

World War, many more people discovered that those responsible for secret intelligence do, in very fact as often as not, behave like characters created by the Marx Brothers" (McCormick 1977, 129).

Another ex-spy, the agent who first learned about Hitler's V-2 rockets, was Bernard Newman, a writer who did much of his research on bicycle tours of Europe. Newman was a highly praised lecturer on spycraft, and his *Spy* (1935) revolved around a British agent playing psychological games on an enemy commander. Early reviewers thought it was an autobiographical account until it was revealed that the story was a hoax (McCormick 1977, 140). Subsequent novels including *Secret Servant* and *Woman Spy* (both 1937) concentrated on European settings capturing the mood of authenticity and topicality of the era. Newman's *Spy Catchers* (1945), a collection of short stories, has been regarded as one of the best books ever written on counter-espionage. In particular, Donald McCormick praised the author's use of radio for coded messages and musical codes, as many suspected the Germans were using these in broadcasts (1977, 140).

Of course, some writers were noted for more fancy than fact in the "Clubland" tradition. The forty books of Francis Beeding (pen name of two authors, John Leslie Palmer and Hillary Adam St. George Saunders) featured patriotic spies in stories such as *The Six Proud Walkers* (1928), one of the few spy novels set against the old League of Nations. One character, Colonel Grandby, often working in France, was Beeding's hero in Secret Service stories such as *The League of Discontentment* (1930) and *Take It Crooked* (1932). Becoming more topical in the late 1930s, the authors introduced a new hero, John Couper, in *The Black Heroes* (1938), in which the ultra-Fascist pirate Society of Black Heroes had a secret submarine, a favorite device of the era. In the same mold, if less prolific, was Sydney Horler, whose *Miss Mystery* (1926), *The Secret Service Man* (1930), and *The Spy* (1931) were highly colored, artificial stories, very popular in the 1930s (McCormick 1977, 99–100). One author with a long career was Dennis Wheatley who wrote the Roger Brooks series of novels set during the Napoleonic era. The character was introduced in *The Forbidden Territory* (1933) and his epic concluded in *Desperate Measures* (1974) (McCormick 1977, 187).

While he is now the writer all critics love to shun, no survey can dismiss Sax Rohmer, who unquestionably peppered his long run of Fu Manchu tales with espionage elements. In an era where foes of

England were either German or diabolical representatives of "The Yellow Peril," no foe was as irrepressible as Dr. Fu Manchu, who first appeared in 1913. During his long reign of terror, Manchu was continually thwarted by Sir Denis Nayland-Smith, a blend of amateur detective, commissioner of Britain in Burma, and controller in the Secret Service and the Criminal Investigation Division (CID), an improbable overlap of legal and independent attributes. Popular encounters included *The Daughter of Fu Manchu* (1931), *The Trial of Fu Manchu* (1934), and finally *Re-enter Fu Manchu* (1958). By all accounts, these books became warnings about what all writers should avoid.

THEMES OF THE FUTURE

According to Peter Wolfe, in his books of the 1960s, Eric Ambler saw changes in the world of espionage and warned:

Actions have begotten reactions of equal force, creating a stand-off. No sooner will a break-through in the area of Top Secret military hardware occur than word of it will leak to the security agencies of other countries. The self-canceling rhythm created by this clash of surveillance and military hardware systems . . . leads to larger, more heavily financed spy networks creating an unstable climate in which spies spend increasingly more time watching each other. This expensive new order will be counter-productive. Rather than stopping treason, it will promote it by fostering a mood of suspicion, swelling the bureaucracy, and relying more and more upon machinery at the expense of people. (Wolfe 1993, 173)

Such comments were both remarkably prophetic and a clear sign that times had changed dramatically since the early years of the twentieth century. By the beginning of the cold war, the profession was far different from a time when an intelligence chief could describe "The Great Game" as "a capital sport." But popular perceptions of spying were influenced by and reflected in media other than the literature of Buchan, Greene, and Creasey. By the 1950s, the realm of espionage had changed in both peacetime and two world wars, along with the technology used in the field and in new means of propaganda. Literature, and principally British writers, laid the groundwork for new forms of entertainment and cerebral musing on the meaning of the covert world. But, in America, far more impact on English-speaking culture could be seen and heard in the airways of radio and the growing industry based in Hollywood.

3

On the Air, on the Screen, and in Word Balloons: Heroes on Radio and Film before the Cold War

There was a suspicion expressed that he might even have cut corners on a map reading exercise. It was one thing to be taught how to stalk an adversary and knife him silently with your hand over his mouth, but to deceive your instructors to avoid an unpleasant night exercise was immoral. . . . But for the officers who ran the S.O.E. . . . a man who cut corners was doubly welcome. They cut corners themselves when they could against their natural enemies, their natural enemies being the Army, the Navy, the Royal Air Force, the weather, the Free French, and a number of ministries and the Chief of Staff's committee.

Ted Allbeury, *The Lantern Network*

In America, espionage wasn't yet an important aspect of popular culture or national security at the beginning of the twentieth century. One indication of Washington's disinterest was that when World War I broke out, the United States had to hire the private Pinkerton Detective Agency to handle counter-espionage and protection from saboteurs for coastal cities. The government sanctioned volunteer groups like the American Protective League and the American Defense Society as quasi-official counter-spy organizations. On a more formal level, Congress passed the first Espionage Act in 1917 after a handful of Justice Department agents from a nameless agency had formed in 1908. Their mandate was to investigate individuals who'd opposed military conscription, sewed dissention within the armed forces, or willfully aided foreign adversaries. These agents were the seeds for the later FBI (Kessler 2002, 4–9).

After World War I, America's first "Red Scare" lasted from 1919 through 1920 when a number of bombs were mailed to U.S. officials. The most famous was the "Palmer Incident," where a terrorist blew himself up on the doorstep of U.S. Attorney General A. Mitchell Palmer. The first to investigate, and to step over the remains, was then secretary of the navy, Franklin Roosevelt (Barson and Heller 2001, 8). But when American fears about anarchists and Communists (few knew any distinction) dissipated, Washington backed away from dealing with spies. After World War I, if the United States had anything close to a national spy agency, J. Edgar Hoover's small Justice Department unit took care of the home front, while the inadequate Office of Naval Intelligence, formerly headed by espionage enthusiast Franklin Roosevelt, attempted to coordinate information about matters abroad (Persico 2001, 3).

During that era, American counter-spies were limited in what they could do. For example, Hoover's agents couldn't carry weapons and had no power of arrest because Congress feared creating a national police force subject to political whims (Kessler 2002, 5–19). Likewise, diplomats, their aides, and attachés were discouraged from intelligence gathering, which was considered unseemly, ungentlemanly conduct (Richelson 1995, 5–9). Much more ominously, in October 1929, Secretary of State Henry Stimpson disbanded the most successful covert office in the United States, Herbert Yardley's "Black Chamber" code-breakers. The new Herbert Hoover administration thought such work was unethical and believed "gentlemen don't read each other's mail." The Russians had other ideas; they established their first espionage network in 1924 with their Soviet Trade Mission. It found wide support from American socialists, who believed East and West should be "sharing information," a euphemism for spying. The work of Yardley's team was relegated to fiction, the basis for a 1935 NBC radio series. *Stories of the Black Chamber* featured future *Here's Lucy* costar Gale Gordon as a master spy (Britton 2004, 18).

Ironically, without intention, many American espionage operations reflected what was going on in the popular "Clubland" novels and stories of the era in which rich adventurers dealt with enemy spies without legal authority or any training in actual spycraft. During the 1930s, harbingers of things to come in fact and fiction could be seen in one unofficial group of "gentlemen amateurs" headed by Vincent Astor of the wealthy and well-connected New York Astor family. "The Room" was a band of businessmen, writers, and adventurers like Kermit Roosevelt, son of former president Theodore Roosevelt, who gathered informally to exchange information gained from their own international contacts (Persico 2001, 10). Among other guests, they invited writer W. Somerset Maugham to come and speak at their meetings, not because of his spy stories, but due to the fact that he had been a secret agent in World War I. All these distinguished dilettantes in espionage shared friendships with Franklin Roosevelt and supported his interventionist policies when he went to the White House in 1933. While their contributions to spycraft were negligible, they were among the president's private espionage network when he could not ask for help from a Congress dominated by an isolationist majority wishing to stay out of European concerns. As the *New York Times* editorialized in 1939, "No secret police is needed or wanted here" (Persico 2001, 10). Overseas intelligence assignments therefore tended to go to officers of independent means serving as military attachés as the depression had made available monies scarce. Roosevelt turned to whomever he could, including novelist John Steinbeck, who'd been asked by the president to spy in Mexico. Steinbeck later recalled that FDR "simply liked mystery, subterfuge, and indirect tactics for their own sake" (Persico 2001, 119).[1]

Because of such issues, America's preparations before Pearl Harbor were fragmented and largely uncoordinated. During the early months of America's involvement in World War II, Astor and John Franklin Carter ran independent operations, while former Pennsylvania governor and playboy George Earl also ran a spy ring for FDR. In 1939, "The Room" changed their name to "The Group," and Astor illegally began looking over telegraph traffic for intelligence. He lobbied hard to become the nation's official spymaster headquartered in New York, the country's commercial capital (Persico 2001, 15–25). John Franklin Carter had similar hopes, and his contacts did contribute to the effort during World War II. For example, Gerald Paxton, Somerset Maugham's secretary and lover, reported to Carter that transatlantic phone calls were a potential source of serious security breaches. As a result, other than embassy communications, this open line was terminated (Persico 2001, 200).

This isn't to say that nothing official was going on. In 1936,

Roosevelt asked J. Edgar Hoover to investigate both Communists and Nazi groups, although such intelligence gathering hadn't been normally in the FBI's purview. The FBI became the official agency investigating subversion, espionage, counter-espionage, and violations of neutrality laws. Hoover felt he had been so successful in building his files that he was certain he had rounded up all foreign spies in America within seventy-two hours after the bombing of Pearl Harbor. This belief led to the incarceration of 110,000 Japanese citizens in detention camps (Kessler 2002, 77). However, the professionals in British intelligence had other ideas. In 1940, Admiral John Godfrey, along with Commander Ian Fleming of the Royal Navy, came to the United States to look over America's intelligence capability. After seeing that the various military agencies weren't interested in sharing information and tended to sensationalize their reports, Godfrey decided, "There is no secret American intelligence service." Prefiguring similar comments regarding the CIA and Cable News Network (CNN) in later decades, the *New York Times*, he pronounced, was more reliable than any other source (Persico 2001, 80). While FDR moved toward abandoning neutrality, the president could not move too far ahead of a largely isolationist public, while Godfrey, Fleming, and Col. William Donovan quietly drafted a model for a centralized service with Donovan at the head. In meetings discouraged by Hoover, among the missions discussed was a plot to infiltrate North Africa and Spain called "Goldeneye," a term that would have several meanings in later James Bond mythology (Lycett 1995, 129–31).

In June 1940, the president finally signed the order establishing the roots of the significant Office of Strategic Services (OSS), the predecessor to the CIA (Persico 2001, 89). But the OSS was resisted by the various branches of the armed forces and the FBI. Again foreshadowing problems seen in later eras, turf wars were as much a part of wartime espionage as investigations into enemy capabilities. Twelve official agencies became involved in intelligence work (Persico 1990, 56). For his part, Donovan sought experts in many fields from academia to industry, including economists, geologists, political scientists, and writers such as the poet Archibald Mcleish (1990, 57). In addition, Donovan reached to Hollywood to create a Field Photographic Branch headed by Oscar-winning director John Ford. One actor involved in the OSS was Sterling Hayden, and future "French Chef"

Julia Child helped decode classified documents. American expatriate Josephine Baker, a popular singer and dancer, helped the French Resistance by carrying secret messages on sheet music (Allen 2002, 4–5).

The stories in this book are told by a former member of the United States Secret Service known as K-7. His adventures in the air as well as on land and sea in many countries is a thrilling document of the intrigue and espionage that exists among the nations of the world. Modesty compels the hero to disguise himself under another name, K-7. But only the principal actors in such gripping dramas could report them in such detail.

Gene Stafford, *Secret Agent K-7*

But before the formation of the OSS, one of the most dominant themes related to espionage broadcasts and films had come in 1935 when the Federal Bureau of Investigation was formally named and the FBI became a brand name. Suddenly there were "G-man radio shows, magazines, comic strips, advertising premiums, toys, and bubble gum cards. Immediately, J. Edgar Hoover eagerly looked to the media to promote himself and his agency. In the beginning, Hoover provided agents as consultants for Hollywood projects to blunt the work of ex-agent Melvin Purvis, who was seeking an income as a film advisor.

In 1935 alone, "Curt Gentry calculated there were 65 movies glorifying the FBI, the most popular being Warner Brothers' *G-Man* starring James Cagney" (Kessler 2002, 38). In a move foreshadowing the bureau's use of Hollywood to get its message out to the public, *G-Man* was viewed as a ploy to encourage public support for FBI agents gaining permission to carry firearms and make arrests, which had been denied them for over a decade (Schatz 1981, 102). A quick master of using celebrity status, Hoover sent information to columnist Walter Winchell, who promoted the FBI on his radio broadcasts, sharing "secret files" with "secret gossip" about film stars. In decades to come, Hoover encouraged photographs of himself with actors from Marilyn Monroe to Milton Berle, providing that no alcoholic drinks were present in the shots. Hoover was so worried about the image his agents presented that he forbade them from drinking coffee to give the public the illusion his G-men were dedicated supermen (Kessler 2002, 38). Hoover appeared as himself in two films, The *Next of Kin* (1942) and *House on 92nd Street* (1945).

On the other side of the coin, Hoover quickly used his position to pressure Hollywood on a number of levels. First, Hoover exercised censorship on film projects. By 1946, one studio censor stated in a letter to Alfred Hitchcock regarding *Notorious*, "I think you know the industry has had a kind of 'gentlemen's agreement' with Mr. J. Edgar Hoover wherein we have practically obligated ourselves to submit to him for his consideration and approval, stories which importantly involve the activities of the Federal Bureau of Investigation" (Gardner 1987, 88).[2] As intended, The FBI benefited in recruiting due to its involvement in Hollywood, as in the case of future agency director Louis Freeh. Before taking the top job in the bureau, Freeh told his father that he wanted to join the FBI because one of his favorite childhood shows was the Efrem Zimbalist, Jr. series, *The FBI* (Kessler 2002, 304).

But an issue that would become controversial in future decades also began in the FBI's formative years. From the beginning, Hoover used his agency to discourage political dissent, mixing his fears of subversion and espionage with violations of Constitutional rights. For example, in 1969, Hoover established the "Intlet" (Intelligence Letter) program seeking items of interest about celebrities for the Nixon White House. He kept files on Martin Luther King, Jr., Marlon Brando, Harry Belafonte, John Lennon, and sports heroes such as Joe Namath, Roosevelt "Rosey" Grier, Muhammad Ali, Joe Louis, and Mickey Mantle (Kessler 2002, 77). This program was an extension of earlier civil rights violations including Hoover's file on actor and director Charlie Chaplin, which had been kept from 1922 to 1952. As a result of the FBI's surveillance, the State Department refused to allow the distinguished director to reenter the United States after a film promotion tour (Belton 1994, 234). In short, Hoover wanted to exploit popular culture to aggrandize himself and secretly strike out at figures not sharing his national vision.[3]

SCIENCE FICTION AND COUNTER-SPIES ON RADIO

Despite his misuse and abuse of the film and broadcast industry, Hoover had good reasons for looking to Hollywood to achieve his goals. Before the advent of television, few Americans knew much about official or private espionage outside of what they heard and saw on popular media. But unlike British Islanders, spies were less often seen between book covers by English authors and more often in movie houses and over the airways. In the United States, Hollywood was far more influential than Fleet Street. Fanciful stories of espionage, often fused with science fiction and playful uses of strange technology, can be seen as far back as silent films. For example, researcher John Baxter noted that in *The Black Box* (1915), a detective invents a device allowing him to see who is calling him on the telephone. *The Secret of the Submarine* (1916) shows the hero and heroine cheating the Japanese out of a device that could extract oxygen out of water (Baxter 1970, 70). Some early silent films catered to popular fears of anarchist uprisings, as in D. W. Griffith's *Voices of the Violin* (1909) in which a gentle German émigré is duped into becoming a saboteur before true love saves him (Porton 1999, 17). Another early film exploiting the anarchist fears was the 1920 *Dangerous Hours* in which Bolsheviks attempt to stir up revolution in shipyards (Barson and Heller 2001, 9). One of the most highly regarded prewar spy films was director Fritz Lang's 1928 *Spione* (Spies). The fast-paced adventure focuses on a criminal posing as a famous banker in a plot to rule the world (Connors and Craddock 1999).

In the beginning of radio's Golden Age, popular magazine publishers used radio to promote their monthly offerings, as in Street and Smith's *Detective Story* featuring a character called "The Shadow," a hero who was no stranger to espionage-oriented adventures. Another important mold first seen in 1929 was *True Detective Mysteries*, the first radio detective show based on a magazine of the same name. This series was so popular it continued into the 1950s and set the stage for similar secret agent "true-life" adventures on film, radio, and television. The first wave of radio spies also came in the 1930s, when many series were broadcast locally before networks were created. In these early cheaply produced experiments, writers with little if any interest in film or literary espionage quickly dashed off formulaic scripts (Britton 2004, 18). Among the first network dramas with a wider audience was the National Broadcasting

Company's (NBC's) 1932 to 1933 *Secret Service Spy Stories*. Another notable early example was San Francisco-based *Dan Dunn, Secret Operative Number 48*. This 1937 fifteen-minute serial imitated the popular comic strip and radio series, *Dick Tracy*. Three new spy serials began in 1938: writer George Ludlam's *Spy at Large*, producer Himan Brown's *Spy Secrets* (both on NBC), and Mutual Broadcasting's four-year success, *Ned Jordon, Secret Agent*. Starring Jack McCarthy as an apparent agent for the FBI, Ned's cover was as a common laborer and accident investigator for a railroad. In this series, the coast-to-coast Federal Express was a major hookup for enemy spies. Each arrest led to a villain being hand-cuffed while hearing, "Uncle Sam wants you!"

While most such shows turned to World War II themes in 1939, seventy-two surviving copies of that year's *Secret Agent K-7 Returns* demonstrate that there was still listener interest in pre-Nazi villains brought down by unknown actors playing unidentified agents in stories narrated by former "number one adventurer" K-7. Apparently retired from his work in "22 countries," K-7 introduced fifteen-minute thinly scripted adventures in which men were always known by code-names (C, Z, B-9) and intrepid women by their first names (Rita, Pat, Yvonne). They all worked in unspecified countries for world peace. Reflecting public notions of the era, these investigators were invariably called "special agents," as the term "spy" was always used to describe enemies of a world that had seen one world war and didn't want another. K-7 began and ended each story with a sermon about the evils of spying as a pipe organ swelled behind his warnings.

Like *Dan Dunn*, another newspaper strip of special interest was the King Features syndicated *Secret Agent X-9*. Its creators were writer Dashiell Hammett, known for his Sam Spade detective stories, and illustrator Alex Raymond, the man behind the Flash Gordon series. According to Don Markstein, "The daily-only X-9 strip began on January 22, 1934," and was clearly inspired by the success of another strip, *Dick Tracy*. Perhaps another influence was the previous year's popular film *Private Detective 62*, based on a series of stories that appeared in the magazine *Black Mask*. Written by Raoul Whitfield, *62* was about a disgraced government agent, Donald Free, who became a private eye. Free was a predecessor to many later ex-agents turned private detectives, especially in the years after the fall of the Berlin Wall, such as television's *The Equalizer*.

From the outset, *Secret Agent X-9* suffered from creative differences between King Features, which wanted a mysterious spy strip, and Hammett, who preferred hard-boiled private investigators. X-9 wasn't given a name or an agency he worked for, although he called himself "Dexter" for a time. Because Hammett's dialog was edited to bring the strip more in line with King's preferences, he left after writing only four stories. Leslie Charteris, creator of "The Saint," succeeded him, but Charteris too stayed only a few months (Markstein 2001). Alex Raymond also moved on to other projects. In 1935, Charles Flanders helped shape the character into a "G-man" for the FBI. From 1940 to 1960, Mel Graff wrote and illustrated the strip, giving X-9 a name—Phil Corrigan. *Secret Agent Corrigan* was the strip's name until George Evans wrote the last episode published on February 10, 1996 (Markstein 2001).

While never a radio drama, X-9 was made into a Universal Studios feature-length movie in 1937 starring Scott Kolk, and a 1945 thirteen-part serial starring Lloyd Bridges. In 1939, Magic Comics began reprinting the strip into comic books (Markstein 2001). Best known for the talent who worked on the stories for more than fifty years, *Secret Agent X-9* was never a major success, but it did demonstrate public attitudes about the covert world. Agent Corrigan's origins were mired in uncertainty about whether or not spies could be heroes at all until Charles Flanders took the strip into the then popular vogue of G-man stories. Later, popular disfavor with the FBI and its director resulted in X-9 again working for an unnamed organization (Markstein 2001). Like James Bond, Phil Corrigan changed with the times, and later versions had little to do with the early serials crafted before both World War II and the cold war.

"You know why he liked old movies?"

"No."

"He thought that if he absorbed popular culture, he'd understand America more. He was proud to be an American. He said he'd lost the feel of being one. Plus, in movies there are clear lines and clean battles. The kind he grew up believing in. Not like in this world."

Two spies remembering a fallen colleague, in James Grady's *Thunder*

Among the many changes in popular thoughts on espionage, one important thread has been the role of women in literature, films, and fact. While director Cecil B. DeMille and Major Russell had fun discussing women in espionage as those likely to be defeated by jealousy and out-of-season petticoats during their 1937 Lux Theatre dialogue, the roles of female agents, both on- and offscreen, wouldn't remain mere laughing matters in popular culture. For many observers, few women could be seen as role models in fictional covert work until the 1960s, when characters like Modesty Blaise, Honey West, April Dancer, Agent 99, and especially Mrs. Emma Peel in television's *The Avengers* shattered the image of lovelorn undercover operatives. However, earlier sisters in spycraft shouldn't be overlooked in any appreciation of the espionage genre, most notably those in the films of Alfred Hitchcock. For example, the character of Pamela Steward, first played by Madeleine Carroll in the film version of *The 39 Steps* and later by Ida Lupino in the Lux radio broadcast, wouldn't fit Major Russell's description of intuitive females driven by passion. A character invented for the film and not in the Buchan novel, Steward keeps pace with the hero (played by Robert Donat in the film) each step of the way, meets him scripted line for witty line in each scene, and outthinks him as often as not. Steward is the one who discovers how to pick the lock of the handcuffs linking the two leads before they decide to marry, despite their preknowledge that they'll be fighting over breakfast, lunch, and dinner.

Of course, *The 39 Steps* wasn't intended to be a turning point in sexual equality, but gender issues were among the film's most discussed aspects for both contemporary and later viewers. As many critics have noted, for Hitchcock, espionage was a cover for his film's real concerns with sexuality. For example, the death of the prostitute/spy Annabella Smith (Lucie Manheim) in the opening scenes is a means to introduce the espionage plot but is juxtaposed against the introduction of Pamela Stewart as the heroine with more moral certainty in her characteristics. As Hannay tries to help Annabella, Pamela helps Hannay (Wood 1989, 274). "The dominant issue is one of trust between a leading man and a woman" (Spoto 1983, 160).

For some critics, *The 39 Steps* was the best synthesis of Alfred Hitchcock's techniques in his English films before his migration to Hollywood, including his best use of McGuffins during the 1930s. For example, the director admitted that, for him, handcuffs provide sexual connotations with a hint of perversion for moviegoers (Truffaut and Scott 1967, 35). One of his simplest McGuffins was the film's search for the enemy agent with the missing finger, a far simpler device than the original idea of having Richard Hannay looking over a hill to discover underground bunkers concealing hidden German planes. Again, sexual connotations have been claimed for the mutilated finger—it might be a symbol of castration. What is certain is that the director decided he couldn't resolve the dilemma that a scene with large bunkers would have presented for his innocent agent. Unlike later films in which pyrotechnics would become almost mandatory, Hitchcock felt Hannay wouldn't be able to blow up a secret air force (Truffaut and Scott 1967, 99). Instead, the story focused on small things and the relationship between his two bantering spies.

But even before Alfred Hitchcock had fun with sexual duels, novelist John Buchan knew well how life had changed for women after World War I. True, his fantasies included casting many "mysterious and evil women with hypnotic, magical properties" and shapely hands with "the suggestion of a curious power like the talons of a bird of prey" (Hitchens 2004, 105). On the other hand, a model for Pamela Steward could well have been Mary Hannay, the wife of the hero of the four Richard Hannay novels. In fact, unlike her husband, she was highly placed in British intelligence and gave her future lover orders during their first missions. In the third of these books, the trustworthy and experienced Mrs. Hannay explodes:

Why women aren't the feeble things men used to think them. They never were. And the war has made them like whipcord. Bless you my dear, we are the tougher sex now. We've had to wait and endure, and we've been so beaten on the anvil of patience that we've lost all of our meekliness. (Buchan 1988, 308)

For some critics, the use of leading ladies like Mary Hannay in spy fiction went beyond literary and film romance. According to Robin Winks, when women were introduced into better projects, the hero often had to accept a wider dimension of responsibility, the women adding meaning and emotional consequence to his actions (1982, 50). But, to be fair, B movies like *After Tonight* (1933), *The British Agent* (1933), *The Emperor's Candlesticks* (1937), and *Espionage* (1937) featured beautiful, if tough and ideological, Russian spies gifted in the use of invisible inks, secret jewelry compartments, and seductive wiles. As Hollywood was often ambivalent about Communist ideology in the 1930s, such stories were merely love-conquers-all yarns. The exotic girls inevitably fell under the spell of English-speaking one-dimensional men of courage and character (Strada and Troper 1997, 22–25).

Romance often won over politics for various reasons. One film about the Spanish Civil War, *Blockade* (1938), was designed to be a warning about the spread of Fascism in Europe. However, distribution of the film was undermined by pressure from the Roosevelt administration which didn't yet wish to be seen taking sides in the war in an era when anti-Fascism was often seen as either a pro-Communist stance or an idea advocated by Communist dupes (Belton 1994, 234). Equally important was the knowledge that romantic entertainment did better at the box office than either subtle or overt propaganda. In the end, the movie was diluted into a simple love story between an idealistic farmer (Henry Fonda) and a beautiful spy (Madeleine Carroll) working for the unstated "other side" (Belton 1994, 234).

Other captivating ladies appeared in World War II projects, such as *Miss V from Moscow* (1943), a seventy-minute B movie with a beautiful Russian spy (Lola Lane) infiltrating the Nazis in Paris armed with brains, guile, and a tight skirt. On radio, Marlene Dietrich's *Time for Love* reportedly included many spy encounters. Ironically, the actual FBI had investigated her to see if she was a Nazi agent, despite the fact that she had recorded a number of pop songs as propaganda for the OSS to be broadcast in Germany (Allen 2002, 5). She was not a Nazi—the bureau only uncovered her lesbian affairs. NBC's 1950 *Top Secret* starred sultry voiced Hungarian actress Ilona Massey as a Mata Hari–style operative before and during World War II in one of the darkest series aired.

In other above-average efforts, women were allowed to come to the fore in spy stories, a genre that didn't always confine the so-called gentler sex to the home, as secretaries in the workplace, or as mere ornamental admirers of male superiority. Espionage yarns took women out of traditional settings and required them to be more than temptresses or second fiddles to James Bond and his imitators. For example, Hitchcock's first spy film, *The Man Who Knew Too Much*

(1934), starring Peter Lorre, Edna Bess, and Leslie Banks, also contained motifs and concepts inspired by Buchan, although the story was adapted from a Bulldog Drummond adventure that, in turn, was based on an actual breakup of an assassination attempt by anarchists involving Winston Churchill (Truffaut and Scott 1967, 63). In the words of Hitchcock's daughter, Pat Hitchcock O'Connell, the Bulldog Drummond inspiration was like "an amateur James Bond" and the film's title was taken from a G. K. Chesterson collection of short stories that had nothing to do with the script. According to Hitchcock himself, Buchan strongly influenced his work before *The 39 Steps* "and some of it is reflected in *The Man Who Knew Too Much*" (Truffaut and Scott 1967, 63). In this script, filmed in just under ten weeks, the Lawrences, a married couple, witness the murder of a friend who turns out to have been a British agent with information about an assassination attempt written on a paper hidden in a shaving brush. The "Fourth Circle," a society using hypnotism and kidnapping to control its agents, blackmail the couple to keep this information secret. In this version of the tale, it's the mother who saves the day, as she is the crack shot in the family. As with *The 39 Steps*, Hitchcock liked the device of ordinary people overtaken by a "sudden eruption of terror," this time in the lives of a couple rather than an individual. The director again sandwiched two concerns together—blending the worries arising about Hitler from news reports coming from Switzerland and audience desires to see light comic relationships. The confusing rumors and vague fears circulating around a hotel dining room gave Hitchcock material to give his story an atmosphere tense with mystery (Spoto 1983, 159).[4]

In 1936, Hitchcock again turned to Madeleine Carroll as his heroine in *Secret Agent*. Based very loosely on two stories by W. Somerset Maugham and a play by Cameron Dixon, this human drama explores how agents can lose their personal identities in the name of a mission or cause. Again, Carroll's female agent is no mere two-dimensional stereotype, although she quickly learns that her primary function is to help provide cover for her fictional husband, Richard Ashenden (Sir John Gielgud). She seeks thrills and excitement in spying and claims not to be the "ministering angel type." She has to be reminded that her mission is to hunt a man, not a fox.

But just who the "secret agent" of the film's title is becomes ambiguous when Gielgud's Mr. Ashenden (clearly not modeled after the character in Maugham's stories) attempts to resign. He states that fighting on the front lines is cleaner work than espionage. However, Mrs. Ashenden's guise as a giddy, neglected wife turns out to be how she stays "three steps ahead" of other agents, and she is the team member to trap the German spy (Robert Young). A precursor to many later espionage outings, *Secret Agent* features a Swiss mountain setting, a train chase, and casino scenes as the hero and heroine chase a Nazi to Constantinople. As it happened, Hitchcock felt *Secret Agent* was largely unsuccessful because the film's ostensible hero is a reluctant agent who considers his mission distasteful. While he admired Maugham's simple writing style, Hitchcock believed audiences couldn't relate to such characters (Truffaut and Scott 1967, 68, 239). Ironically, the director's remarks were made in 1967 during a decade when such characteristics were becoming a dominant trend in spy films and fiction. But when the film was originally released, it was criticized not for the characters but for what Graham Greene saw as too much melodrama. To be fair, Greene disliked most of Hitchcock's films of the era, believing the director had ruined *The 39 Steps* because Hitchcock had an underdeveloped sense of realism (Greene 1980, 1). In the case of *Secret Agent*, Greene thought the audience should laugh at the sequence of unlikely scenes, as in the occasion when a spy loudly shares his orders in a voice easily overheard by anyone passing by (Greene 1980, 74–75).

On the other hand, 1938's *The Lady Vanishes* is still regarded as one of the director's best films of the period, although Hitchcock had little to do with the script for a movie filmed in but five weeks (Spoto 1983, 191). Based on a book by Ethel White, *The Wheel Spins*, the plot involves Iris Henderson, a young English girl (Margaret Lockwood) who meets a charming old lady, Miss Froy (Dame May Whittey) on a train. Froy disappears, Iris seeks to find her, but everyone on the train claims never to have seen any such lady. It turns out that Froy is a counterespionage agent carrying a secret message and the train is full of spies. Iris discovers the plot with the help of a young musician, Gilbert (Michael Redgrave). According to the director, this film was one of his best uses of "implausibles"—why would anyone entrust a vulnerable, helpless woman with an important message encoded in bars of a song (Truffaut and Scott 1967, 94)?

Of course, not all of Hitchcock's spy films dealt with gender issues. When Hitchcock came to America before the outbreak of World War II in Europe, he claimed he had trouble making adventure films because, at that time, Hollywood relegated such projects to "B movie status," which meant the best actors and writers were rarely available to him; they had been in England, where such films were held in higher regard (Truffaut and Scott 1967, 96, 109). For example, when Hitchcock completed the script to *Foreign Correspondent* (1940), he approached Gary Cooper, who turned down doing any thrillers. Instead, Joel McCrea took the lead as reporter Johnny Jones sent to Europe in 1939. He joins a loose group of "gifted amateurs" who take out a spy ring with limited help from professionals. The "McGuffin" is a secret clause in a peace treaty which, it turns out, becomes meaningless when World War II erupts in the final moments. As would become typical of Hitchcock thrillers, unused scenes from Buchan's *The 39 Steps* were incorporated into the script. Praised by Charles Higham as perhaps Hitchcock's best American film, distinguished by William Cameron Menzies's art direction, "Hitchcock has seldom equaled its parade of brilliantly inventive set pieces—the famous assassination of the phony diplomat from Holland with a gun hidden in a camera, the sinister windmill, its sails revolving as a signal to a plane . . . the death of Edmund Quinn falling to his doom in an attempt to push Joel McCrea off Westminster Cathedral," and the final plane crash, "a marvel of special effects" (Higham and Greenberg 1968, 99). While designed as entertainment, the film's final scene was reshot with McCrea pleading over a radio broadcast for American intervention in the war. In 1940, this topical reference turned out to be a case of art again foreshadowing reality (Spoto 1983, 244).

Unmasking the man behind your back.
From a promotional poster for *Saboteur*

Hitchcock's *Saboteur* (1942) was a film stressing the message that there are "traitors among us." Hitchcock believed that *Saboteur* had few virtues since he had little control in casting. In that film, largely a remake of *The 39 Steps* with the hero crossing America instead of England, a young worker in a munitions factory (Robert Cummings) is wrongly accused of sabotage. In this ordinary manhunt adventure, Cummings was badly cast as the hero, an actor more suited for light comedy and unable to convey anguish on the screen (Truffaut and Scott 1967, 104). Unlike most of Hitchcock's other spy projects, *Saboteur* was made during wartime, so the espionage elements superceded human relationships (Wood 1989, 274). The director wanted the story to point to the evil of a group called the "American Firstists," actually a Fascist group, but was forced to settle for a more traditional heavy, as he couldn't hire a first-class actor in the villain role.[5]

While Hitchcock believed that Priscilla Lane was also unsuitable, she is remembered for helping out at the dramatic scene at the Statue of Liberty, a clear precursor to the Mount Rushmore climax in *North by Northwest* (Truffaut and Scott 1967, 104–45). Still, *Saboteur* had above average comic moments provided by writer Dorothy Parker, notably the circus freaks on the train, and one nod to sexual equality. Both the hero and heroine are seen escaping as individuals before teaming up for escapes as a pair.

It's worth observing that the British director was able to make such quality efforts even in often exploitative subgenres of espionage films. According to John Baxter, *The Whip Hand* (1952), a germ warfare horror flick, was the last gasp of the Nazi Spy cycle, which ran from 1940 to 1950. In the case of *The Whip Hand*, the Nazis were improbably working for the Communists (led by Red agent Raymond Burr) as they devised a deadly bacteria in the Wisconsin woods. Baxter claimed that the Korean War ended the fashion for movie stories about German communities plotting revenge in isolated country towns, Nazi beasts planning for a comeback, and the ferreting out of concentration camp commandos in Argentina (1970, 66). While the cycle lasted, notable efforts included Hitchcock's highly regarded *Notorious* (1946). On one level, Ben Hecht's screenplay was a character study of a love affair between a stoic American agent (Cary Grant) and a disreputable daughter of an American Nazi (Ingrid Bergman). The film played on the "patriotic spy" motif, with Bergman's Alicia Huberman claiming that such spies wave the flag with one hand while picking pockets with the other. Still, Huberman works for her country despite mixed motives, and nearly dies for her efforts, forced to marry a German agent in Brazil seeking secrets to build an atomic bomb.

As much a love-triangle story as an espionage yarn, Hitchcock admitted that he looked for simplicity in the film's production. "As a rule, there's a good deal of violence in movies dealing with espionage and here we tried to avoid that" (Truffaut and Scott 1967, 121). The attempted murder of Bergman's heroine was by means of arsenic poisoning, a commonplace device used in countless mystery tales. "Usually," Hitchcock said, "when film spies are trying to get rid of someone, they don't take so many precautions. They shoot a man down, or take him for a ride in some isolated spot and simulate an accident . . . here there was an attempt to make the spies behave with reasonable evil" (Truffaut and Scott 1967, 122).

As it happened, *Notorious* was a film that both flaunted and bowed to censorship pressures of the era. While Hollywood held a thirty-second limit for on-screen kisses, Hitchcock had Bergman pecking on Grant while he was on the phone for nearly three minutes. According to Gerald Gardner, "Hitchcock managed to inject a healthy dose of sex into a genre where it seldom found a home, the counter-spy adventure" (1987, 86). Under a pervading atmosphere of menace, Bergman uses her sex appeal to invade a den of Nazis although, as Gardner noted, the "Madonna-faced" Bergman was cast because studio censors wanted to play down the call-girl characteristics that writer Ben Hecht had in the original script. The role of Alicia Huberman was "scrubbed clean" from a prostitute to a gold-digger. In the final version, Bergman relies more on her wits than her body. Still, one group of censors banned the picture because of its casual treatment of marriage, the film portraying a woman marrying to uncover secrets while carrying on an immoral relationship with her lover (Gardner 1987, 88).

Notorious was also important because it predated the trend for "atomic bomb" films, going into production before the first blasts that ended World War II. The uranium ore and "atomic sands" in the film might have been typical Hitchcock "McGuffins" with no meaning in their use, or, as Michael Grost suggests, they were indeed means to convey social commentary. For example, Hitchcock returned to then current fears in the atomic age in two of his last films, *The Torn Curtain* (1966) and *Topaz* (1969) (Grost 2003). However, Hitchcock claimed he used the McGuffin as a last resort. According to Hitchcock, the original idea was to have the Nazis building a secret army of German refugees, but he couldn't figure out what they'd do with such an army. He decided that he could create a visual device with uranium ore in wine bottles despite objections from the studio (Truffaut and Scott 1967, 120–21). While the director was aware of work on the atomic bomb before the first tests, few Hollywood executives knew of these plans. According to Hitchcock, he'd have been willing to substitute industrial diamonds used to cut weapons—as usual, the device wasn't important to him (Truffaut and Scott 1967, 121). Ironically, after the film's release, he visited an atomic laboratory and asked about the size of an atomic bomb. After being warned that such information was top secret, the director said the FBI placed him under surveillance for three months (Truffaut and Scott 1967, 121). Later documents cast doubt on Hitchcock's fears, but it was true the film's producer, David O. Selznick, had received a letter from the State Department stating that any movie using American agents would have to be cleared by the government before it could be exported, a primary reason the film's McGuffin was minimized (Spoto 1983, 301).

On another level, *Notorious* has been seen as an early example of the film noir movement reflecting a dark postwar mood in America. Such films focused on sexual ambiguity and the changing roles of women, fears of atomic annihilation, and a new ideology casting Communists as the symbols of alienation and dehumanization (Schatz 1981, 112). Other such films that year included director Fritz Lang's *Cloak and Dagger* (1946). Another notable effort cited by Thomas Schatz from 1946 was *The Stranger* starring Edward J. Robinson, Loretta Young, and Orson Welles as Professor Charles Rankin who is actually ex-Nazi Franz Kindler hiding out in Hartford, Connecticut. The small-town atmosphere didn't suffer from the small budget that was given the film, and the script revitalized the dropping reputation of Welles (Connors and Craddock 1999). But the genre of hidden Germans in sleepy American towns largely disappeared from the big screen, while ex-Nazis and neo-Nazi story lines continued until the 1970s.

MORE BRITISH SPIES ON THE LARGE SCREEN

Lest anyone think Alfred Hitchcock stood alone in the forefront of pre–World War II spy filmmakers, quality undercover adventures were created by other British directors such as Michael Powell, Carol Reed, and Tim Whelan, the man behind the popular *Q Planes* (1939). (Later, actor Patrick Macnee claimed that Ralph Richardson's role in *Q Planes* was one influence on his portrayal as John Steed in television's *The Avengers*.) Such films tended to mix thrills with comedy, especially comedies of manners, avoiding the puzzle plots of mystery and detective movies (Grost 2003). Notable exceptions included overt propaganda films such as Powell's 1939 *The Spy in Black*, retitled *U-Boat 29* in the United States. Starring Conrad Veidt, Valerie Hobson, and Sebastian Shaw, the plot (based on the novel by J. Storer Clouston) revolved around a German submarine commander assigned to spy on the British in the Orkney Islands (Connors and Craddock 1999). Powell's follow-up film, *Contraband* (1940), reflected the trend for realist motifs like those in hard-boiled detective stories (Grost 2003).

At last we had the screws on Harbin and we twisted them until he squealed. This kind of police work is very similar to secret service work. You look for a double agent whom you can really control and Harbin was the man for us.

Graham Greene, The Third Man

Carol Reed, of course, is best known for his 1949 film version of Graham Greene's *The Third Man* (1950) set in postwar Vienna when the city was occupied by the four Allied forces—American, British, French, and Russian. Noted for many outstanding classic movie moments, such as the memorable Anton Karas dulcimer title theme, the underground sewer sequence, and the introduction of Orson Welles as black-market drug dealer Harry Lime, the movie remains a major portrayal of national loyalties during the cold war (Connors and Craddock 1999). *The Third Man*, as a film, was something of an anomaly in the process of dramatizing a Greene story for the screen. As the novelist admitted, the movie was better than the book. One important change was dropping a scene where the Russian secret police kidnap Harry Lime's girlfriend, Anna Schmidt. Both Reed and Greene worried that this would make the movie seem like a propaganda piece (Greene 1977, iii). "We had no desire," Greene wrote, "to move people's political emotions. We wanted to entertain them, to frighten them a little, to make them laugh" (Greene 1977, iii). Because of such alterations from Greene's short treatment, the film had fewer espionage elements and instead used Vienna as an atmospheric backdrop. Still, "spycraft" was evident in the secret means Lime and others used to make contacts, disappearing in the sewers to escape to the Russian zone which evoked similar escapes in another occupied city—Berlin.

The film and book had little to do with two later radio series employing either Greene's characters or simply the famous title. Orson Welles continued the Lime character in one radio series of short stories that was published by the News of the World in adventures set before Lime's death in the movie. Later, another *Third Man* starred Hollywood heartthrob, Douglas Fairbanks, Jr. He played a variety of nameless "silent" risk-taking federal agents from 1951 to 1952. He worked for the Departments of Commerce, Immigration, and the Postal Service, but mostly anonymous secret agencies (Dunning 1998, 50).

Greene and Reid collaborated on other films, including *Our Man in Havana* (1960) starring Alec Guinness, Noel Coward, Burl Ives, Maureen O'Hara, and Ralph Richardson. One unlikely reviewer for the film, Ian Fleming, took the opportunity to discuss the changes in fictional espionage. In Fleming's words, the old-fashioned idea of spying where the codebook is always purloined by the embassy valet is dead. Today's secret services didn't need to uncover the numbers of tanks or design of bombs; weapon details were known. "Therefore," Fleming said, "any book or play about the secret service had to be either incredible or farcical." Fleming observed of the man then giving him useful literary business advice, Greene "takes the splendid myth of centuries and kicks it deliriously downstairs" (Lycett 1995, 362). Other Greene stories to be filmed included *This Gun for Hire* (a.k.a. *A Gun for Sale*), which first appeared in print in 1936. The first movie version was released in 1942, directed by Frank Tuttle, starring Alan Ladd, Veronica Lake, and Robert Preston. Director James Gagney's version came out in 1957, and a television movie was broadcast in 1991 starring Robert Wagner. *The Ministry of Fear* (1944), directed by Fritz Lang, starred Ray Milland, Marjorie Reynolds, Carl Esmond, and Hilary Brooke. The 1939 novel, *The Confidential Agent*, became a film in 1945 starring Charles Boyer, Lauren Bacall, and Peter Lorre. Greene's *The Quiet American* (1955) was another story reworked by various directors. Joseph Mankiewicz's 1958 version starred war hero

Audie Murphy, Michael Redgrave, and Claude Dauphin; Phillip Noyce tried the story again in 2002, featuring Michael Caine and Brendan Fraser.[6] In October 2004, Turner Classic Movies broadcast a documentary, *Shadowing the Third Man*, as part of their 100th anniversary celebration of Greene's birth. Along with airings of the film, seven other Greene movies were broadcast, including *Ministry of Fear* and *The Confidential Agent*.

During his career, Graham Greene was not only a novelist and scriptwriter, he was also a noted film critic for *The Spectator*. He had little praise for spy films of the 1930s, including British director Anthony Asquitch's *Moscow Nights* (1935), which Greene saw as a film riddled with worn-out cliches. These included Volga boatmen and quaint gypsies in this tale of an elderly, genteel spy (Athene Syiler) getting secrets in a hospital (Greene 1980, 35–36). The film was released in the same year in the United States as *I Stand Condemned*. For some critics, it was perhaps an indication that something was askew in the Russian judicial system (Barson and Heller 2001, 19). In the same year, Greene damned *The Second Bureau*, a film about dueling French and German secret services for much the same reason. Like other films of the era, the script included the obligatory car chase and a beautiful Russian spy falling in love with an English agent. For Greene, the film overflowed with melodrama, with two murders, a suicide, routine destruction in the opening sequence—an overabundance of violence. Such films, Greene wrote, would be better if they were satirical rather than bungled romance (Greene 1980, 36). For this reason, he preferred the film with the unlikely title, *The Sequel to the Second Bureau* (1936) in which German spies stole a weapons cartridge from the French. In the plot to recover the cartridge before the Germans can analyze it, in Greene's opinion, the film had light charm and malicious humor, as the audience knew the weapon had limited importance.

Thus, all the maneuvers to protect it were clearly overdone (Greene 1980, 136–7). Greene had little interest in *Dark Journey* (1937), a World War I love story about a fashionable dressmaker and double agent (Vivien Leigh) working for the French in Sweden. Wanting to escape the lies of her double life, she falls in love with a German spymaster, Conrad Veidt. In the end, he winds up in French prison after rescuing her from a German submarine (Greene 1980, 140–41). One

1947 effort, *British Intelligence*, was apparently missed by Greene. It starred Boris Karloff as a butler-spy in one of the best dramas of the period.

THE AMERICAN SPIN

Graham Greene wasn't alone in his criticism of spy movies of the 1930s and 1940s. Of course, by design, many World War II endeavors were cranked out to satisfy government interests in supporting the war. Few studios expected large revenues from them. According to Charles Higham, while British producers tended to mix propaganda with quality productions, "Hollywood responded [to the war] with spy melodramas that often bordered on the surreal spinning over into a comedy that was sometimes intentional, sometimes not" (Higham and Greenberg 1968, 99). In one intentionally comic effort, Hitchcock collaborator Ben Hecht took a turn at lampooning Communists in *Soak the Rich* (1936) in which the forces of good opposed the Society for the Preservation of Monsters (Porton 1999, 23). Actress Joan Crawford, in Charles Higham's opinion, starred in two films with less obvious intentions, *Reunion in France* (1942) and *Above Suspicion* (1943). In the former, she stars as a Parisian who stoically gives as good as she gets to the German overlords. In the latter, she partnered with Fred MacMurray in "a hairbrained expedition to southern Germany to discover a magnetic mine formula." Information was exchanged in a bookstore, "always a reliable venue for espionage activity" (Higham and Greenberg 1968, 102–103).

Other German-set adventures included Vincent Sherman's *Underground* (1941), which had Mona Maris rifling Hermann Goering's private desk for incriminating papers. The same director's *All Through the Night* (1942) featured Humphrey Bogart and Judith Anderson in a "side-splitting domestically located German spy yarn" with a brilliant auction scene (Higham and Greenberg 1968, 102). *World Premiere* (1941) was another "comic masterpiece" featuring German subversives sent to Hollywood to disrupt the film industry. Starring John Barrymore and Frances Farmer, the film's spies, played by the diminutive Fritz Feld and the giant Sig Rumann, subdue a lion by tying a knot in its tail. One scene in which they slip a "mad Kraut propaganda film into cans containing producer John Barrymore's latest celluloid sensation had an inspired zaniness" (Higham and Greenberg 1968, 105).

During the 1940s, many spy adventures first appeared as serials, shown in parts so that audiences would return to theaters each weekend to catch up with the adventures of heroes left in cliff-hangers the week before. One example was *Spy Smasher* (1942), which was originally shown in twelve parts. In the story, a war reporter uses his supposed death and his twin brother to go underground and try to destroy the German economy. The same year, *Spy Smasher Returns* starring Cane Richmond, Marguerite Chapman, and Sam Flint was released as a full motion picture. However, it was not a sequel, but rather a condensation of the serial (Connors and Craddock 1999).

One film that rose above the pack was *House on 92nd Street* (1945), the title taken from the address of a German spy leader. Shot in documentary style, with newsreel footage inserted to augment the film's realism, the story centered on a federal investigator named George Briggs (Lloyd Nolan) aiding a German student contacted by Nazis. A precursor to similar outings in the 1950s, an atomic bomb scientist is a Nazi agent, merging concerns of a war winding down and one about to begin. The production was clearly intended to reassure the American public that J. Edgar Hoover's agents were ready to stop the nefarious hidden threats to America, both those recently past and now beginning to seep up from under the woodwork.

Russia is a never-never land of steppes, samovars, and spies. Beards, bears, bombs, and borscht where almost anything can happen and usually does.

Prologue to *Comrade X*

In a decade when enemies shifted dramatically from Pearl Harbor to the aftermath of VE day, moviemakers were occasionally caught up in major political demands. During World War II, Hollywood's contributions to the war effort included *Confessions of a Nazi Spy* (1939), which at first blasted Russia's invasion of Finland. In the story, German agents in Scotland, Germany, and America operated in an implausible plot to kidnap German Americans and send them back to the Fatherland. In the script, German girls were pressured to do their maternal duty for the state (Greene 1980, 229). But after the Soviet Union became an ally in the war, the film was withdrawn and then edited with offensive scenes cut. Likewise, *Mission to Moscow* (1943) was an unusual propaganda film inspired by President Roosevelt's desire to stimulate interest in a land-lease program to benefit the Russian military (Strada and Troper 1997, 43). The script was based on the 1941 best-selling memoir of the same name by former ambassador to the Soviet Union Joseph E. Davies, who was played by Walter Huston in the movie. The book was also a clear plea to support Stalin despite Davies' eyewitnessing of the results of Stalin's bloody purges (Barson and Heller 2001, 9). Other pro-Soviet films included *Comrade X* (1940) starring Clark Gable, and the aforementioned *Miss V from Moscow* (1943). During the war, the Soviet embassy was invited to look over these scripts before filming. After the war, these efforts had to be reedited and retitled when former allies became the new enemies (Strada and Troper 1997, 49). When the McCarthy era was in full stride, the crafters of propaganda found themselves having to defend their wartime efforts when Communists replaced Nazis as the new breed of international warmongers. Less controversial were some films set in the recent past, as in 1946's *O.S.S.*, starring Alan Ladd as John Martin, a would-be spy for the World War II Office of Strategic Services. Geraldine Fitzgerald plays his female partner, who parachutes with him into France to destroy train tracks as the Gestapo chases them. The actual OSS allowed Paramount to look over their files for story ideas, and ex-agents acted as film consultants (Connors and Craddock 1999). Ironically, former OSS chief "Wild Bill" Donovan provided an introduction for the film, and his notes would have been written at the same time President Truman was making it clear that Donovan wouldn't be his choice to head the coming CIA.

In the same year, the OSS also provided realism by providing actual footage for *13 Rue Madeleine*, a film starring James Cagney leading a group of French fighters battling the Gestapo in Paris. The small band (played by Annabella, Red Buttons, and E. G. Marshall) looks for a secret Nazi missile base while worrying about which one of them is a dirty double. Like similar projects, the script blended realism with propaganda, notably the early scenes showing agent training. But this film was more controversial than the Ladd vehicle, as one scene has a French Resistance operative knifing a Nazi in the back. This was not only unsportsmanlike, but the situation mirrored a real stabbing in which an actual German was considered more honorable than his fellows in occupied France. In another scene, Cagney machine-guns unarmed soldiers, reflecting his monologue earlier in the film in which he states that this new war isn't for gentlemen. Richard Hannay would not have approved.

ROBIN HOOD WAS A NAZI

One startling revelation that came out years after World War II was the role of actor Errol Flynn in espionage. According to one source, Joseph Persico, Flynn was barred from service in the OSS after the swashbuckler wrote FDR claiming he'd be a useful spy in Ireland because of his unique fame. "If I were to go there openly as a Hollywood figure in an American Army uniform," Flynn allegedly wrote, "I would be far less suspected of gathering information than the usual sort of agent" (Persico 2001, 187). But, according to Persico, Flynn had shown past sympathies with Nazi figures, and Irish neutrality was in continual question. However, according to Charles Higham's detailed and well-researched *Errol Flynn: The Untold Story* (1980), which didn't mention the FDR letter, Flynn was a Nazi spy of both long duration and of some importance. Using his star status, Flynn reportedly manipulated Eleanor Roosevelt to block deportation of a Nazi agent. He likely drove the same agent to Mexico to avoid arrest. From 1933 on, British intelligence maintained files on Flynn, and observed that while the actor was working on *The Adventures of Robin Hood* in 1937, he made a trip to Berlin where he allegedly met with Rudolf Hesse and Martin Bormann and began work as a subagent, that is, a collaborator helping set the groundwork for Gestapo agents in California.

A number of unusual circumstances surrounded Flynn before the war years. U.S. Naval Intelligence was nervous about Flynn and his employers, Warner Brothers, and tried to block access to their San Diego base for filming the ostensible propaganda film, *Dive Bomber*. But because of Flynn's White House connections, the secretary of the navy overruled these objections. The final cut of the movie included scenes shot on the base, as well as Flynn's own camerawork around Pearl Harbor. Possibly, the Japanese found these reels useful in their plans to bomb Pearl Harbor along with Flynn's observations on harbor and shore conditions (Higham 1980, 22, 210, 213). During the war, Hoover was suspicious of Flynn's activities and had the actor under FBI surveillance for years, but withheld any action for reasons uncertain and undocumented.

At the time, Nazi sympathizers weren't hard to find in Hollywood, Higham reports, and "strong elements" tried to stop production of *Keeper of the Flame*, one anti-Nazi production (1980, 131). While Warner Brothers promotions said otherwise, Flynn avoided military service, ignoring a summons from Winston Churchill when hostilities erupted in England. Instead, Flynn joined the leading men ostensibly doing propaganda work in movies such as *Desperate Journey* (1942). In one of the many ironies surrounding Flynn, the actor bitterly complained when future Cold Warrior Ronald Reagan stole a scene in which a brave American stood up to Raymond Massey's sneering Gestapo interrogator. In *Edge of Darkness* (1943), Flynn plays a Norwegian fisherman leading a local underground with the help of his loyal fiancée Ann Sheridan. Based on the novel by William Woods, the film is remembered for its troubled set but better-than-average performances (Connors and Craddock 1999). Before America joined the war effort, Flynn apparently also worked as a secret agent for Spanish Nazis, a real-life foreshadowing of his 1952 radio series, *The Modern Adventures of Casanova*, lover Christopher Casanova that is. Trying to live down the reputation of his famous Italian ancestor, Christopher was a secret agent with a secret identity familiar with the drawing rooms of the rich and famous for "Worldpol," the "World Criminal Police Commission" (Britton 2004, 19). Flynn also played spymaster Mahbub Ali in *Kim* (1951), filmed in India in 1948.[7]

Returning to Ronald Reagan's Hollywood work, it's worth noting that some observers in the 1980s and beyond wondered if another Reagan film, *Murder in the Air* (1940), might have influenced the creation of the president's "Star Wars" defense shield policy. In the script, secret agent "T-Man" Brass Bancroft (Reagan) impersonates a dead saboteur to find out his mission. Turns out, he is to board the USN airship *Mason*, which is testing the super secret Inertia Projector, which can destroy all incoming bombs before they hit the United States. In the film, Reagan saves the device. It worked in the film—why not in real life? Actually, the movie was Reagan's second outing as an airborne spy. In 1939, he also starred in *Secret Service of the Air*.

Black warfare. Espionage. International intrigue. These are the weapons of the OSS. Today's story . . . is suggested by actual incidents recorded in the Washington files of the Office of Strategic Services. A story that can now be told.
Opening narration to radio drama *Cloak and Dagger*

Perhaps the greatest changes shown in both fiction and fact came with innovations in technology in ways beyond scripts and how they were delivered on broadcast media. According to intelligence expert John Keagan, the beginning of real-time espionage—that is, gaining information in sufficient time to use it—began at the advent of radio, when war on sea and air changed in World War I (Persico 2003, 10). By World War II, the power of this medium was important in several ways.

First, when World War II began, radio broadcasting had become a competitive industry. Scripts and production values were a far cry from the earlier experimental local offerings. One important trend was quasi-realism, which helped give radio shows credibility and an excuse to use violence in the name of public information. Every fictional hero from Sherlock Holmes to Tom Mix was called to do battle with "Gerrys" and "Japs" as part of wartime propaganda. In addition, broadcast codes asked radio stations to censor newscasts, ad lib or audience talk shows, and foreign language shows in German or Italian to ensure that secret messages weren't being sent via the airways (Macdonald 1985, 10).

Among radio's less-moralistic efforts during the 1940s and 1950s were series like *The Man Called* X (CBS, 1944–1952) starring Herbert Marshall as Ken Thurston, an American intelligence agent sent around the globe to deal with foreign intrigue. As the show's narrator said each week before a live studio audience, Thurston travels today "where you and I will travel tomorrow." Mister X's sidekick, Pagon Celdschmidt (Leon Belasco), was a comic character that evolved during the series. Thurston liked seductive women with mysterious pasts; Celdschmidt was a larcenist who worked when the money was right (Dunning 1998, 344). Realism wasn't the point. When the pair traveled to Lisbon, the Portuguese women had clear midwestern accents. The concept made for a short-lived syndicated television series in 1956 starring Barry Sullivan. Known for intrigue rather than romance, one fondly remembered episode featured X taking on a gang of female spies (Britton 2004, 22).

From 1943 to 1944, Brian Barry (Jay Jostynn) and Carol Manning (Vicki Vola), the former leads in the popular *Mr. District Attorney*, took on the Gestapo in *Foreign Assignment* for Mutual. Taking its cue from Hitchcock's *Foreign Correspondent*, this series established the format of reporters as spies (Dunning 1998, 275). Similarly, the very popular radio show *Counterspy* was aired on NBC, CBS, Mutual, and the Blue Network from 1942 to 1957. In the series, David Harding (Don MacLaughlin), assisted by Peters (Mandel Kramer), is the head of U.S. counterintelligence, seeking out Gestapo agents, members of the Japanese Black Dragon, and criminals on home soil. The series featured guest agents always identifying themselves as "counterspies," even when investigating drug smugglers or other crimes not related to espionage. In the pre-Miranda era, these agents often beat their prey to get information or confessions. One possible reason for the series' longevity was its tendency to upstage news stories. One October 1945 plot about a racket to abuse families of missing war heroes aired two days before an actual case hit the headlines. Another story about a German Mata Hari aired two days before the arrest of an actual Nazi spy who was also seductive and had a photographic memory (Dunning 1998, 182). *Counterspy* producer Philip Lord, who established the recurring tone of praise and tribute for law enforcement agents, created many such shows employing real-life FBI agents providing introductions and narrating audio wanted posters for these series.

After the war, other radio dramas included *Cloak and Dagger*, which ran for twenty-two episodes in 1950. Based on a book of the same name by Cory Ford and Alister McBain, each adventure was a fictionalized account of World War II operatives going on dangerous missions for the OSS. Starring the occasional characters of the Hungarian giant (Raymond Edward Johnson) and Impy, the elf (Gilbert Mack), this series most often featured guest stars describing human dramas behind enemy lines. Always worried about their shortwave radios being discovered, the agents are such squeaky clean "ordinary people" that one reveals he is under duress by cursing over his radio. He alerts headquarters of his danger by saying "darn" over and over. Known for avoiding formulas, the tense dramas occasionally starred future television spy Ross Martin (*Wild Wild West*) and invariably began with a question by Johnson: "Are you willing to undertake a dangerous mission for the United States knowing in advance you may never return alive?" Earlier, the juvenile serial, *Don Winslow of the Navy*, which began its network run in 1937, starred Johnson in its 1942 season as a young naval officer assigned to wartime intelligence. Originally, Winslow and his buddy, Red Pennington, battled the evil worldwide organization headed by the Scorpion before going to war against the Japs and Nazis (Dunning 1998, 206).

In the spirit of then popular anthology series showcasing Hollywood talent, *Intrigue* (1946) cast notable character actors like Vincent Price in a variety of spy outings. *I Love Adventure* was a brief spin-off of the long and successful *I Love a Mystery*. In 1948, the primary character, Jack Packard (Michael Laseto), formerly of American intelligence, is sent to London to work for the top secret "21 Old Men of 10 Gramercy Park." These keepers of international peace meet behind a large two-way mirror where Jack can hear but never see them. On his missions, Jack is accompanied by his friends from *I Love a Mystery*, Reggie York (Tom Collins) and Doc Long (Martin Yarborough) (Dunning 1998, 340).

In 1950, radio stalwart Jack Armstrong became *Armstrong of the S.B.I.* for one season, working as a counter-spy for the Scientific Bureau of Investigation. In the NBC comedy mystery *Three Sheets to the Wind* (1942), Jim Lockwood (Helgan Moray) worked for British intelligence, and actor John Wayne was Dan O'Brien, an American agent posing as a drunk (Dunning 1998, 672). In a more realistic vein, *Secret Missions* (1948–1949) was based on a book of the same name by Rear Admiral Ellis N. Zacoriase, who narrated the anthology series about adventures in naval intelligence. Likewise, *Spy Catcher*, a 1960 to 1961 BBC radio series, was based on the memoirs of Lt. Col. Oreste Pinto of Allied Counterintelligence Services. Perhaps the strangest of all was ABC's *Tennessee Jed* (1945–1947) starring Johnny Thomas as Tennessee Jed Sloane, a singing and yodeling agent sent by President Grant to roam the Wild West. In between searches for the perfect mate for his horse, Smokey, and helping out "heap good" Comanche chief Gray Eagle, Jed battles whip-cracking Nick Dalton and his henchman, the killer "Rat." They plan to start a new war between the states and take over the government.

A number of Hitchcock films beyond *The 39 Steps* were adapted for radio. *The Lady Vanishes* was broadcast on the Philip Morris Playhouse starring Errol Flynn in 1940. On January 26, 1948, the Lux Radio Theatre adapted *Notorious*. In that broadcast, Ingrid Bergman reprised her role from the film, while Joseph Cotten played the part of Devlin. On July 24, 1946, the House of Squib Academy Award broadcast its adaptation of *Foreign Correspondent* starring Joseph Cotten in place of Joel McCrea, who wasn't available for the broadcast.

NEW COMIC BOOK SPIES

Before moving into cultural shifts after the war, it's worth noting that the 1930s and 1940s were regarded as the "Golden Age" in another popular media—comic books. As with radio, espionage had an important influence on the formative years of costumed heroes. For example, in 1939, Joe Simon and Jack Kirby created *Captain America*, the only man injected with "Super Soldier Serum" because a Nazi spy had killed the scientist with the formula. Isolationists had complained about the first cover, a drawing of Cap's fists meeting Hitler's jaw, which some felt was an overt attempt to reach young readers. This was likely. Seven months before Pearl Harbor, Captain America fought an unnamed Asian country trying to destroy the American Pacific fleet. Then, in 1941, intelligence officer Steve Trevor crash-landed on Paradise Island, which inspired the secretive group of Amazons to provide *Wonder Woman* in the war against Hitler. Diana Prince's alter ago was something of a predecessor to James Bond in that she too relied on special gadgets—bullet-bouncing bracelets, a lie-detecting rope, and an invisible plane. In this series and in the 1970s television versions of the story, Trevor was probably the most inept secret agent with a cleft chin. He never suspected that the strongest woman on earth hid her secret from him by merely putting on horn-rimmed glasses.

AFTER THE WAR

Without question, the 1950s were dominated by real and fictional spies targeting the new menace of Communism in a very changed climate from earlier decades. Still, some changes came slowly. For years, it was difficult for FBI agents to run covert surveillance due to Hoover's strict dress code that made agents easy to spot. More importantly, after World War II, the OSS was disbanded as Congress, yet again, disliked the fact that Communists had been employed, that some feared it was but a tool of British intelligence, and that it might become an American Gestapo. Still, four months after Harry Truman disbanded the organization, on January 24, 1946, the president held a whimsical ceremony in the White House presenting Rear Admiral Sidney Sowers with a black cloak, black hat, and a white dagger before making him the nation's first director of the Central Intelligence Group which metamorphosed into the CIA.

In July 1947, Truman signed the executive order creating the Central Intelligence Agency, charged with countering the spread of Communism using Stalin's own methods: propaganda, payments to dissenting political parties, sabotage, funding guerilla movements, and engaging in all-out spy wars—in short, fighting fire with fire (Hitz 2004, 37). The first generation included charter members who'd served in the OSS. Drawing from elite schools like Yale and Princeton (the OSS had been known among insiders as "Oh So Social"), the new agency preferred secrecy to propaganda. But events in Washington, D.C., and Hollywood, not to mention London, Moscow, and a divided city called Berlin, made the 1950s known far more for espionage on the open stage rather than behind closed doors.

4

McCarthy, Television, and Film Noir: The Russians Arrive

> For we wrestle not against flesh and blood, but against principalities, against powers, against the rulers of the darkness of this world, against spiritual wickedness in high places.
>
> Ephesians 6:12

In one episode of the 1980s television series *The Equalizer*, one supporting character is captured and brainwashed. At the end of the hour, the rescued man asks Robert McCall (Edward Woodward) how much of what he had been told during his experience had actually happened. The ex-Cold Warrior, "The Equalizer," answers that nothing since October 1957 was true. While not specified in the dialogue, McCall must have been referring to October 4, 1957, the date when Russians launched Sputnik, the small satellite that energized the American government into the "Space Race," a renewed furor in cold war dualities, and, not coincidentally, an explosion of funding in public education.

Whatever scriptwriters intended for this oblique reference to a moment thirty years in the past, without question, the events of the 1950s had important shadows long after entering history books. But cold war turning points had taken place before the launch of Sputnik. For example, in February 1950, revelations came to light that the Soviets had gained atomic secrets due to the spying of Klaus Fuchs. Immediately, the media began to sensationalize stories of his work, including one report that stated Fuchs had betrayed the secret of a hormone ray that could feminize enemy soldiers. Equally sensational were accounts of twelve FBI plants that began testifying before the House Un-American Activities Committee (HUAC) that became a lightning rod throughout the decade (Leab 2000, 41). The following year, the fears of Communism spread at the same time as the growing importance of a new medium—television. The public trials of Harry Gold, Klaus Fuchs, and the capture of U-2 pilot Gary Powers put actual espionage into the living rooms of America.

Most dramatic of all, in 1954, Americans watched the Army-McCarthy hearings for thirty-six days, which launched a new era in public affairs awareness. These hearings demonstrated that rooting out traitors was a murky concern. In addition, the death sentences for Julius and Ethel Rosenberg led to a controversy that lasted for decades—was Ethel Rosenberg guilty of treason, and if her involvement was less than claimed by prosecutors, did she warrant execution? Similarly, the trials of Alger Hiss led to the elevation of Richard Nixon into the national consciousness. But Hiss cast doubt about his convictions, leading to speculation for more than forty years before it became certain that he was the traitor he'd been accused of being. During these years, the methods of the prosecutors in many trials and hearings led to long worries about who was worse—the protectors of American democracy or the reputed circles of spies operating at the highest levels of U.S. government.

Other themes of the era with a long reach included the demonization of the Soviet Union. In the twenty-first century, the Supreme Court heard a protest from Americans who felt that the phrase "under God" in the Pledge of Allegiance was unconstitutional. For critics, this phrase, inserted in the Pledge in 1954, was a relic of cold war fears when President Eisenhower heard a sermon saying the phrase would differentiate the United States from "the godless Communists." Congress agreed, saying "the dependence of our people and our Government is upon the Creator, and deny the atheistic and materialistic concept of communism" (Greenberg 2004, 9). This aspect of culture wars was also seen in Hollywood nonsense. Actor Peter Graves, later to join the cast of *Mission: Impossible*, appeared in a series of low-budget B movies such as the melodramatic cold war science fiction *Red Planet Mars* (1952), regarded then and now as one of the worst of the breed. In that odd adventure, orthodox Christians defeated Nazi-turned-Communist agents pretending to be Martians to upset the U.S. economy. It was not coincidence that the first CIA agents were sometimes called "soldier priests," and spying for God was an aspect of both fact and fiction in cold war espionage.

The growing public fears also fanned the flames of "McCarthyism," a term coined by *Washington Post* cartoonist Herbert Bloc—known as Herbloc—and the subsequent blacklist of Hollywood writers and producers. During the 1950s, collusion between Hollywood and law enforcement went far beyond studio appeasement of J. Edgar Hoover. For example, bringing both commercial and governmental pressures together on Hollywood, former navy intelligence officer Vincent Hartnett, an advisor to the *Gangbusters* radio series, became a subversion consultant compiling lists of suspicious leftist writers and directors. He sold his list to sponsors who in turn pressured the industry to drop or cancel radio and television series with "questionable" ties to Communism. A number of writers and directors were unemployed, not because networks doubted their loyalty to the United States, but because they wished to avoid controversy. One reason for the Western becoming popular in Hollywood was that studios felt it was a genre safe from the glare of McCarthyism (Gorman 1998, 5). Radio and television spy movies and shows of the era went to great lengths to demonstrate their prodemocracy themes and portray Communism as the dark side of black-and-white programming. Another source for the collusion between Washington and Hollywood was NBC founder and Brigadier General David Sarnoff, a powerful executive keenly interested in military intelligence and how broadcast technology could assist anti-Communist efforts. As a result, in 1952, NBC trained CIA operatives in overseas propaganda efforts in Europe and the Far East (Barnouw 1990, 190). Another outgrowth of these efforts was "Radio Free Europe," an allegedly private organization, which was in fact supported by the CIA.

As it happened, most government agencies were willing to cooperate with broadcasters because real intelligence gatherers weren't nearly as successful in their aims. During the 1950s, Western powers knew very little about the eastern bloc and in fact exaggerated the true extent of Soviet missile capability. The CIA orchestrated its first coup, reinstalling the shah of Iran on his "Peacock Throne" in 1953. This incident set up the first instance of "blowback" in cold war history, that is, creating unintended consequences for international meddling. As with efforts in South America to preserve the commercial interests of the United Fruit Company, the Iran coup showed that U.S. policy would often be more motivated by self-interest than more credible intentions. The Iran situation, of course, set the stage for the ongoing Middle East crises beginning in the 1970s.

In the 1950s, the United States moved ahead of the Russians with satellite technology; the KGB in turn outdid the CIA with human assets due to a wide number of enthusiastic American volunteer agents. After this era, the KGB specialized in blackmail, threats, and "Honey Traps" ensnaring Western diplomats with the time-honored ploy of pillow talk. As the public knew little of this, the media served both to heat up fears of the cold war and make claims for the new CIA that were far more fancy than fact. It can be said this decade was the time when the purpose of spying changed. Before the cold war, the reason for intelligence was to gain information before military or political operations; quickly, the purpose of most operations became to gain intelligence.

The spy role, despite my aversion to Communism, frightened me no end. It would be foolhardy for me to say otherwise. When all is said and done, Communists know no flag but the Red flag. They sneer at God, and being Godless, they have no compunctions about resorting to brutal, horrible torture and murder tactics of the most hardened, sadistic criminals.

Matt Cvetic, *The Big Decision*

One story that pulls together many of the themes of counter-espionage in the 1950s is the life of Matt Cvetic, an informant for the FBI from 1943 to 1950. According to Cvetic, FBI agents approached him in 1941 because of his knowledge of Slavic languages and his job in the U.S. Employment Office in Pittsburgh. That position, he wrote, gave him access to files of Communists seeking jobs in local industries, a target of the northeastern American Communist Party. He stated that the bureau liked his brief background in criminology and the fact he'd applied for work in U.S. army intelligence during World War II but was turned down because he was too short for military standards (Cvetic 1959, 5). Later, he claimed to have attended close to three thousand secret meetings and provided the FBI with fifty thousand documents, a claim likely close to fact. During his seven years working for the FBI as a low-level official of the Communist Party, his record showed continual praise from his supervisors. Even J. Edgar Hoover himself noted Cvetic's work was excellent. But after Cvetic surfaced in 1950, feeling the time had come for some recognition of his work, the bureau quickly distanced itself from him. While local FBI officials favored his request, Hoover refused, saying somewhat disingenuously that going public would be bad policy in all such cases. Despite this disenfranchisement, Cvetic became an important, if tarnished, witness at federal, state, and local deportation and loyalty hearings. On top of this, Cvetic had a quick flash of fame as a celebrity "professional anti-Communist," inspiring a film and radio series very loosely based on his undercover work.

What makes Cvetic's story of special interest is how he both used and was used by a media looking for heroes and voices against Communism in the same years Sen. Joseph McCarthy took the center stage of American culture. The myth began in 1950, when West Pennsylvania right-wing groups sponsored an interview with Cvetic for a Pittsburgh paper. This story led to a subsequent heavily scripted radio broadcast of both interviews and dramatized scenes portraying Cvetic as a heroic counter-spy whose adventures were more dramatic than any fictional radio drama (Leab 2000, 81). The show began, "This special broadcast tonight is being aired in the hope that you, the listening public, will become more aware of the dangers and the workings of the Communist Party" (Leab 2000, 75). Another such program was simulcast on television and radio on July 14, 1950, on Gulf Oil's popular *The People Speak* program, which again emphasized Cvetic's heroism and the terror and suspense of his work. Cvetic described himself as an ordinary guy asked by his government to do a job. "A guy who was scared, but a guy who couldn't say no" (Leab 2000, 86).

For the rest of his life, Cvetic parroted these words, repeatedly claiming his double life led to his divorce from his wife, Mary, and that he sacrificed his family in the name of national service. These claims expanded when the *Saturday Evening Post* ran a multipart version of his accounts, which led Warner Brothers to produce a film based on Cvetic's self-aggrandizing and melodramatic story, *I Was a*

Communist for the FBI. Described by Daniel Leab as a tacky, lurid B movie in the gangster tradition, the film was intended by the producers to fit the mold established by the widely praised *Confessions of a Nazi Spy* (1939) and not as a didactic propaganda piece. In a move to recapture moviegoers now finding other entertainments, Hollywood studios were seeking new genres to sell while retaining old formulas. At the same time, Hollywood couldn't afford to ignore the urging of politicians like HUAC member Richard Nixon declaring that Hollywood had "a positive duty" to make anti-Communist movies (Leab 1996). Scriptwriter Crane Wilbern and director Gordon Douglas were therefore asked to sell a story with danger and romance. Douglas had earlier directed *Walk a Crooked Mile,* one of the first anti-Communist films in 1948 in which the FBI and Scotland Yard teamed up to catch a gang of Commie spies. For Douglas, both *Walk* and *I Was* were mere jobs, not a means to address political concerns. Radio actor Frank Lovejoy was given the role of Matt Cvetic and Dorothy Hart was the romantic interest. Ironically, according to Matt Cvetic, Jr., the woman she was loosely modeled on wouldn't approve of the script unless the studio promised not to use the real names of her two twin boys, Matthew Jr. and Richard.[1]

As the treatments and screenplay developed, executives noted that the film would be "no *House on 92nd Street,*" then regarded as the best documentary-style spy effort to date. Cvetic himself had little to do with shaping the movie. When filming began on January 6, 1951, with less than half the script completed, Cvetic was touring the East Coast doing one-night appearances. He spoke at women's luncheons, civic groups, in school gatherings, graduations, and on radio broadcasts (Leab 2000, 89–102). But, as even a friendly Pittsburgh reporter declared, Cvetic had "a hard time" staying away from "booze and babes" (Leab 1996). On one such night, he was jailed for drunk and disorderly behavior, an embarrassment to Warner Brothers. His publicists later claimed they'd created a monster. The FBI agreed; they approached Warner Brothers and warned them about some of Cvetic's charges, such as the possibility that a Commie operative was in a position to poison the water supply of a California city. Quickly, J. Edgar Hoover sent out a memo to all FBI offices saying the bureau had nothing to do with the film and told agents to be polite but distant from the project (Leab 2000, 91).

Without question, this movie embellished Cvetic's story and added a level of evil to the Communist Party, whose membership and activities were far more mundane than Hollywood was interested in portraying. In one section, Cvetic has a sincere interest in a schoolteacher who declares she will name names when she realizes she has been duped. The party orders her liquidation, and Lovejoy's Cvetic saves her in a shoot-out with Communist Party thugs, a scene not even touched on in Cvetic's memoirs. In another scene, Red goons use lead pipes wrapped in Yiddish newspapers to beat and silence union leaders (Leab 2000, 99). Like other projects of the era, the party tried to enflame racial tensions for its own ends. Reds boasted that they would infiltrate churches, force American women to work in brothels to service Red occupiers of the country, and all Americans would live in harsh labor camps while being brainwashed in the doctrines of Marx, Lenin, and Stalin. While most critics blasted the movie, reviewers tended to get in laudatory words about Cvetic himself, making him something of a noble folk hero (Leab 2000, 100–102). Inexplicably, the movie was nominated for an Oscar as the best full-length documentary of 1951.

The subject of the film, however, wasn't happy. He didn't make the money he hoped for, as all his various managers took large chunks from his earnings. But Cvetic's fortunes got a second wind when, between 1952 and 1954, popular actor Dana Andrews starred as Cvetic in radio's version of *I Was a Communist for the FBI*. Andrews had earlier starred in *Behind the Iron Curtain* (1948), another effort among the first Hollywood films fusing actual espionage files with early cold war propaganda. *Curtain* was a grim, dull film loosely based on the actual case of Igor Gouzenko (Andrews), a young Russian code clerk at the Soviet Embassy in Ottawa, Canada. He'd defected in September 1945 and, in the film, tripped up ten Russian agents (Strada and Troper 1997, 85). In his new radio role, Andrews's voice was heard in a series of seventy-eight episodes, enjoying one of the biggest budgets of its day, with scripts by the likes of playwright Robert Lee, later known for such dramas as *Inherit the Wind*. Producer Frederick W. Ziff found untypical sponsors; the American Legion, chambers of commerce, unions, and veterans organizations considered sponsoring the series as a public service, even if the adventures had no basis in fact. In one episode, Cvetic saves the life of a liberal editor who learns he's been duped by the Party, and in "The Little Red Schoolhouse," Reds provoke a riot while a female agent tempts Cvetic to test his loyalty. In such scripts, Cvetic said he learned nothing about women. "Why not? Because the women who join the Reds aren't interested in being women." One FBI agent monitoring the show described it as "the eeriest kind of cloak and dagger stuff" with poor writing, loose plots, and juvenile endings (Leab 2000, 111). Once again, Hoover insisted that there be no connection between the FBI and the series. Again, Cvetic's public statements while the series was broadcast overreached reality, as in his belief that China was asking the United States to intervene on its behalf with Russia and that he personally helped the FBI capture a Nazi spy, a story he retold in his *The Big Decision*.

At the same time, Frederick Ziff promoted another related venture, the syndicated television show *I Led Three Lives*, based on the 1952 best seller built on the actual files of undercover FBI agent Herbert Philbric. Like Cvetic, Philbric had surfaced in 1949 after serving as a middle-level Communist Party official in New York. From 1953 to 1956, and in reruns well into the 1960s, 117 half-hour adventures were broadcast over 600 stations in an overt attempt to take anti-Communism into mass culture. One week before its 1953 debut, it was reported that the show was scheduled on more stations than even network offerings (Grace 2003, 22). Unlike Cvetic's projects, the FBI supported *I Led Three Lives* and Philbric had the bureau look over the scripts. To Cvetic's distress, Philbric enjoyed a longer level of fame because he didn't have the image problems Cvetic brought on himself. Not only did Philbric gain a reputation with his lectures, but the star of the show, Richard Carlson, also gained an extra income by speaking about his role (Leab 1996).

I Led Three Lives ended up being the trendsetting television spy series of the decade. In scripts written by future *Star Trek* creator Gene Roddenberry, "Those sweet little old ladies who lived in the house on the corner were, it turned out, evil-doing reds; the elevator operator was a Commie, too; so were the butcher, the baker, and the candlestick maker. If the percentage of Communists to the total population had actually been as high as portrayed on that series, the Communists could have elected the president and held a majority in Congress" (Grace 2003, 22). While American watchers might have missed this breed of overkill, international viewers did not. When the show was aired in Mexico, the Russian embassy filed an official complaint. The series was barred from distribution in Hong Kong, Australia, Argentina, Venezuela, and Columbia. The British House of Commons debated over the implications of the series (Britton 2004, 23–24). Later, the series was mentioned in the Warren Commission report when the half-brother to accused Kennedy assassin Lee Harvey Oswald told the commission that Lee watched the series faithfully each week, even into reruns (Marrs 1989, 98).[2]

Through it all, the FBI proudly touted Philbric as one of their own, and had him host *What Is Communism*, an early 1960s short now regarded as a "B movie classic" (McKee 2003). The script had two points: to praise J. Edgar Hoover and demonstrate the dangers of Communism by, among other techniques, showing viewers footage from Communist work camps that resembled Nazi concentration camp film. According to Marty McKee, Philbric emphasized and dissected nine key words to understand Commies: "Lying. Dirty. Shrewd. Godless. Murderous. Determined. International Criminal Conspiracy."

Cvetic's jealousy over the FBI's treatment of Philbric was but one reason for a decade full of personal problems. Cvetic checked into rehabilitation centers to deal with his alcoholism resulting in electric-shock therapy, a condition the Communist press happily capitalized on. In 1954, he tried to run for Congress but lost the primary to a more respected Republican candidate. In a time when first-person memoirs from informants and agents were filling bookshelves, including those of Philbric, Elizabeth Bently, and Whittaker Chambers, Cvetic talked with various publishers about a book of his own. After a series of rejections, Cvetic issued *The Big Decision* himself in 1959. Again, the FBI wanted nothing to do with the manuscript, fearing both claims of censorship and claims that they had authorized it. While critics felt, largely unfairly, that the book was influenced more by the film and radio show than the true story of Cvetic's undercover work, *The Big Decision* benefited from Cvetic's late-life associations with right-wing groups like the John Birch Society and the Christian Crusade, who promoted Cvetic in their publications. Again, Cvetic was largely a pawn for the interests of others—in this case, political fringe groups. Cvetic wrote articles for the *American Mercury*, where he accused comedian and *Tonight Show* host Steve Allen, former first lady Eleanor Roosevelt, and Dr. Linus Pauling of Communism (Leab 1996). All this occurred long after the heyday of McCarthyism, and Cvetic was therefore unable to stir up much interest in his diatribes.

Before his death in 1962, many of Matt Cvetic's earlier claims about himself and his official testimony also became matters of debate. His theme of self-sacrificing patriotism was challenged when critics noted that Cvetic was guilty of avoiding child support, spousal abuse, and beating his sister-in-law (Leab 2000, 18). While his sons still believe his motives were patriotic, Matt Jr. remembers his mother's complete disbelief that her husband worked for the government and said he turned in Reds to save his own skin. She refused to call Matt Jr. by his given name. "She called me Murray," he said. He remembers the family discord seemed more a matter of his father being away most evenings to go to meetings and remembers his mother's anger over all the *Daily Workers* lying around.

According to Daniel Leab, no Cvetic supporter, Cvetic liked intrigue and began his work as a patriot with a minimal stipend, but as time progressed he pressed the FBI for larger sums of money (Leab 1996). It seems the bureau valued what he provided and continued to give him raises as the years went by. Technically, of course, Cvetic was not a trained FBI agent but more accurately a "confidential informant," a term not always clear in subsequent reports on his activities. The fact that he lacked any experience or education in his work and that he was largely left to his own devices during his years as a double agent should earn him a level of respect and sympathy for his burdens. Still, while not publicly known until 1991, the FBI fired Cvetic before he rose to fame, apparently because his alcoholism and indiscretions revealed his work to clergy, family, and friends (Leab 2000, 2). While there seems little question that Cvetic was a valuable plant in Pennsylvania Communist operations, his use in subsequent trials and hearings is less praiseworthy. Even as his name came to national prominence in the media, his testimony was often questionable and led, like many other such hearings, to innocent victims being brushed with labels they didn't deserve. Matt Jr. recalled seeing people coming by the Cvetic home begging not to be added to the lists given to authorities, although most records indicate the provided names were already well-known to investigators.

All these aspects of Matt Cvetic's career point to key characteristics of the 1950s beyond adding a sad twist to the old motif of the "patriotic spy" as seen in Cooper's *The Spy* and Major Russell's comments in the *39 Steps* radio broadcast. (The series of FBI informants also serve as real-life examples of "amateur spies" in a grimmer realm than the fiction of Buchan and his breed.) First, America's fears of a Communist takeover were fanned by the likes of Cvetic and Philbric, who were first spies, then public informants in Congressional hearings, and finally media-driven spokespersons during the Red Scare. Whatever the value of their undercover work and testimony afterward, they became central figures in the media who took their spycraft and rewrote history for clearly commercial purposes. As books, films, television series, and radio shows beat the drums against the Red Menace, figures like Cvetic and Philbric gave credibility to the myths that grew around them as they made public appearances in every venue possible. They put a face to the abstractions of the fears of atomic war.

CIVIL DEFENSE

Beyond the exploits of undercover informants during the 1950s, reminders of fear in the new atomic age weren't hard to find across America. Buildings with sturdy basements plastered brown and yellow signs on their outside walls proclaiming they were authorized civil defense fallout shelters. Homeowners were encouraged to build such shelters in backyards equipped with provisions to feed their families after any nuclear attack. In schools, students were drilled in air-raid exercises, with girls sitting along hallways with boys standing guard over them, their palms pressed protectively against the lockers. After school and on Saturday-morning cartoons, children watched live-action and animated adventures featuring young spies in the 1956 syndicated anthology series, *I Spy*, and as helpers for the syndicated *Jet Jackson, Flying Commando* (based on the long-running radio show, *Captain Midnight*). Adult role models starred in 1953's *Atom Squad*, a weekday serial in which three government agents thwarted Communist plots. From 1959 to 1964, and in syndicated reruns for decades afterward, Rocky the flying squirrel and his buddy, Bullwinkle T. Moose, fought Boris Batenoff, Natasha Fatale, and Fearless Leader,

all agents of an East European country called Pottsylvania with suspicious accents (Britton 2004, 27).

Young people were also barraged by a wide number of free comic
books distributed nationwide by various organizations. On one hand,
champions of decency blasted comics as a Communist conspiracy; on
the other, the same voices exploited the medium to spread fear. As "a
result of this forced hysteria," a self-regulating comics code was insti-
tuted to reduce violence and horror and mandated that comic books
uphold moral values (Barson and Heller 2001, 8). As on radio shows,
however, violence seemed a viable solution when dealing with
Commie thugs. Pumping the theme of "this could happen here,"
"teens for America" groups were created to enlighten young people
about the dangers and to have high schoolers spread the word (Barson
and Heller 2001, 8). Likewise, pulp magazines issued a curious mix of
stories about evil Reds and imperiled babes for their all-male readers,
tales essentially the same as during the Nazi era with criminals wearing different uniforms (2001, 8).

All of this, according to Eric Barnouw, contributed to the major
premise that Americans lived in a world of unscrupulous conspiracies
that required a response in kind, allowing fictional secret agents to
employ the same means of deceptions and violence used by the enemy
(Barnouw 1990, 369). To create this atmosphere, the free world was
always seen in danger and therefore in need of extraordinary
guardians. As Jeremy Black noted, in Ian Fleming's second Bond
novel, *Live and Let Die* (1954), while James Bond is on a mission seeking gold coin smugglers, he observes that New York is covered with
civil defense warning signs about what to do in case of enemy attack.
While his case has nothing to do with such matters, he tells his contact "this must be the fattest atomic bomb target in the world" (Black
2001, 11). In such a climate, secret agents had to be free to be as de-
ceptive as their opposition. While some saw spy films as aggrandizing
a contemptible business, one May 1952 *Sunday Times* reviewer noted
that such movies were perfect vehicles in which "lone heroes could
wander at will in any disguise, through any social milieu, and in which
acts of violence and promiscuity were vaguely condoned by the fact
that the heroes were always fighting for 'our side,' " without need for
elaborate explanation (Shaw 2001, 57). In an era of such fervor, with
the ambiguities seen in film noir efforts, and cultural shifts setting the

stage for the upheaval of the 1960s, clearly spy projects of the 1950s would be quite different from what had been seen before.

See how a psychopathic love-starved woman defies the law! See how a man is driven to suicide rather than bend to the yoke of tyranny! See how a man is brutally murdered because he challenges gangster rule!

Ad for Republic Pictures' 1949 *The Red Menace*

In the 1950s, many of Hollywood's efforts at propaganda were both critical and popular flops, particularly because the Communists were so evil that no true human drama could be explored (Gorman 1998, 8). During this era, more than thirty-five movies dealing with domestic Communism were produced, peaking in 1952 with twelve titles released in one year (Strada and Troper 1997, 95). In early 1948, entertainment magazine *Variety* reported that on-screen anti-Communist plots had become "the hottest topic" (Leab 1996). Throughout the early 1950s, "second- and third-class performers such as hillbilly star Judy Canova, Roy Rogers ('King of the Cowboys'), and erstwhile *Tarzan*, Johnny Weissmuller appeared in films fighting subversion and villains named Ivan and Boris" (Leab 1996). At a time when *Life* magazine warned of "waves of Red bombers descending on the American heartland via the North Pole and Canada," serials like *Canadian Mounties vs. Atomic Invaders* (1953) and *Red Snow* (1952) played on such themes (Leab 1996). Likewise, *Rocket Attack USA* (1959) had spies racing to stop Russians from nuking New York.

Other examples of such fare include *Red Menace* (1949), narrated by an actual Los Angeles councilman. That same year, in *Conspirator*, Elizabeth Taylor is shocked to learn her husband, Rod Taylor, isn't the British agent he pretends to be, but is instead a Russian plant blackmailed to reveal atomic secrets. *Five Steps to Danger* (1957) featured Ruth Roman, who knows there are spies in a nuclear plant, but finds herself accused of mental instability for her whistle-blowing. *Big Jim McLane* (1952) starred John Wayne as an FBI agent tracking down Communist spies in Hawaii with his buddy, James Arness, later television's Matt Dillon on *Gunsmoke*. In the film, they work for the House Un-American Activities Committee, whose members are thanked in the end credits (Belton 1994, 245). One unique project began when the CIA's Office of Policy Coordination funded the landmark 1954 animated film, *Animal Farm*, a masterstroke of anti-Communist propaganda (Shaw 2001, 119–23).

With some irony, Howard Hughes's 1957 *Jet Pilot* was withheld for seven years by RKO studio executives fearing the comic plot might be seen as too soft on Communism. Hughes, the eccentric millionaire and sometimes movie mogul, was far from the political Left and in fact closed RKO for several years to clean house and ensure no such creators were on his payroll. One Hughes film, at first titled *I Married a Communist*, was initially yanked and then released in 1949 with the less-polarizing title *The Woman on Pier 13* because it had Americans outfoxed by Russian agents (Barson and Heller 2001, 52). *Jet Pilot*'s plot was more about aerial stunts, but became more outdated because of the seven-year lag than the spy versus spy subplot in which another beautiful Russian agent (Janet Leigh) was charmed by American pilot Jim Shepard (John Wayne).

Not all Hollywood, or British, projects were so didactic. In 1951, *My Favorite Spy* was comedian Bob Hope. The foot-stomping musical *Silk Stockings* (1957), a remake of the 1939 *Ninotchka*, had leggy Cyd Charisse as a Russian agent going after three comrades seduced by the West. Of course, she is herself seduced by Fred Astaire dancing to the hit tunes of Cole Porter. One British film, *Top Secret* (1952), had a sanitation engineer mistaken for a top scientist. *Down Among the Z Men* (1952) was a film vehicle for the Goons radio team lampooning British governmental structures and espionage in a lighthearted vein (Shaw 2001, 21). Not all this comedy pleased high-level officials. When scripts were drafted to turn Graham Greene's 1958 *Our Man in Havana* into a movie, the British film board at first refused to issue a certificate. It didn't want any satires of the British Secret Service stirring up controversy (Shaw 2001, 176).

> What do I know about Commies? I don't know a thing. I just know I don't like them.
>
> Mo in *Pickup on South Street*

Praised efforts of the period included Samuel Fullers *Pickup on South Street* (1953), a Brutal New York drama starring Richard Widmark as

Skip McCoy, a weasely, "shifty as smoke" petty crook who steals a wallet containing microfilm from Candy (Jean Peters), an inadvertent Communist courier. FBI agents and Red conspirators chase McCoy, an individualist seeking money and revenge, not patriotic reward in a paranoid world (*Movie Guide* 1998, 523–24). Based on the book *Blaze of Glory* by Dwight Taylor, the story line was originally a straightforward drug-peddling crime drama, but director Fuller decided to politicize the story. Thelma Ritter, the over-the-hill police informant Mo, was nominated for an Oscar for best supporting actress in the film.

According to Joseph Krebbs's May 2004 review of the DVD release of *Pickup*, the film maintains its value for new audiences. In Krebbs's view, the film is "80 minutes of hard-boiled plot, an oddball mix of cynical, lower-depth realism and anti-Commie flag-waving" filled with colorful grifters and "muffins too dumb to be hookers. And these are the good guys" (2004, 97). The fact that such characters were "the good guys" was part of the film's deeper meaning. In his commentary for the DVD release, Fuller noted that his Communist agents weren't true Reds—there are those who will sell anything for money. Claiming these types were based on his own days as a street reporter, he sold studio head Darryl Zanuck on his premise of antisocial types as being human even if they weren't the normal sort of heroes audiences root for. Skip, Candy, and Mo were, in his mind, apolitical, not caring about such matters and weren't impressed by FBI agents waving the flag. Avoiding what he called "phony Cold War" motives, Fuller said his characters moved into action for purely emotional reasons, as when Skip decides to avenge the beating of Candy.

Still, the film was released against the backdrop of news headlines announcing that Klaus Fuchs had sold his secrets using microfilm, making the device something more than a mere "McGuffin" in the film, although it's never clear what secrets are on it. When the film was released in France, censors changed the crime back to drug peddling in order to avoid offending the Russians. The script made it clear that even street cons who'll sell information about each other at the drop of a dime have to draw the line somewhere, and Reds were on the other side of the line. Even the remorseless policemen realize the difference between crooks and traitors. Ironically, in two meetings with studio head Darryl Zanuck and J. Edgar Hoover, Fuller claimed that Hoover didn't like the script, saying the FBI did not work with the New York Police Department. Hoover also didn't like the use of the term "God damn" in one line, and this suggestion was adopted. Slightly more worrisome was actress Jean Peters's chauffeur, who kept close watch on her love scenes with Widmark. As it turned out, he was no mere chauffeur, but her boyfriend, Howard Hughes.

She was a jerky Red. She owned all the trimmings and she was still a Red. What the hell was she hoping for, a government ordered to share it all with the masses? Yeah. A joint like this would suddenly assume a new owner under a new regime. A fat little general-ranking secret policeman, somebody sure it's great to be a Commie.

Mickey Spillane, *One Lonely Night*

For very different reasons, *Kiss Me Deadly* (1955) was lauded for its art direction, which led to its becoming something of a cult classic. Ralph Meeker played Mickey Spillane's famous private investigator, Mike Hammer, who rescued a nearly naked Cloris Leachman in the opening moments of the movie. As violence plays a role in nearly every subsequent scene, the "Neanderthal" Hammer finds a mysterious key to a mysterious box that reveals a nuclear conspiracy. Despite its overuse of viciousness—Hammer gains information by slamming informants' fingers in desk drawers and we see the death of Leachman in the image of her bare legs hanging in the air—for years to come, the film was described as an important example of the coldest aspects of paranoia, existential angst, and deep-rooted fears in the atomic age (*Movie Guide* 1998, 50).

Whatever the merits of such fare, most discussion of the era included the worries about Communists somehow taking control of America's entertainment industry. Ironically, for the most part, Russian spymasters actually considered Hollywood far removed from their centers of operation on the East Coast. Paramount music director Boris Morris flimflammed the KGB into subsidizing a number of fruitless ventures, planted one Soviet spy in Paramount's Berlin office, and helped transfer monies for the NKVD (the predecessor to the KGB) in between work for Fred Astaire, Ginger Rogers, Laurel and Hardy, and Bing Crosby (Hayes and Klehr 1999, 200). Morris asked for funds to set up a company that would create music specials for film and television showcasing Russian composers. But the KGB correctly discovered the project would have been more to Morris's personal advantage than any espionage efforts.

Ultimately, Morris became a double agent for the FBI and helped indict a trio of Soviet contacts. In the spirit of the times, he wrote his own melodramatic memoir, *My Ten Years as a Counterspy*, and saw his self-aggrandized accounts turned into the film, *Man on a String* (1960) starring Earnest Borgnine as Morris. "I hated everything the Communists stood for," he told interviewers, "and had to play a role more difficult than any of my actors played in the movies" (Weinstein and Vassiliev 1999, 113–19). In addition to Morris, KGB agent Steven Laird used his position as an RKO film producer as cover for his travels in the 1940s. But this is not to say that the Soviet Union was uninterested in the growing efforts in media anti-Communism. The Russians were well aware of the effects of such American propaganda against them. In one Soviet spy's 1950 report, declassified in 1993, Moscow was advised that American "expansionist circles" were "setting middle-class Americans against the USSR and People's Democracies with the help of anti-Soviet, anti-Communist propaganda through the press, radio, cinema, and the church" (Weinstein and Vassiliev 1999, 120).

HITCHCOCK IN THE 1950s

Of course, not all Hollywood efforts were locked into Red Scare formulas. While Alfred Hitchcock had made many pointed references to dangers from Germany in his black-and-white English adventures, he clearly wished to distance his Hollywood work from cold war themes in the 1950s. For example, when he remade *The Man Who Knew Too Much* in 1956, he never specified whether or not the country that the diplomat slated for assassination represented was a democracy. "I didn't want to commit myself to any country," Hitchcock claimed, "We simply indicated that by killing the ambassador, the spies hope to embarrass the British government" (Truffaut and Scott 1967, 170). In the 1934 version, the consequences could have been world war; in the remake, the "elementary political statement is suppressed and the assassination becomes a matter of internal politics and personal ambition" (Wood 1989, 360). This choice foreshadowed films and television series of the 1960s and beyond, when adversaries like SPECTRE, THRUSH, and KAOS were diversions from the cold war and not reflections of it. The 1956 film is considered as being far superior to the 1934 original because of the casting, new script, and Hitchcock's more sophisticated abilities. James Stewart and singer Doris Day were both praised for their performances, and Day's career enjoyed a boost when one song from the film, "What Will Be (Que Sera Sera)" became her signature tune and won an Oscar as best song of the year.

Not surprisingly, Hitchcock created perhaps the most important spy film of the era, 1959's *North by Northwest*. As Michael E. Grost observed, *North by Northwest* was another example of Hitchcock's mix of travel to exotic locations, use of unusual set pieces, and suspenseful climaxes atop high landmarks as the director had done in *Foreign Correspondent* and *Sabotage* (Grost 2003). In *Northwest*, Hitchcock continued his theme of reluctant loners as alienated and nearly lifeless until they became "quickened" by their experiences into more active, passionate humans (Mogg 2004). Such a "faceless nobody" was Richard Hannay, as was Roger Thornhill (Cary Grant) in *Northwest*. He began the film as a cipher, mistaken for an agent who didn't exist. But he exclaimed in the final moments, "I've never felt more alive!" (Mogg 2004). At the same time, Eve, the female secret agent (Eva Marie Saint) was redeemed as she finally placed loyalty and love over murky duty. For critic Robin Wood, this movement transformed both leads—Thornhill, an aloof businessman and Eve, a ruthless spy—into accepting order and responsibility (Wood 1989, 140–43).

In Hitchcock's own opinion, *Northwest* was something of a remake of *Saboteur*. In *Northwest*, Hitchcock said he had his best McGuffin of all his movies. At the scene in the Chicago airport, the intelligence man (Leo G. Carroll) tries to explain to Thornhill the truth about the primary villain, played by James Mason. After Thornhill asks "The Professor" what the enemy spy does, Carroll's character responds, "Let's just say he's an importer and exporter." "What does he sell?" Thornhill asks. "Oh, just government secrets." According to Hitchcock, this exchange "boiled down [the McGuffin] to its purest expression. Nothing at all" (Truffaut and Scott 1967, 100). There was more meaning in the last scene, when we see a train disappearing into a tunnel, an overt phallic symbol.

It's also important to note how many have seen the Bond films and 1960s spy phenomena as extensions of what Alfred Hitchcock created. For example, Francois Truffaut observed in 1967, "the James Bond series . . . is nothing else than a rough caricature of all Hitchcock's work, and *North by Northwest* in particular" (Truffaut and Scott 1967, 14). For some critics, 007 suffered by the comparison. Feminist Robin Wood dismissed *Goldfinger* as mindless light entertainment; on the other hand, *Northwest* was also light, but with purpose (Wood 1989, 130–31). For Wood, *Northwest* was superior to Hitchcock's earlier *Saboteur* and *The 39 Steps* because the situations of the reluctant agents weren't organic to their lives, whereas Roger Thornhill's predicament was (Wood 1989, 133). The character played by Eva Marie Saint, a spy falling in love against her will, was dealt with in more depth than the quick seduction of Pussy Galore in *Goldfinger* (Wood 1989, 136). (Perhaps the best term for this transformation would be "flippant"?) *Northwest* was influential on such films as *From Russia with Love* (1963), as the crop-dusting scene in the earlier film, created by scriptwriter Ernest Lehman, was repeated when Sean Connery's 007 ran from SPECTRE's helicopters. One scene from the 1936 *Secret Agent* was also repeated almost line for line in Roger Moore's first Bond adventure, *Live and Let Die*. In both films, the male lead checks into a hotel to learn from the desk clerk that a fictitious wife is already in his room. In both films, the surprised "husband" finds his spouse in the bath. In turn, Hitchcock said his 1966 *Torn Curtain* reflected what he didn't want to repeat from the Bond films. Spy films, he said, were all beginning with a scene with a man getting a mission. "I just didn't want to repeat that scene again. You have it in every one of the Bond pictures" (Truffaut and Scott 1967, 234). In addition, *Northwest* had an important impact on 1960s television; if nothing else, it gave screen credit to three future television spies: Leo G. Carroll (*The Man from U.N.C.L.E.*), Martin Landau (*Mission: Impossible*), and Edward Platt (*Get Smart*). The creators of *U.N.C.L.E.* admitted that their Napoleon Solo was based on the Cary Grant lead, and they liked the device of innocents being pulled into dangerous situations. And, before James Bond came to the silver screen, British producers Ralph Smart and David Tomlin created a television series that was to be part Ian Fleming, part Hitchcock. The result was *Danger Man*, retitled *Secret Agent* when the series debuted in the United States in 1966 (Britton 2004, 94).

1950s SPIES ON TELEVISION

Before the spy explosion of the 1960s, fictional spies came to television during the McCarthy era, and the earliest series were primarily live-action radio dramas with visuals. In 1951, the same year *I Love Lucy* changed American entertainment, three spy shows were pioneer efforts: *Dangerous Assignment* (syndicated, 1951–1952), *Doorway to Danger*, a.k.a. *Door with No Name* (NBC, ABC, 1951–1953), and *Foreign Intrigue* (NBC, syndicated, 1951–1955).[3] *Dangerous* had been an above-average NBC radio series (1948–1953) starring Brian Donlevy as "colorful, two-fisted government agent Steve Mitchell" who went on fast-paced adventures around the globe. In one radio outing, Mitchell foiled a plot in Brazil where a pseudorevolutionary army faked UFO sightings; the next week, Mitchell hid in secret tunnels in Morocco to find an assassin who looked like him. A precursor to the later *Wild Wild West* was Russell Hayden and Jackie Coogan's *Cowboy G-Men* (syndicated, 1952–1953) in which government agents worked on the open range. A similar endeavor was *Mackenzie's Raiders* (syndicated, 1958–1959), which returned Richard Carlson to television, this time as Col. Ronald Mackenzie. He headed a frontier unit under the secret orders of President Grant and Gen. Philip Sheridan. Based on fact, the raiders were a special unit thwarting the activities of Mexican bandits even if it meant illegally crossing the border (Grace 2003, 22). In the thirty-nine episodes, this group kept their secret to avoid an international incident, knowing if they were caught, they'd be disowned—shades of the later *Mission: Impossible*. In this series, Carlson was allowed to be more of a swashbuckling figure in a series known for "Stealthy attacks and shiny swords" (Brooks and Marsh 1999, 669).

Future *Gilligan's Island* skipper, Alan Hale, Jr., was a businessman who spied in *Biff Baker, U.S.A.* (CBS, 1952–1953). Other independent operators included two versions of *Hunter* (CBS, 1952; NBC, 1954), the former starring Barry Nelson, who would become the first actor to play James Bond in 1954's *Casino Royale*. One radio stalwart to move from radio to the small screen was The *Adventures of the Falcon* (syndicated, 1955) starring Charles McGraw as a "famous secret agent." Another series noted for romance and seen as a precursor to the glamorized series of the 1960s was *Passport to Danger* (syndicated, 1954–1956) starring the world-wise Cesar Romero.

As the decade progressed, both agents and the organizations they worked for came to the fore, as in *Pentagon U.S.A.*, later *Pentagon Confidential* (CBS, 1953), *Secret Files USA* (syndicated, 1954–1955), OSS (ABC, 1957–1958), and *The Man from Interpol* (NBC, 1960). Such shows moved toward cold war themes, becoming as much propaganda as adventure, as in Brian Keith's *Crusader* (CBS, 1955–1956) and Bruce Gordon's *Behind Closed Doors* (NBC, 1958–1959). Ironically, no one could have predicted the importance of science fiction in espionage in both films and on television in the 1960s. In particular, B movies created the vogue of low-budget sci-fi stories that became cautionary tales of misuses of science in the atomic age. Drawing on story lines first popularized in pulp magazines and radio serials, a plethora of mad scientists sought revenge and world domination using every imaginative device and gimmick scriptwriters could invent. The two television series that most obviously set the stage for later fanciful efforts were British-made children's shows. Ralph Smart, producer for the subsequent *Danger Man*, a.k.a. *Secret Agent* was responsible for the first television *Invisible Man* (syndicated, 1958–1961) starring unknown actors to give the show a measure of mystique. The device had been tried earlier in *The Invisible Agent* (1942), a film in which a transparent spy (John Hall) battles Nazis. Special effects were also the hallmark of *World of Giants* (syndicated, 1959–1960) in which Marshall Thompson plays a six-inch FBI operative.

HISTORY, FANCY, AND LITERATURE

One ongoing genre in spy fiction, film, and broadcast media included stories about World War II operations that were told after the end of the conflict. Most were set in Europe and few in the Pacific Theatre, largely because of the work of the OSS in France, Italy, and Germany. One unique story began with the publication of Sir Alfred

Dove Cooper's *Operation: Heartbreak* (1950), a fictionalized account of the *Man Who Never Was* ploy used by the Allies before the invasion of Italy. The publication was a breach of the Official Secrets Act, which inspired reporters to root out the truth hidden in government files. Ultimately, the whole story came out in the nonfiction account *The Man Who Never Was* (1953) by Lt. Cdr. Ewen Montagu (McCormick 1977, 55). Another book with a similar title, L. C. Moyzisch's *Operation Cicero*, also published in 1950, had a wide influence as well. In 1951, the book was adapted as a film, *Five Fingers*, starring James Mason. A television series of the same name aired on NBC in 1959 to 1960 starring David Hedison, the only actor to later play James Bond's American buddy, Felix Leiter, in two films (*Live and Let Die, License to Kill*). For fifteen episodes, Hedison played Victor Sebastian, an American counter-spy posing as a theatrical booking agent in Europe (Britton 2004, 26). His ongoing romance was with Luciana Paluzzi, another actor to appear in a 007 film (*Thunderball*).

While women authors were few, one novelist of note was Sarah Gainham, who began her career as a socialist sympathizer before she witnessed the Soviet takeover of Hungary, which turned her into a staunch anti-Communist. Her four spy stories were each set in different European locations. *Cold, Dark Night* (1957) was about life as a reporter in Berlin in 1954; *Mythmaker* (1957) was set in Vienna; *The Stone House* (1959) was set in Prague; and her spy books concluded with *Silent Hostage* in 1960 (McCormick 1977, 82–83). On the other side of the literary spectrum, Ann Bridge created Julia Probyn, a self-effacing, alluring character unofficially connected with MI6 in books that blended romance and espionage. Probyn's adventures included *Peking Picnic* (1950) and *Dark Moment* (1952) (East 1983, 43).

One author with a distinctive pen name, Sea Lion, was Capt. Geoffrey Martin Bennett. After publishing a number of naval adventures, Bennett created secret agent Desmond Drake, who appeared in *Meet Desmond Drake* (1952), *Damned Desmond Drake* (1953), and *Desmond Drake Goes West* (1956) (McCormick 1977, 161–62). Another writer to launch a new hero before the Bond books was Desmond Cory, creator of agent Johnny Fedora. While later critics said the Fedora stories were worthy of replacing 007 for readers looking for spy adventures after the death of Ian Fleming, Fedora actually appeared in 1951 in *Secret Ministry*. The piano-playing spy, along with sidekick Sebastian Trout, starred in a number of tales, including *Johnny Goes East* (1958) and *Sunburst* (1971).

Other writers to begin new spy series included Simon Harvester, a novelist now largely forgotten, but with important credentials in the 1950s. His twenty-six novels, largely featuring his character Dorian Silk, were praised by at least one intelligence officer as being the most realistic of the period. One CIA listening post was surprised when a series of Russian agents ordered a number of copies of Harvester's books (McCormick 1977, 96). The novels that intrigued the Communists began with *The Bamboo Screen* (1955) followed by the "Road" series, including *Unsung Road* (1960), *Silk Road* (1962), and *Siberian Road* (1976), the last of the series. In a similar vein, Edward S. Aarons introduced CIA agent Sam Durrell in *Assignment Dossier* (1955), the first of the "Assignment" series. The agent from the fictional "K Section" of the agency was featured in books ranging from *Assignment to Disaster* (1955) to *Assignment: Sulusea* (1964). Credited for being among the first series to look into the background of the CIA, the best of the lot is considered to be *Assignment: School for Spies* (1966). As time progressed, the series went to forty titles written by a number of authors (East 1983, 7–14).

Another new writer of the period who is still highly regarded was William Haggard, an intelligence officer in India during World War II. His best-known character was Col. Charles Russell, security executive, appearing in stories described as a mix of spying and diplomatic interplay based on Haggard's own experiences in Whitehall (East 1983, 131). Critically praised but never a major success in the United States, the Russell books were also seen as continuing the Clubland characters of the upper class who joke with social know-how (Winks 1982, 75). In addition, Russell is viewed as a transitional figure as he got along with his opposite numbers in enemy services (McCormick 1977, 94–95). Russell first appeared in *Slow Burner* (1958) and later in *The Arena* (1961), *The Unquiet Sleep* (1962), and *The Antagonist* (1964), among others. According to Robin Winks, novelist Eric Ambler can be said to have moved spy fiction to the Left, Haggard and then William F. Buckley shifted the direction to the Right (Winks 1982, 75).

> When you get back to London, you will find there are the Le Chiffres seeking to destroy you and your friends and your country. M will tell you about them. And now that you have seen a really evil man, you will know how evil they can be and you will go after them to destroy them in order to protect yourself and the people you love. You know what they look like now and what they can do to people . . . Surround yourself with human beings, my dear James. They are easier to fight for than principles, but don't let me down and become human yourself. We would lose such a wonderful machine.
>
> Mathis to James Bond in *Casino Royale*

Of course, the writer to change everything was Ian Lancaster Fleming, whose 1953 *Casino Royale* was the first of his fourteen James Bond books, seven of which appeared in the 1950s. Some commentators believe it all began when Fleming intuitively realized that it had become time to move away from the straightforward moralizing aspects of cold war anti-Communist G-men and return to the gentlemen heroes of Buchan, Ambler, and Sax Rohmer that had fascinated him during his own childhood reading (Pearson 1966, 11). Without question, Fleming had been steeped in fantasy from an early age. Bulldog Drummond tales had been read aloud to him at school, although he professed to have preferred Edgar Allen Poe and Sax Rohmer before stating near the end of his life that the most influential writer on his work, and society as a whole, was Graham Greene (Lycett 1995, 11, 391). Some of his literary connections to past masters were on a personal level, as in his long friendships with W. Somerset Maugham and Eric Ambler, who had a weekend cottage next door to Fleming's "Goldeneye" Jamaica home (Lycett 1995, 193).

Some connections to the literary past seem obvious, as in the character of "M," who can be seen as a Clubland hero, a country squire who has aged and become a father figure to his younger agents (Sauerberg 1984, 121). Sports imagery returned with cards (*Casino Royale*), chess (*From Russia with Love*, 1957), and golf (*Goldfinger*, 1959). Villains were noted for their tendency to cheat. Hugo Drax couldn't be a gentleman because he cheated at cards in *Moonraker* (1955), and Auric Goldfinger was dishonest with both cards and golf (Lindner 2003, 63).

One insightful critic, Kingsley Amis, himself one of the later authors to take a turn at writing a 007 novel, pointed to important elements of the books in his 1965 *The James Bond Dossier*. In his introduction, Amis claimed the books were "more than simple cloak and dagger stories" and were more complex and ambitious than contemporary reviewers allowed (1965, ix). He correctly stated that Bond wasn't a spy per se, not "a man who steals or buys or smuggles secrets of foreign powers." Bond's only true literary "spy adventure" was 1957s *From Russia with Love*, in which the Russian SMERSH file on Bond used the term "spion" to describe 007, a word equally applied "to any undesirable not actually in an enemy uniform" from conspirators to deserters (1965, x). Bond more often acted as counter-spy in *Casino Royale*, *Moonraker*, *Live and Let Die*, *Goldfinger*, and *Man with the Golden Gun* (1965, 1).

While the 007 of the movies would rarely be considered a man showing deep feelings in either romance or on the job, Amis wrote that Fleming added emotional levels to a profession in which his agent was a member of a mundane "British government subdepartment" (1965, 3). For Amis, Bond was a relief from the tradition of the "gifted amateur" and instead a resilient, resourceful professional (1965, 10). While not dwelling deeply and at length with moral issues, Bond indeed questioned his actions, as "if he were running with the moral hounds and hunting with the homicidal hares" (19). The major distinction between 007 and his adversaries was that he happened to be on the right side. Most telling, in the later books, Bond has been worn down and shows signs of frailty and vulnerability. He pays the cost of torture and brainwashing in *You Only Live Twice* (1964) and *Man with the Golden Gun* (1965, 20).

During the 1950s, when human weakness was demonstrated in such books, reviewers complained about the torture and sadism, as in Owen Dudley Edwards's comment that Fleming's debt to Sax Rohmer's Fu Manchu stories was nothing more than a move "from crude to lewd" (Bold 1988, 44). Despite Paul Johnson's famous 1958 "New Statesman" article in which he coined the phrase, "sex, sadism, and snobbery," Kingsley Amis claimed that such scenes were merely signs of changing times. After World War II when the German Gestapo and death camps had become part of public consciousness, fantasy torture had to move beyond mere thumb-crushing episodes as seen in earlier Bulldog Drummond stories (Amis 1965, 13). Later, Christoph Lindner added to this notion, saying "with atrocities such as trench warfare, the Holocaust, Stalin's purges, and the dropping of atomic bombs over Japan, the first half of the 20th Century witnessed war, destruction, and genocide on an unprecedented and previously inconceivable scale" (Lindner 2003, 87). All this background, in Lindner's view, made Fleming's world-threatening situations, if not possible, at least plausible.

Some have noted that Bond changed the face of fictional espionage by being a member of a bureaucracy clearly on the side of the angels, with supporting characters like "M," "Q," and Miss Moneypenny, all parts of an international organization giving 007 legitimacy and power. Most of 007's time wasn't spent fighting extraordinary threats. In Fleming's words, "There was only two or three times a year that an assignment came along requiring his particular abilities. For the rest of the year, he had the duties of an easygoing senior civil servant. Elastic office hours from around ten to six, lunch generally in the canteen, evenings spent playing cards in the company of a few close friends" (*Fleming* 1955, 1). As Kingsley Amis first observed, Bond appeared at a time when professionals needed to replace amateurs. New threats now required training, information, and understanding of new technology.

From another view, the later Bond books and their imitators appeared at the end of the 1950s when the USSR was going through the "Khruschev thaw." Briefly, the change in the regime from Stalin to Nikita Khruschev promised to replace military confrontation with legitimate economic competition. Before the Soviet premier's 1960 U.N. appearance where he pounded his shoe on his desk and proclaimed, "We will bury you," the West saw the new leader's denunciation of Stalin as a window for discussion. Whatever the fears during the 1961 showdown, the Cuban Missile Crisis led to an opening of direct communications between Washington and Moscow. Against this background, it began to seem possible that the superpowers could cooperate on questions of mutual security. Reflecting this shift in outlook, the 007 films, unlike the books of the 1950s, didn't exploit the cold war themes of Western versus Soviet spheres but diverted us from them as "all the world's intelligence agencies battled technologically crazed pirates capitalizing on the rift between the East and West" (Sauerberg 1984, 8). Bond and his ilk, especially in the films, were a new mythology, a reassuring presence on the cold war scene. As Cynthia Baron noted, the entire spy genre acted as a "safety valve" for tensions after the years dominated by the dueling personalities of Stalin, McCarthy, and all they represented (Lindner 2003, 135).

On top of this need for a shift in culture, what made the Bond phenomena most remarkable, believes John Cawilti, was the speed at which James Bond permeated popular culture. Like Elvis Presley and the Beatles, Bond uniquely enjoyed a "transformed significance" by passing through the cycle of person to hero to phenomenon to institution without taking decades to become so integrated in our collective consciousness. Clearly, mass media has accelerated such processes, but few can predict what or who can make such leaps (Cawilti 1987, 122). All this, of course, blossomed in the 1960s, a decade that showed a dramatic spike in public interest in espionage.

"Cloak and Swagger": James Bond and the Spy Renaissance in the 1960s

No matter how many times you repeat the obligatory repudiation of Bond and all he stands for, there is not a spy alive who did not sign on without a Bond complex, the vaguest fantasy that he or she would not have something of the same experience, nor a rookie recruit who does not have to curtail a swagger mimicked from Sean Connery. . . . You can denigrate him all you want, but there is no denying his place as a cultural icon with resonance far beyond the domain of espionage. There is not another profession that can point to a single fictional representation that is so universally recognized.

Former spy Todd Hoffman in John Le Carré's *Landscape*

DEFINING THE CINEMATIC JAMES BOND

From the onset of the Bond phenomena in the early 1960s to the present, critics of every stripe have tried to determine just what has made 007 and his progeny so fascinating and durable. One answer seems obvious. Throughout the run of Fleming's novels and the following film series, neither Bond nor the world in which he operated can fairly be seen as static or merely formalistic. For example, Lars Sauerberg claimed that Fleming was originally more of the realistic school of writers until his novels from 1959 to 1961, when he moved toward sensationalism. He realized that the extreme aspects of his cold war stories were becoming anachronistic (Sauerberg 1984, 11). In the first books, Bond battled overt operatives of foreign powers, then he fought

Communists, as much criminals as agents, and finally, in the 1960s, he struggled with independent organizations without political allegiances, notably Ernst Stavro Blofeld, the creator of SPECTRE. By making SPECTRE the representation of evil itself, Fleming "responded to the general mood of restlessness, insecurity, and loss of clear political issues" (Sauerberg 1984, 169).

On a more pragmatic level, when Fleming moved to dealings with SPECTRE, his style also changed because he anticipated his stories becoming movies. Just before his death in 1964, Fleming showed how he was influenced by the films. In *On Her Majesty's Secret Service* (1963), he mentioned Ursula Andress, the ultimate Bond girl in *Dr. No*, as a visitor to Piz Gloria. More significantly, Fleming hadn't identified Bond's genealogy until after he'd seen Scottish-born Sean Connery. In *You Only Live Twice* (1964), Fleming announced that Bond's father, Andrew Bond, was a Scot. In the closing lines of *The Man with the Golden Gun* (1965), Bond turns down a knighthood saying, "I am a Scottish peasant and I will always feel at home being a Scottish peasant" (Fleming 1965, 183), shades of Richard Hannay. Of course, Fleming was also of Scottish blood and may have used himself as a model for this claim. Whatever the case, in fact, the first international superstar was rarely played by a true-blue Brit. After Connery, 007 was played by an Australian (George Lazenby), a Welshman (Timothy Dalton), and a son of Ireland (Pierce Brosnan). As of 2004, only Sir Roger Moore was a full-fledged British Islander.

Despite these castings, no figure has been so widely identified with queen and country, and there's an important irony in England's desire to claim 007 as its own. At the beginning of the 1960s, Great Britain's role in the cold war was far different than films or novels typically showed. Most importantly, the disillusionment of the British Empire made England one of many secondary players in the new era. All NATO allies, under the umbrella of America's nuclear stockpile, were now essentially countries squeezed between the interests of two superpowers. In the book version of *You Only Live Twice*, Bond is shocked when Japanese secret service chief Tiger Tanaka tells him that the Communists don't rank Britain as being any more significant than Italy or Belgium. In the film, *Diamonds Are Forever* (1971), Blofeld laughs when Bond is sent to represent the global community—

his "tiny island" hadn't even been threatened. In fact, British diplomacy of the era primarily dealt with relations within its own former colonies and their quest for independence. Fictional agents like television's John Drake (*Danger Man*) thus found themselves working in proxy battles in the international cold war.

Only in fiction could Britain be in the center of events, and Bond was thus both a means for national propaganda and a source for commercial revenue. According to Tony Bennett and Janet Woollacott, in the Fleming books, Bond's cover was as an agent of the universal import/export company (later the Transworld Consortium), which means the idea that Bond is as much "supersalesman" as "superspy" can be traced to 007's origins (Lindner 2003, 32). James Bond was equally successful on both fronts. In the 1960s, spy thrillers weren't only part of popular reading, they were the center of it. Spy films, books, and television series were a significant part of British exports including pop music, Carnaby Street fashions, and the "Swinging London" baby boom subculture that kept England in the eye of the world. After the movie debut of *Dr. No* in 1962, the merchandising of the Bond franchise exploded with games, models, and an endless variety of products for younger viewers more interested in films than books. For older readers, American publishers' long-standing sales of paperbacks were said to have become popular in England after British publishers followed this trend with Bond books. Before 007, they had historically only issued hardcovers preferred by libraries (Lindner 2003, 27). As time progressed, Bond became a spokesman for Western commerce with product placement and promotional tie-ins for everything from BMW cars to Omega watches. Fleming's oft-noted use of brand names in his fiction had led to his books being branded "snobbery," but clearly he had the last laugh at such accusations. And if wish fulfillment was what Bond is all about, then his strongest selling point was another theme of his detractors—sex.

It was just as she'd thought. These Secret Service people always seemed to have time for sex however important their jobs might be. But her body obstinately tingled with the shock of the kiss and the golden day seemed to have taken on a new beauty.

Ian Fleming, *Moonraker*

———————

For the next few weeks, you will be most carefully trained for this operation until I send for you and tell you exactly what to do in all contingencies. You will be taught certain foreign customs. You will be equipped with beautiful clothes. You will be instructed in all the arts of allurement. Then you will be sent to a foreign country somewhere in Europe. There you will meet this man. You will seduce him. In this matter, you will have no silly compunctions. Your body belongs to the State. . . . Now your body must work for the State. Is that understood?
Rosa Klebb to Tatania Romonova in *From Russia with Love*

One book and film, *From Russia with Love*, is an interesting case study of the presence of Bond in the early years. *Russia* was the only Fleming novel for which he wrote a preface pointing to the realism in the story and that the situations and characters were not entirely fictional. Ironically, the plot of *From Russia with Love* wasn't a direct threat to England but a Russian scheme to discredit the image of Bond himself and thus the British Secret Service. In this conspiracy, SMERSH plans to use film when Soviet agents photograph Bond and Tatiana Romanova together in bed. Before this rendezvous, Bond has been shown a photograph of the girl and told that like a film star, the girl has a crush on him and will defect with a code machine if Bond comes to get her. Doubting the veracity of the story, M still tells Bond that he has to live up to the expected image Romonova has of him. Again, fact meets fancy in this setup—this unlikely scenario is a twist on one of the KGB's most successful ploys for decades: employing seductive "swallows" in "Honey Traps." In fiction, of course, Bond gets both the girl and machine, and the sign of victory in the closing moments of the 1963 movie (when SPECTRE replaced SMERSH) is the shot of Bond's hand tossing the film into a canal in Venice. Beyond the ironic imagery of film-within-film—in this case, pornography within mainstream cinema—the theme of sexuality and cultural expectations in gender roles was something quite different from previous decades.

For some critics with a feminist bent, the new emphasis toward overt sexuality transformed the themes seen in films like those of Hitchcock, where patriarchal heads of criminal gangs and Nazi cells had been domestic models of doting fathers and husbands. These apparent paragons of proper home life were juxtaposed against young, unmarried heroes, a contrast that created moral ambiguities for viewers (Wood 1989, 279). For other observers, one reason for the success of the Bond phenomena was that 007's sexual independence mirrored contemporary shifts in post–World War II attitudes. U.S. president John F. Kennedy later recalled that the late 1950s and early 1960s were good times to be a bachelor, especially after 1960, when the Food and Drug Administration (FDA) authorized the birth control pill, ushering in the "Sexual Revolution." This warmth for freedom, independence, and romance in the mode of the new playboy culture clearly favored unmarried secret agents. Unlike Sherlock Holmes who advocated bachelorhood so he could rise above and be immune from human weaknesses and passions, the new breed of heroes could enjoy sexual encounters without encumbrance, as close involvements were dangerous and made agents vulnerable. As M tells Bond in the novel of *From Russia with Love*, he doesn't want a woman hanging on Bond's gun arm. According to Glenn W. Most, secret agents in the 1960s mold had to be able to move confidently through every stratum of society and were usually single or divorced, their parents rarely mentioned, and childless. This freedom allowed them to see clearly through the workings of other characters, although they were enigmas outside of the rules that bind families (Bold 1988, 140). Were a spy to be married, as in the television series *I Led Three Lives*, the agent would be forced to keep his secrets on a variety of levels. This situation would become an important theme in subsequent decades, when family duties and relationships indeed complicated the private lives of fictional secret agents.

In the 1960s, the emphasis on sexual independence was more than literary romance. For example, CIA director Allen Dulles was a widely known womanizer who could get away with his amours in the days before Congressional hearings targeted men for such peccadilloes (Srodes 1999, 130). While many would see such "sexcapades" as mere eye candy on large and small screens, Robert O'Neill believed figures like Honeychile Ryder and Pussy Galore represented important changes in culture. In his view, these women were at least allowed to express their sexuality. "In some way, at least, this is a victory for women in that female sexuality is actually recognized." In the 1970s,

O'Neill claimed, the realism of John Le Carré was something of a step back in that women again adopted the "mantles of moral purity" (Bold 1988, 171). Reviewer Peter Wolfe agrees, saying Bond films represented a progression from the early books of Eric Ambler where women had little place in the stories. Wolfe believed women would have cluttered up story lines with relationships inconvenient for the plot (Wolfe 1993, 25). As it happened, both the first edition of *Casino Royale* and the first issues of *Playboy* magazine appeared in 1953. In many later interviews, *Playboy* publisher Hugh Hefner has frequently pointed to how 007 films and his magazine were mutually supportive endeavors. Beyond sexual roles, Fleming's snobbery in the form of worldly knowledge of fine cuisine, *Gentlemen's Quarterly* fashions, and sexy cars—all also celebrated in the pages of *Playboy*—easily translated surface sophistication into pop art in *Our Man Flint*, *Honey West*, *The Avengers*, and the Matt Helm series starring "Rat Pack" swinger, Dean Martin.

RE-CREATING BOND

Of course, Ian Fleming's inception began to be shaped by a variety of other creators almost from the beginning. One year after the appearance of *Casino Royale* in 1953, the novel was adapted for television for Climax Theatre starring Barry Nelson as an obviously Americanized "Jimmy Bond." The earliest parody came in 1955 by Daniel George, who had Bond "pitched from a cyanide super-charged gravity-resisting helicopter into a herd of elephants looking for valuable radioactive mud" (Lycett 1995, 271). Bond's popularity went into its upswing in 1957, when the *Daily Express* serialized *From Russia with Love* and began a daily comic strip illustrating Fleming stories. These strips were reprinted in Denmark and Sweden and a separate strip appeared in Yugoslavia (Lindner 2003, 23). To capitalize on the fame of Bond's creator, Fleming himself was approached to play M in the first film, as he was a well-known commodity in his own right (Lindner 2003, 127).

After Fleming's death in the heyday of the Bond phenomena, his literary executors, Glidrose Productions, commissioned a series of authors to keep the world's most famous secret agent alive and well between hardcovers and on the screen. One interesting effort was Fleming biographer John Pearson's 1973 *James Bond: The Authorized Biography of 007*, in which Pearson tells the story of Bond's early years using clues from Fleming's books. Along the way, Pearson made the case that Bond is a real person who did, in fact, perform much of what Fleming narrated. Pearson maintained that Fleming was contacted by British intelligence to help in an elaborate propaganda project using Bond's exploits to enhance public support for MI5 and MI6. In the final chapter, the author even interviewed Bond, now in retirement, getting the agent's opinions of the movies based on his life.

Nineteen sixty-eight was an interesting year for the literary Bond. For one matter, Kingsley Amis, under the pseudonym of Robert Markham, issued *Colonel Sun*, the first of the authorized novels sanctioned by Glidrose.[1] This was Amis's single contribution to the series, but publicity for the book was almost outshadowed by the publication of a Bond novel by an unlikely source. In 1966, Bulgarian novelist Andrei Gulyashki was hired by a Soviet press to create a Communist agent to stand against James Bond because of Russian fears that 007 was in fact an effective propaganda tool for the West (McCormick 1977, 93). The book, *The Zakhov Mission* (1966), appeared after the story was serialized as "Avakoum Zakhov vs. 07" in a Russian youth edition of *Pravda*. In 1968, the English version was released in a translation by Maurice Michael. Reviewers, and comments by Gulyashki in interviews, noted that his Avakoum Zakhov was far more proletariat than Bond, preferring boiled cabbages and noodles to 007's gourmet cuisine (McCormick 1977, 94). To avoid copyright infringement, the publishers could only use "07" to refer to Bond who, naturally, loses to Zakhov in the final moments.

But Andrei Gulyashki was but one, and far from the first, writer to take potshots at the new espionage icon. In 1965, so many spy films came out of Italy that United Artists threatened legal action for breach of copyright. The following year, more than thirty such films were released (Lindner 2003, 23). For some observers, the numerous parodies of the secret agent genre in the 1960s were an exercise in the redundant. In particular, from the outset of James Bond's screen life, no one in the production team expected viewers to confuse the world of 007 with reality. In his DVD commentary for the special edition of 1964's *Goldfinger*, director Guy Hamilton noted that Sean Connery's first appearance in the film, rising from the water with a bird on his head, stripping off a wet suit to reveal a perfectly tailored tuxedo, set the tone for the movie in particular and the 007 universe in general.

As the Bond movie series progressed, the humor became more than puns and double entendres. Bond smashing up the entire Las Vegas police force in *Diamonds Are Forever* (1971), Bond cutting up speedboats and leaping over bridges in *Live and Let Die* (1973), and 007's capturing a midget in a footlocker in *Man with the Golden Gun* (1974) were clearly more comedy than drama. For many fans, the Roger Moore films can be dismissed as the "James Bond comedies," best exemplified by the clown face disguise that Moore used in *Octopussy* (1983). The era of Timothy Dalton brought with it a feeling of relief as the over-the-top antics of Moore were replaced by the more Flemingesque tone of *The Living Daylights* (1987) and *License to Kill* (1989). These films, in a sense, cleansed the palate of moviegoers before they quickly clamored for a return to humor and fantasy in the series. But back in the 1960s, when spies appeared in every guise imaginable, humor was prevalent in a genre no one was supposed to take too hard or too much to heart. For the most part.

THE IMITATORS

Before Moore's antics, *Our Man Flint* (1965) and *In Like Flint* (1967), with music by composer Jerry Goldsmith, featured ultimate secret agent Derek Flint (James Coburn) attempting to take over Connery's place at the center of the superspy boom. In both films and a television movie sequel, Flint worked for Z.O.W.I.E. (the Zonal Organization for World Intelligence and Espionage). He rescued women who were brainwashed by hairdryers, and was revived from deathlike comas by a watch that resuscitated his pulse. Like many other films and television series, he acted as the extreme independent man fiercely opposed to rogue scientists with utopian dreams. Initially, producers feared that Coburn's star power wasn't enough to sell the first film. They scripted radio promos around the Americanness of the agent without mentioning the star's name. (In 2002, Mike Myers paid homage to the Flint films by having phones in *Goldmember* ring with the musical strains used in the Flint ventures.)

In the British film *Carry on Spying* (1964), Dr. Crow controlled S.T.E.N.C.H. (the Society for the Total Extermination of Non-Conforming Humans). The heroes were Desmond Simpkins (Kenneth Williams) and James Bind (Charles Hawltry) with Honey Butt, a.k.a. Agent Brown Cow (Barbara Windsor), a clear takeoff of *Dr. No*'s Honeychile Ryder. In 1965, the British romantic comedy *Hot Enough for June/Agent 8 ¾* was yet another quickly forgettable parody of the Bond boom. Its primary contribution to spy history was providing screen credits for actors more known for other secret agent projects, including Leo McKern (*The Prisoner*), Richard Vernon (*The Sandbaggers*), and Noel Harrison (*The Girl from U.N.C.L.E.*). The plot involved an out-of-work writer who speaks Czech and so is sent to Prague on a secret mission by MI6. Naturally, his opposition number is a sexy chauffeur with whom he falls in love. One odd nod to John Le Carré was *The Spy with a Cold Nose* (1966). Actors Laurence Harvey, Daliah Lavi, and Lionel Jeffries took a backseat to the star of the show, a bugged dog passed between Russian and British intelligence.

David Niven, the actor Ian Fleming had in mind for the official cinematic James Bond, starred in *Where the Spies Are* (1965), which included references to the spy craze. For example, Niven's character was given a gimmicky wristwatch with the inscription, "With love, from Uncle." Wolf Mankowitz wrote the script, the man who had introduced Harry Saltzman to Albert R. Broccoli, thus helping the James Bond series get off the ground. Similarly, *Operation: Kid Brother* (1967) had overt Bond connections. It was a cheap knockoff starring Neal Connery, younger brother of Sean. The credits were spiced with Bond veterans Daniela Bianchi, Lois Maxwell, and Bernard Lee.

Some parodies resulted from authors like John Gardner who, in those days, frankly hated Bond. In 1964, Gardner developed his send-up of Bond, creating his character Boysie Oakes for *The Liquidator* as a joke. Gardner's Oakes was fearful of violence, prone to airsickness, and afraid of heights (McCormick 1977, 83). Two years later, *The Liquidator* (1965) was released as a film with Oakes as a cowardly cybernetic assassin for British security. His reputation was based on the success of the hit men he hired to do his jobs for him. Oakes appeared in a series of novels including *The Amber Nine* (1966), in which he still passed his assignments off to gangsters. But by *Understrike* (1973), the formula was beginning to wear. After his *Werewolf Trace* (1977) and *Dancing Dodo* (1978), Gardner would take on a new role in 1981—as a true-blue Bond novelist. One contemporary novelist, Anthony Burgess, published his own spy spoof, *Tremors of Intent* (1966), before trying his hand at writing a Bond screenplay. Unlike Gardner, the author of *Clockwork Orange* wasn't able to craft a story deemed worthy of the 007 universe.

Clearly, one main goal of the parodists was simply a means to cash in on the Bond bonanza. Charles Feldman, owner of the rights to Fleming's *Casino Royale*, found himself shut out of the Bond franchise when the Albert Broccoli-Harry Saltzman team made Sean Connery the walking definition of 007. To make use of his property, Feldman brought in five directors who turned the Bond formula on its head. In the script, the true, original Sir James Bond (David Niven) came out of retirement, complaining about the sexual acrobatics of his name-sake. Rigidly moral and celibate, Sir James reformed, not seduced, fe-male spies who retired into convents. To fight the unknown Dr. Noah (Woody Allen), Niven's 007 sent out five different James Bonds to confuse the enemy including Ursula Andress, the former Honey Ryder. In the opinion of most critics and audiences, gratefully, the whole cast was blown up in the last scene.

Another set of comic outings began with *Salt and Pepper* (1966) starring Sammy Davis, Jr. as Charles Salt and Davis's "Rat Pack" buddy, Peter Lawford, as Christopher Pepper. The lightweight comedy made overt references to both Bond and an obvious television inspi-ration, the biracial pairing of *I Spy*. The concept was successful enough to result in a 1970 sequel, *Let's Do It Again*, in which the ostensible nightclub owners-turned-secret agents lamely bantered their way through another slight effort. Ironically, the films were inspired by one appearance Davis and Lawford did together on the television series *The Wild Wild West*. They enjoyed the experience so much that they asked the episode's director, Richard Donner, to direct *Salt and Pepper*. Later, after directing for *Get Smart* and *The Six Million Dollar Man*, Donner said his *Salt and Pepper* experience led to his Hollywood ca-reer, including films like *Superman* and the *Lethal Weapon* series (Britton 2004, 152). While Lawford and Davis didn't know it, they were under actual FBI surveillance at the time, along with buddy Frank Sinatra for their Mafia and political connections.

Of course, there was money to be made producing fare largely intended for then-popular Saturday afternoon matinees and "all-nighter" marathons of B movies at drive-in theaters. One implausible would-be teen heartthrob, Frankie Avalon, left his beach blanket romances to defeat the nefarious *Dr. Goldfoot and the Bikini Machine* (1965). One 1968 Italian example of such nonsense had two titles, *Danger! Death Ray* and *Nest of Spies*, yet another excuse for bikini voyeurism in the spirit of a sister film from the same year, *Danger! Diabolik*. *Death Ray* starred former Hercules and Tarzan lead John Phillip Law as a spy with the unlikely name Bart Fargo. Later, the film was lampooned on the television series *Mystery Theatre 3000*, with scenes of a helicopter landing on the deck of a submarine filmed in a bathtub with tubby toys. The distinctions between the original and the parody are slim. Another target for *Mystery Theatre* was *Agent from H.A.R.M.* (1966) starring Peter Mark Richman as Adam Chance and Barbara Bouchet, a Bond girl in *Casino Royale*. To get this acronym to work, the scriptwriters had to reach. H.A.R.M. stood for Human Aetiological Relations Machine. Aetiology? Well, it is a British variant of etiology that is the branch of medical science concerned with causes and origins of diseases. In this case, the baddies had a spore that turned people into goo.

The spy boom was not limited to novels and feature films. In print, *Mad* magazine not only parodied each television series in its monthly send-ups, but also each month a one-page minidrama pitted "Spy vs. Spy." Inevitably, the spoofing wandered into popular music as well. Nancy Sinatra, who'd crooned the Bond theme to *You Only Live Twice*, also produced a *Thunderball* parody, "The Last of the Secret Agents," the theme for a vehicle for the comedy team of Martin and Rossi. While some television stars issued singles capitalizing on their spy connections (Patrick Macnee and Honor Blackman did "Kinky Boots" and Barbara Feldon performed the embarrassing "Max" and "99"), record companies took sales seriously. In 1965, the *Goldfinger* soundtrack went to number one in the states, knocking the Beatles out of the top slot. The score made composer John Barry and guitarist Vic Flick the most influential musicians in what became the spy music genre. In 1967, during the "Battle of the Bonds" when the sanctioned

You Only Live Twice competed with the parody *Casino Royale*, Connery won at the box office but *Casino* scored with record sales (Lindner 2003, 129). Composers saw not only vinyl albums with their scores for films on the charts, but television tie-in soundtracks also became popular, often with music never used on the small screen. Title songs for Bond films became a staple on both album and singles charts, along with television themes for series like *Mission: Impossible* and *Secret Agent*. Budget record labels tossed out albums with spy themes performed by a variety of orchestras, and rock groups like The Ventures released versions of secret agent themes along with their own compositions with spy-related titles.

My real name is Helm, Matthew Helm, and certain unofficial records have me cross-filed under the code-name, "Eric." But for the evening, I was James A. Peters, employed by Atlas Enterprises. . . . The nature of the company and my exact position with them remained carefully unspecified on the identification I carried. Anyone who became really interested, however, interested enough, say, to send a set of finger-prints to the Chicago police would be informed that I was known locally as Jimmy "The Lash" Patroni, the man with influential friends and an unsavory reputation. In other words, I wasn't, for the record, a very nice guy and it was just as well. The job wasn't a very nice job.
Donald Hamilton, *Murderer's Row*

While having a "00" meant having a license to kill, assassination was rare in fact, at least in American and British services. After revelations of rather fantastic but failed attempts on Fidel Castro during the Kennedy administration and rumors of CIA/Mafia involvement in Kennedy's Dallas murder, the possibility was made illegal in the 1970s. Western services weren't unhappy, as none wanted to be tarred with the practice of killing. As would be seen in the endless blood-letting of the Israeli/Palestinian conflict, violence leads to violence (Hitz 2004, 116). Not until 9/11, when President George W. Bush authorized the use of airborne "predators" against Al Qaeda, was the concept a serious concern in terms of official Western agencies.

In fiction, however, sanctioned killers on the government payroll were a dominant thread from 007 onward. One prime example originated from the typewriter of Swedish-born author Donald Hamilton, whose Matt Helm became one of the longest-lived and most successful heroes in the history of the genre. Hamilton's role in literary espionage is central because he both drew from the past and then influenced later generations of thriller novelists while being credited with being among the breed of writers who popularized paperback originals in the late 1950s (East 1983, 101). According to Donald Skinner, Hamilton was inspired by Dashiell Hammett, Ernest Hemingway, Raymond Chandler, and Leslie Charteris. Many see strong influences of both John Buchan's *The 39 Steps* and Geoffrey Household's *Rogue Male*, as Hamilton's early books showed a marked fondness for "everyman" characters drawn into danger (Skinner 2004). After the success of the Helm series, crime writers such as Loren Estleman, Bill Crider, Ed Gorman, James Sallis, and Skinner himself consider Hamilton a primary influence on their writing.

During the 1940s and 1950s, Hamilton began his writing career with early spy novels that reflected two of the novelist's most recurring threads: an affection for edged weapons and a disdain for bureaucracy (Skinner 1998). In 1960, Fawcett Gold Medal publishers approached Hamilton because they were looking for a counteragent who would work against foreign spies within the boundaries of the United States to emulate the success of Edward S. Aaron's "Assignment" series (Skinner 2004).

In the first novel, *Death of a Citizen* (1960), Helm was introduced as a Buchanesque regular guy, happily married with children, an avid outdoorsman and hunter, and an accomplished writer and photographer (Skinner 1998). But the former wartime killer was brought back to his past by chance at a social gathering and a transformation begins. Before novel's end, Matthew Helm is working for a mysterious boss named "Mac," is code-named "Eric," finds himself beginning a pattern of adultery, and loses his wife, Beth, to become a full-time assassin.

Hamilton's Helm was often compared to Bond, who was not yet a cinematic sensation when Fawcett first approached Hamilton to create a hard-boiled American agent. In the books of both authors, love affairs dramatized the hardness of the main characters as the ladies most often were agents of the opposition doomed to early graves. The first series of Helm books included, among others, *The Silencers* (1962),

The Terminators (1975), and *The Retaliators* (1976). In 1977, Hamilton published what many feared was the last Helm novel, *The Terrorizers*, in which Helm pursues a gang of American terrorists. In the final pages, Helm seems overwhelmed by the violence in his life. The hospitalized agent is apparently unsure of his future and is at least considering the possibility of a high-level desk job. For five years, Hamilton moved to other projects, notably *The Mona Intercept* (1980). According to Robert Skinner, this novel brought together Hamilton's most recurring themes: "Women, both ineffectual and stalwart, are on display. Non-violent Everymen driven to violence by criminal attack and bureaucratic indifference outnumber, but do not quite supplant ruthless government agents. There are also criminals who sacrifice themselves in a noble attempt to atone for their tragic flaws" (Skinner 2004).

Matt Helm reappeared in *The Revengers* (1982), a book more complex and different in tone from the earlier pulp novels. He is less ruthless, less willing to kill, and more sentimental about the women he meets (Skinner 1998). His role in Mac's secret agency has changed, now working as a company troubleshooter more than as Mac's favored skillful assassin. This somewhat subdued Helm appears in *The Annihilators* (1983), *The Infiltrators* (1984), and *The Damagers* (1993), among others. Reports circulate that Hamilton wrote one final Helm novel, but has been unable to find any publisher interested in a character some consider dated and out of popular favor. However, DreamWorks Productions announced plans in 2003 to begin a new Helm film series based closer in spirit to the books than the campy Dean Martin vehicles in the 1960s.

There's a whole new breed of scientist today. They smoke, drink, and swear, but they won't answer one simple question. How do you destroy Washington D.C.?

Carl Malden as Julian Wall in *Murderer's Row*

Speaking of Martin, the comedian/singer's Matt Helm film series—*The Silencers* (1966), *Murderer's Row* (1966), *The Ambushers* (1967), and *The Wrecking Crew* (1968)—featured an alcoholic, womanizing, and bubbling Helm whose cover was as a world-famous fashion photographer. This version of Hamilton's character burst into song at incongruous moments, singing about the dangers of a sweetheart with a pistol under her pillow. Like his compatriot, Derek Flint, Martin's Helm was a reluctant agent, but not for the usual reasons. Superspies in the Helm/Flint mold were too busy enjoying life to the fullest to be bothered with worldwide calamities until adversaries unwisely attacked them personally. *Murderer's Row* employed one device typical in spy fiction, that of a spy working on his own because his supervisor knows there's a traitor at headquarters and only the irreverent outsider can be trusted to get the job done.

Later, *Matt Helm*, a 1975 television attempt to recreate the character as a retired spy turned private sleuth, aired for fifteen episodes. Starring Tony Franciosa, the series had nothing to do with either Hamilton's gritty novels nor Martin's over-the-top silliness, despite the fact that Irwin Allen produced both the films and the pilot. Still, the lightweight pilot (featuring ex-Avenger Patrick Macnee) foreshadowed themes more characteristic of projects in the 1980s and 1990s. In Sam Rolfe's script, Helm—once an agent of a now discredited "The Machine"—told another ex-agent that he'd left the covert world because the battles had become habit without principles. For this far more moral version of Hamilton's assassin, the cold war had lost its purpose. Of course, such scruples didn't prevent him from remaining on the books as eligible for emergency call-ups, which allowed Helm to call on the government to help him out with files and information.

Dark themes were also evident in other significant and popular spy books and films of the 1960s. Very much in the spirit of Donald Hamilton, novelist Andrew York created his own memorable and popular assassin, Jonas Wilde, who appeared in ten successful books. The first, *The Eliminator* (1966), was filmed as *Danger Route* (1968). In a similar vein, longtime pulp magazine detective Nick Carter was resurrected in a new series of paperbacks. Working for the U.S. government, Carter was now known as "Killmaster," and the name sums up the books, all of which were written by a series of unattributed authors.

According to Donald McCormick, author Steven Coulter had helped Ian Fleming shape the casino scene in *Casino Royale*; in turn, Coulter wrote his own spy fiction under his own name and with his pen name, James Mayo (McCormick 1977, 55). As Mayo, his novels featured his agent, Charles Hood, most notably in *Hammerhead* (1967). Produced by Irving Allen (who'd broken his partnership with Albert Broccoli because he didn't like the Bond novels), the book was filmed with Vince Edwards, the former television doctor *Ben Casey*, as Hood. Follow-up novels included *Let Sleeping Girls Lie* (1965) and *Shamelady* (1967). Under his own name, Coulter produced *The Stranger Called the Blues* (1968), *Embassy* (1969), and *Account to Render* (1970).

Another critically acclaimed writer debuting in the 1960s was Ross Thomas. His twenty-five books, occasionally under the pen name Oliver Bleeck, began after he spent twenty years as a reporter, publicist, and political strategist. His first novel, *The Cold War Swap* (1966), written in six weeks, introduced his most famous duo, McCorkle and Michael Padillo. They reappeared in four books, including *Cast a Yellow Shadow* (1967) and Thomas's last novel, *Ah, Treachery!* (1994).

Before his death on December 19, 1995, Thomas was known for entertaining, quirky looks into Washington corruption, as in *If You Can't Be Good* (1973). Equally sleazy fictional California cities were the settings in *The Fools in Town Are on Our Side* (1970) and *Chinaman's Chance* (1978), which Introduced Thomas's second colorful duo, Artie Woo and Quincy Durant, who returned in two later novels.

According to Thomas himself, plots weren't his strong suit, but his books were noted for clever opening scenes, sly political wit, and quirky character names. His books were considered "bawdy, bloody, complex, minutely crafted and very American" (Winks 1982, 65). An example of his humor is the name of one organization interested in political soft money—VOMIT (Victims of Military Intelligence Treachery). When one character sees an episode of *Scarecrow and Mrs. King*, she dismisses it as "James Bond meets Irma Bombeck."

According to his wife, most of Thomas's novels were too complex to be made into movies with one exception, *The Procane Chronicle* (1972), adapted into the film *St. Ives* (1976) starring Charles Bronson, John Houseman, Maximilian Schell, and Jacqueline Bisset (East 1983, 293). Two of his novels won Edgars, the most prestigious award for mystery fiction: *The Cold War Swap* (1966) and *Briarpatch* (1984).

Perhaps the most successful and critiqued woman writer of the era was Helen MacInnes, whose spy novels began with *Praise for a Brave Heart* in 1955. Described as the "Queen of Spy Writers" for best sellers like *The Venetian Affair* (1963) and *The Double Image* (1966), one critic saw her style as "satin smooth," as she wrote about "unscathed heroes" who were always amateurs (McCormick 1977, 124). Other observers didn't place her in espionage royalty, saying her books featured agents known for luck so clearly good against enemies so clearly bad that their novels were little more than formulas (Cawilti and Rosenberg 1987, 202). In this view, MacInnes's characters were "embarrassingly domestic" in their Manhattan middle-class apartments and Long Island summer homes. The stories are "so consistently naïve in tone as well as the thrust of the plot that invoking MacInnes as a serious force is often a problem" (Cawilti and Rosenberg 1987, 202). Such reviews have a point. When MacInnes wrote of Communist cells in Europe, she tended to make their leaders rich capitalists without ideology, which made her attempts for realistic topicality suspect and obviously contrived. The movies based on her books fared little better. *The Venetian Affair* (film, 1967), in particular, should have benefited from the star power of Robert Vaughn, fresh off his popularity as *The Man from U.N.C.L.E.* His leading lady, Elke Sommer, was then much discussed as a new screen sex symbol. Vaughn's character, Bill Fenner, was an alcoholic, depressed journalist, which led some critics to see the movie as having a touch of film noir. Partially shot in Venice, the cast also included notables such as Boris Karloff, Edward Asner, and Lucianna Paluzzi. However, the dry script and low-key execution contributed nothing to any participant's reputation.

For your information, the television series entitled *The Man from U.N.C.L.E.* is fictitious. There is no government agency which performs the functions portrayed in this program.
Letter from J. Edgar Hoover to those asking about joining U.N.C.L.E. in the 1960s

Early in the 1960s, espionage television shows flooded small screens on the then three networks. In the beginning, entertainment was clearly the point. When the watershed spy series *The Man from U.N.C.L.E.* (1964–1968) debuted on NBC on September 21, 1964, reviewers quickly saw that something fresh was on the airways. But even new concepts owed much to the past. Bill Ornstein's review for the *Hollywood Reporter*, which appeared the day after the show's premiere, was typical. Ornstein claimed *U.N.C.L.E.* contained "Shades of Herbert Rawlinson in *The Black Box* and Pearl White in the *Perils of Pauline*, which would offer audiences "spoofing in a serious way" (Ornstein 1964, 3). Ornstein noted one obvious connection between the new show and old-time Saturday matinee serials of the Rawlinson-White era. The show's opener was "divided into four chapters, each having a separate heading to get you into the dime movie-plus serial era. It's novel, to say the least, to bring this idea out of the misty past, and can very well be the beginning of something" (1964, 3). Two years later, when the spin-off *The Girl from U.N.C.L.E.* joined its parent show on NBC, other reviewers saw what *Man* had started. Again for the *Hollywood Reporter*, Hank Grant invoked a catchphrase from the parody-of-parodies, *Get Smart*, "Would you believe . . ." describing the latest secret agent outing. "Would you believe . . . Batman is no longer the only 'put on' series extant. In many respects, the plot devisers of this series have *Batman*'s beat, and once you realize even the straight scenes are gags, it's rather enjoyable—if thoroughly unbelievable" (Grant 1966, 10). After all, Grant noted, who would believe that secret antidotes could be smuggled via fleas on a dog?

Nineteen sixty-five was dubbed "Year of the Spy," as secret agents in the U.N.C.L.E. mold popped up in prime time on every night of the week, with imitators including *Amos Burke, Secret Agent* (ABC, 1965–1966), *I Spy* (NBC, 1965–1968), *Wild Wild West* (CBS, 1965–1970), and *Get Smart* (NBC, CBS, 1965–1970). In 1966, the British exported *The Avengers* (ABC, 1966–1969) and *Secret Agent* (CBS, 1966). In the same year, America offered one-season wonders like singer Robert Goulet in *Blue Light* (ABC), comic Red Buttons in *The Double Life of Henry Phyfe* (ABC), *The Girl from U.N.C.L.E.* (NBC), and *U.N.C.L.E.* producer Norman Felton's *Jericho* (CBS). The year's most important contribution to the genre was producer Bruce Geller's *Mission: Impossible* (CBS, 1966–1973), which survived a series of cast changes, was brought back on ABC from 1988–1990, and renewed again for several Tom Cruise vehicles in the 1990s. As if to demonstrate that the genre was not out of gas, 1967 saw the ambitious *The Man Who Never Was* (ABC) starring Robert Lansing and the sci-fi oriented *The Prisoner* (CBS), which came to the United States in 1968 featuring former *Secret Agent* Patrick McGoohan. On top of all this, few television series could avoid spy connections, from *Flipper* the dolphin to *Secret Squirrel* to *Lancelot Link, Secret Chimp* to the talking horse, *Mr. Ed.*

During the boom, a merchandising bonanza yielded a wide variety of tie-ins to television spies including novels (*U.N.C.L.E.* had twenty-three), magazines, board games, dolls, guns, lunch boxes, bubblegum cards, and walkie-talkies. Perhaps the strangest outgrowth of it all was the number of viewers who blurred fact from fiction. In the spirit of shows from the 1950s, which often expressed gratitude to actual law enforcement agencies for their help, the producers of *The Man from U.N.C.L.E.* tagged a note to their end credits as a joke: "We wish to thank the United Network Command for Law and Enforcement, without whose assistance this program would not have been possible." To everyone's surprise, J. Edgar Hoover wasn't amused when letters poured into not only the FBI but the United Nations. For a time, the U.N. hired a secretary whose only task was to answer U.N.C.L.E. correspondence. In the 1990s, a researcher looked through FBI files and found letters from the United States, England, Canada, and Ireland (Pringle 2000). For most responses, Hoover sent a terse note disclaiming any connection with U.N.C.L.E. and gave would-be spies booklets entitled "What It's Like to Be an FBI Agent" and "Should You Go Into Law Enforcement?" Some replies had to be more formal. In 1966, someone from the office of California representative John V. Tunney, the son of boxing champion Gene Tunney and later a senator, called the FBI on behalf of an unnamed individual interested in U.N.C.L.E. After a note from Hoover and a visit from a CIA agent, Tunney reported to his constituent that "although we have no colorful U.N.C.L.E. agents around, we do have some tenacious investigators who don't think it is below them to give a good answer to a citizen who asks a valid question" (Pringle 2000).

For the most part, all this was good fun, with producers doing their best to distance themselves from cold war connections by sending their agents out to do battle with the likes of THRUSH and KAOS, and strange masterminds like Dr. Migeleto Loveless on the *Wild Wild West*. But as the decade became more and more politicized, espionage shows began to reflect more serious concerns. In particular, Patrick

McGoohan's *The Prisoner* dealt with a covert world in which good vs. evil dichotomies were rarely cut-and-dried, and that the West's motives and actions were no different than the opposition. For example, in a *TV Guide* interview, McGoohan described the inspiration for his fantastic setting in his seventeen-episode program, stating "What do you do with defectors, or with people who have top-secret knowledge of the highest order and who, for one reason or another, want out? Do you shoot them? I know there are places where these people are kept. Not voluntarily, and in absolute luxury. There are three in this country—let someone deny it! I know about them because I know someone who used to be associated with the service" (Barthel 1968, 13). Such fears were also evident in shows apparently created for lighter purposes. In the opinion of *Get Smart* creator Mel Brooks, agents 86 and 99 spoke to a general feeling of disbelief in the government that was less than honest about Vietnam and other actions creating the "Credibility Gap" in President Lyndon Johnson's administration. For Brooks, one of the points of *Get Smart* was to make fun of government boondoggling and propaganda. According to fellow Max Smart creator Buck Henry, viewers could "see government espionage for what it really is, an idiotic enterprise glamorized by Hollywood" (Green 1993, 5). Thus, some films, books, and television series dealt less with the "reality" of espionage, and more with themes of what we feared it might be.

Ironically, metaphors about the cold war came to television largely in the guise of science fiction. In the 1950s, B movies about genetically altered mutants were parables about the misuse of atomic power. Most of television's 1960s spy shows were what scriptwriter Danny Biederman called "Spy-Fi," that is, entertainment fusing fantastic villains and weaponry with stories of heroic agents saving the world week after week. On the other side of the street, however, straightforward science-fiction shows often looked at the cold war with more thoughtful purposes, and espionage was often a device used in their stories. For example, spy plots and backdrops could be seen in three ABC shows, *The Outer Limits* (1963–1965), *Voyage to the Bottom of the Sea* (1964–1968), and *The Invaders* (1967–1968).[2] *Mission: Impossible* writer Allan Balter worked on both *The Outer Limits* and *Voyage*, providing an anti-Chinese communist episode for *Outer* in 1963, titled

"The Hundred Days of the Dragon." Another episode, "The Invisibles," depicted an undercover CIA agent infiltrating a secret subversive organization. "The Chameleon" focused on an ex-compromised CIA agent turned into an alien to spy on a UFO.

One reason for creative overlaps was the work of writers and producers working on both secret agent and sci-fi series. For example, important producer Joseph Gantman worked for both *U.N.C.L.E.* and *Mission: Impossible*, as well as *Voyage* along with Allan Balter and his writer associate, William Read Woodfield. As a result, *Voyage's* first season reflected the international anti-Red crusade in many stories clearly as much espionage as fantasy oriented. Quinn Martin's *The Invaders* also had spy connections, including sharing *U.N.C.L.E.* producer Anthony Spinner and *Mission: Impossible* producer Laurence Heath along with a director for both series, Sutton Roley. A precursor to *The X-Files*, the concept was about conspiracy and subversion in the government and industry.

Over the years, one series noted for cold war metaphors was *Star Trek*, from its original run through its movies to eventual sequels. The film *Star Trek VI: The Undiscovered Country* (1991), in particular, was an obvious metaphor for the aftermath of the breakup of the Soviet Union in the guise of a similar fate for the Klingon Empire. But even in the 1960s, such connections were part of the show's production. One directive read, "From a series point of view, if the Klingons are going to appear regularly as villains in stories, then they need to be 'controlled' villains. That is, the situation should be equivalent to the American-Russian cold war of the fifties" (Gerrold 1973, 33).

COMIC BOOK SPIES

One continuing influential media for the young, of course, was comic books, and spies took a prominent role in the 1960s. In Marvel Comics, *The Fantastic Four* got their powers as they went on an unauthorized rocket trip because "we have to beat the reds." Marvel's version of the Norse god, *Thor*, dealt with a Castro-like dictator in his second adventure and later went to Vietnam, a setting avoided in most films, television series, and comics.

One heavy influence was on Marvel's *Iron Man* in which Soviet leaders (and later Castro) were shown ordering a hit on Anthony Stark (the superhero's secret identity) because his company supplied high-tech weapons to the U.S. government. The Soviets were seen in their own attempt to have a superhero "arms race" by building their answer to Iron Man, the Crimson Dynamo. Marvel imitated *U.N.C.L.E.* by having their World War II hero, Nick Fury, become head of S.H.I.E.L.D. and battled their worldwide foe, Hydra. (It was later revealed that Spiderman's parents were S.H.I.E.L.D. agents killed on a secret mission.) Other comic book lines had their own acronym agencies, from T.H.U.N.D.E.R. to C.H.I.E.F., for which radio stalwart "The Shadow" reported. Of course, alphabet names weren't merely relegated to color pages for the young—for those into prurient tastes, books and films featuring the girl from L.U.S.T., the man from O.R.G.Y., and the man from T.O.M.C.A.T. weren't hard to find.

One comic strip, which led to a series of novels and one feature film, is worthy of an honorable mention here. According to writer Peter O'Donnell, he was approached in early 1962 by the cartoon editor of the *Express* group of newspapers. They wanted a new strip featuring a woman star who was both feminine and capable of traditionally masculine action adventure. O'Donnell recalled a refugee girl he'd seen in 1942 when he was a noncommissioned officer (NCO) in charge of a mobile radio detachment line of observation posts in Iran. He'd been charged with giving warning if German forces moved to seize the oilfields, when he saw the earthy, scrawny girl passing through the line ("Peter" 2004). Using this image as a starting point, O'Donnell created "Modesty Blaise," who first appeared in comic form in 1963 in the *London Evening Standard*. In 1965, O'Donnell began his long series of novels, which ended with 1996's *Cobra Trap*. Modesty's popularity in America also began in 1965 with the release of the film *Modesty Blaise*, starring Monica Vitti.

In the beginning, Modesty was a survivor of many international adventures before she became head of the criminal "Network" where she befriended her longtime associate, Willie Garvin. After the pair retired from crime, Sir Gerald Tarrant, head of a secret British agency, recruited them for their skills, asking for their assistance in solving problems outside of his "legal" realm. Thus, Modesty Blaise was a character reminiscent of Leslie Charteris's Simon Templar ("The Saint") who'd also been a thief recruited by the British government, in

Templar's case, by Sir Hamilton Dorn in 1935. Modesty was a bit more fantastic than Templar—she could run backwards—but her chief importance was as an example of the emerging feminist ideal that the Bond girls represented in the 1960s.

THE "STAINLESS STEEL RAT"

Even more fantastic than Modesty was "Slippery Jim" DiGriz, a.k.a. the "Stainless Steel Rat," who first appeared in two 1957 short stories by Harry Harrison. These tales were later developed into the novel *The Stainless Steel Rat* (1961), introducing the intergalactic criminal turned secret agent 33,000 years in the future. As various critics have noted, Harrison brought the picaresque adventures of eighteenth-century English and French novelists into the interplanetary scope of science fiction.[3] He mixed these elements with the characteristics of James Bond and Leslie Charteris's Simon Templar, preceding many television and movie spies who were former criminals turned into secret agents like Modesty Blaise.

Many of DiGriz's adventures, especially the later books such as *The Stainless Steel Rat's Revenge* (1970), were tongue-in-cheek reworkings of terrestrial spy adventures. Harrison expanded the settings of earth-bound international Robin Hoods from global crises to intergalactic power plays. Moving from planet to planet, most settings were earth-like worlds with primarily power-hungry human adversaries instead of alien creatures. Most stories were an episodic series of captures, near captures, attacks, escapes, and judo fights, as DiGriz took on galactic counterparts to Latin American dictators, future Nazis, and societies modeled on cold war Communist states as in *The Stainless Steel Rat Wants You* (1979). In these books, Harrison described mechanical gadgets and the obstacles DiGriz overcomes, parodying the special machines and weapons made famous by James Bond and his imitators.

DiGriz's escapades were mainly quirky action-adventure stories told with a wry, sardonic tone, largely seen in DiGriz's disdainful, outsider attitudes told in the first person. As the books progress, the "Rat" becomes a moral criminal in an uncaring "stainless steel" galaxy. Like many Robin Hoods before and after him, DiGriz continually shows his rebellious attitudes toward a society and legal system he finds beneath him.

A few books include topical satire and slapstick situational comedy not present in earlier books. For example, Harrison's 1999 *The Stainless Steel Rat Joins the Circus* includes one passage that would have worked well in a *Get Smart* script. In this adventure, the sometime agent for the intergalactic Special Corps is shown a new protective device called a "Surveillance Detector Detector," which can, of course, detect what someone else is detecting. These devices can be countered with a "Surveillance Detector Detector Detector." "Continuing down this road," the Rat observes, "only leads to madness." Harrison's humor also appeared in non-Rat stories, such as "The Man From P.I.G." featuring a galactic troubleshooter and his porcine sidekicks.

THE OTHER SIDE

Of course, the 1960s had more than Bond, pulp fiction, and parodies. As reviewer Laura Miller put it, spy stories can be seen as "The preposterous and the disillusioned," and the latter are often described as correctives to the former (Miller 2004, 39). In the 1960s, not only did we see the debuts of "corrective" authors like John Le Carré, Len Deighton, and Adam Hall, but Hollywood offered films that treated espionage as in days of yore, as epic tales of men and women in war and as commentary on themes beyond pure entertainment. Such projects were rarely intended as diversion but rather reflections of what both insiders and critics thought actual espionage was all about. The romantic aspects of Ian Fleming and the realm revolving around 007 was one arena in popular culture; headlines and an anti-Fleming movement created another.

6

From George Smiley to Bernard Sampson: The Counter-Fleming Movement

So far as I can ever remember of my youth, I chose the secret road because it seemed to lead straightest and furthest towards my country's goal. The enemy in those days was someone we could point at and read about in the papers. Today, all I know is that I have learned to interpret the whole of life in terms of conspiracy. That is the sword I have lived by and as I look around me I see it as the sword I shall die by as well. These people terrify me but I am one of them.
George Smiley in John Le Carré's *The Honorable School Boy*

While many literary and film spies of the 1960s created the illusion that the good guys always won in the end, the actual intelligence community was frequently more disturbing than THRUSH, KAOS, and SPECTRE combined. According to John Cawilti and Bruce Rosenberg, as revelations about the secret world became more widely known, many viewers of film and television and readers of both newsprint and new novels began to believe that all intelligence agencies of all countries acted much the same. The CIA, MI6, KGB, or Israel's Mossad were just as likely to assassinate enemies; steal hardware of military and strategic importance from friends, neutrals, and enemies; manipulate public and private events; finance revolutions; and make deals with the enemy (Cawilti and Rosenberg 1987, 188–89).

Inside the actual spy community, one theme seemed to dominate all others—paranoia. CIA counter-espionage chief James Jesus Angleton, an admirer of *The Manchurian Candidate*, created the phrase "a wilderness of mirrors" to define his implausible, and largely fictional, belief that the KGB had a "Master Plan" that led to his failure to recruit any Russian agents. He feared that they would invariably be plants and unreliable. Even after his departure, the agency had little success recruiting Soviet agents beyond walk-ins and defectors offering their services of their own accord (Hitz 2004, 19). For a time, Angleton even suspected his boss, CIA director William Colby.

But, as if to prove Angleton's fears were on target, in 1963, one of the most notorious traitors of the twentieth century, Kim Philby, eluded MI6 and escaped to Moscow, which gave the Soviets a propaganda bonanza. In 1968, Philby published *My Silent War*, which received widespread media interest, including excerpts in Western news magazines of Philby's condescending summations of both American and British intelligence chiefs. One reader who later claimed to be influenced by the book was FBI traitor Robert Philip Hanssen (Hitz 2004, 29). Hanssen wanted to be both Philby and James Bond. Like many agents, he owned a Walther PPK (pocket pistol). (Later revelations proved that Hanssen couldn't have read Philby's book when he was fourteen, as he had claimed; he was twenty-four when the book appeared [Wise 2002, 76].)

Alongside fears of what the Soviets were up to, new worries about Western agencies led to another kind of secret being buried. According to James Bamford, U.S. government cover-ups extended well beyond the Vietnam theater, where the North Vietnamese far outpaced the CIA with successful intelligence operations. When revolutions broke out in Ethiopia and Yemen, in Bamford's opinion, both America and Britain were less concerned with the fate of civilian populations than they were with the prospect of losing their eavesdropping listening posts in those countries. Between 1965 and 1969, the British drove out an entire native population from an East Indian island to set up a surveillance post for the Americans (Bamford 2001, 177). In 1967, during the Arab-Israeli War, the Israelis massacred the defenseless crew of the U.S. spy ship *Liberty* because they feared the Americans knew about similar atrocities the Israeli army was committing in their unprovoked attack on Egypt. President Lyndon Johnson imposed a news blackout and labeled the incident an accident. In an election year, he didn't wish to antagonize pro-Israel voters and said he didn't care if the ship sank so long as an ally wasn't embarrassed (Bamford 2001, 166).

In the same year, North Korea captured the equally unlucky spy ship *Pueblo* and held the American crew prisoner for eleven months. American television viewers watched as the Koreans paraded the captured officers in front of cameras; they beat and tortured them when the propaganda machine was turned off. As it happened, John Walker began his long career as a Soviet spy at the same time the Russians poured over their *Pueblo* bonanza. From that point on, the U.S. Navy held few secrets from the Soviets. Before anyone knew of this, scriptwriter D. C. Fontana took the *Pueblo* situation as her inspiration for "The Enterprise Incident," an episode of *Star Trek* in which Captain Kirk and company steal a cloaking device from the Romulans. Reportedly, Fontana wanted to tell the story as close to reality as possible, with the Romulans winning the battle (Gerrold 1973, 257). But networks, unlike governments, have more power over entertainment than headlines. Still, in one venue, so-called realism flourished in the 1960s. As usual, literature led the way, most notably in the works of John Le Carré:

When I first began writing, Fleming was riding high and the picture of the spy was that of a character who could lay the women and drive the fast car, who uses gimmickry and gadgetry and escape. When I brought back, but did not invent, the realistic spy story, it was misinterpreted as a great new wave. The old wave had a tidal force. (John Le Carré, quoted in Bold 1988, 9)

Since his debut in 1961, the novels of John Le Carré (pen name for David Cornwell) have been examined as both examples of high literary quality and ostensible windows into British intelligence and the English class system. On a literary level, Le Carré admitted he drew stylistic techniques and approaches from his readings of Joseph Conrad, John Buchan, Sir Arthur Conan Doyle, and Graham Greene (Bold 1988, 51; Bloom 1987, 4–5). Le Carré stated that his creative desire was to be credible, not authentic, using the "furniture of espionage" to deal with the literary themes of doubts, paranoia, morality, honor, and decency in questionable circumstances (Hoffman 2001, 41–43). In Le Carré's view, espionage provides great tension because people pretend to be something they are not. In commentary for the DVD release of *Smiley's People*, Le Carré said the secret world is under the world in which we live, our national subconscious. For him, the "metaphysical secret world" addresses the universals of real life, as in the conspiratorial relationships we all have with spouses and employers.

With such themes, Le Carré has been embraced by critics and reviewers as a writer who simply employed espionage as a device to explore, as the novelist claimed, more universal concerns. But such notions cannot separate or elevate Le Carré out of the spy genre from which his reputation was built. Many of the author's claims were part of his own "disinformation" public relations campaigns. In the 1960s, much was made of Le Carré's involvement in World War II espionage, but Le Carré insisted for decades that his literary success was more based on writing skills than any drawing from experience. He repeatedly stated that any semblance between his fictional "Circus" in British intelligence with fact were but illusion (Bold 1988, 8). However, in the 2000 BBC documentary *The Secret Service*, Le Carré broke some of the silence he'd maintained over the years. "At Lincoln College, he apparently kept his eyes open for possible agents recruited by the Soviet Union. Later Le Carré moved from MI5 to MI6, and he was in Berlin when the wall was erected" ("John" 2003). His was one of the names Kim Philby gave his Russian masters. Le Carré's experiences led to his writing *Call for the Dead* (1961), which, at that time, alienated the author from his former colleagues. In 2000, he recalled that publication of the book led him to be included in the "ranks of other shits like Compton McKenzie, Malcolm Muggeridge and J. C. Masterman, all of whom had betrayed the Service by writing about it" ("John" 2003).

Outside of the British intelligence community, other readers had different reactions. The media took to Le Carré in a big way with the success of the 1964 *The Spy Who Came in from the Cold*. One reviewer praised its "atmosphere of chilly hell," Graham Greene considered it the best spy story he had ever read, and the novel won Le Carré the Somerset Maugham Award ("John" 2003). Starring Richard Burton, Claire Bloom, and Oskar Werner, the story became a highly regarded, harshly photographed black-and-white film in 1966. Subsequent movies of the decade included *The Deadly Affair* (1966), based on Le

Carré's first novel, starring James Mason, Simone Signoret, Maximilian Schell, and Harriet Andersson. The 1965 book *The Looking Glass War* was filmed in 1969 starring Christopher Jones, Pia Degermark, and Ralph Richardson. Of these, *The Spy Who Came in from the Cold* was first seen as an antidote to James Bond and his imitators and later as an indication of themes Le Carré would explore in more depth.

For example, in both the book and film, Alex Lima (Burton) is no heroic agent in the Bondian sense. His moment of seeming courage occurs when he allows himself to be gunned down at the Berlin Wall after he learns he's been betrayed by his higher-ups. His mission had been to protect the identity of an East European double who was unlikable and despicable. As his job progresses, Lima becomes convinced that the wrong man was saved by impersonal and uncaring forces. To reach this human understanding, he faces his girlfriend Liz (Claire Bloom), demanding to know—which side is he on, good or evil? He responds that, for governments, secrets are far more important than people and any sacrifice is worth the cost (Hitz 2004, 41), adding:

What do you think spies are? Priests, saints, and martyrs? We're a squalid profession of vain fools. Traitors too. Pansies, sadists, and drunkards. People who play cowboys and Indians to brighten their rotten lives. (Lima in Hitz 2004, 41–42)

Such downbeat portrayals of spies continue throughout Le Carré's career, most notably in the projects involving George Smiley. Unlike the "organization man" of James Bond, Smiley dressed badly, didn't drive fast cars, and was a symbol of "the meek who do not inherit the earth." For most readers and critics, these characteristics were part of a literary mythology far removed from Fleming-flavored fiction. As Alan Bold noted, Le Carré's use of British intelligence had more to do with moral uncertainties than sex and gadgetry. For one thing, Smiley never got the girl. For the dumpy, short-legged Smiley, women were haunting memories, deceivers and betrayers personified in his unfaithful wife, Ann, who'd been seduced by the Soviet mole, Bill Hayden, on Moscow's orders. Beautiful women were supporting characters in a world of men, a means to power and perks, while others were mainly mother figures (Bold 1988, 70–77). On another level, Le

Carré can be seen as writing "anti-thrillers" because he doesn't follow the formula of exalting the hero when the villain is conquered. In the case of George Smiley, his survival was the only sign of victory, the validation of his sacrifice and the questionable ends and means he must use (Sauerberg 1984, 50).

The issues dominating Le Carré's work came to the fore when two BBC miniseries, *Tinker, Tailor, Soldier, Spy* (1979) and *Smiley's People* (1981), made actor Alec Guinness synonymous with George Smiley (Britton 2004, 214). Before the device became commonplace after the fall of the Berlin Wall, *Tinker* dealt with the theme of aging spies. In this instance, Smiley was pulled out of forced retirement because operatives in government agencies were so suspect that an independent investigator had to go it alone to find the ultimate mole in the Secret Service. Reviewers for both the book and series such as Brendan Kenny saw Le Carré as using the secret "Circus" as a microcosm of both British intelligence and English society as a whole—secretive, manipulative, class-structured, emotionally sterile, and materialistic. All branches of the British government, including intelligence, seemed under the control of a public school and Oxford educated elite retaining power within a restricted clan (Bold 1988, 35).

When the novel was televised, *Tinker*'s popularity was partly attributed to revelations that year that Sir Anthony Blount, the queen's supervisor of her art collections, was the fourth member of Kim Philby's "Cambridge Spy Ring." It was soon learned that the traitor Smiley tracked, Bill Hayden, was based on Philby.[1] Moles in fact and fancy seemed to mirror each other, while conservative critics blasted the grayness of the series, attempting to block its airing (Bold 1988, 36). According to some, Le Carré saw patriotism as an ideal now an institutional steamroller more likely to betray than protect. Le Carré's "circus" worldwide organization of spies didn't reflect high morals or singular purpose but was instead a perverted, corrupt family. Democratic power seemed on the decline with a rise in manipulative bureaucracies whose means were more important than the ends (Cawilti and Rosenberg 1987, 175). In these efforts, and many other Le Carré books and films, the higher-ups wore cloaks to protect themselves from their political masters and used their daggers on their own subordinates (Bloom 1987, 40). In Le Carré's view, this was one reason Americans took to George Smiley when the books were so clearly a commentary on English matters. In the DVD edition of *Smiley's People*, Le Carré claimed that America responded to Smiley because he is anticorporate. In the midst of those who succeeded in climbing the class ladder, the drab Smiley represented a professional man but clearly flawed human being.

The tragic humanity of Smiley was most evident in the last scenes of the important "Search for Carla Trilogy" (*Tinker, Tailor, Soldier, Spy*; *The Honorable School Boy*; *Smiley's People*) by less than heroic means—blackmailing his Russian adversary with news about his daughter. Smiley's shame was based on the fact that the West had adopted too much the methods of its Soviet enemy; on the other hand, Smiley's Russian archenemy had succumbed to the humanitarian appeals of the West. In *Smiley's People*, Smiley interrogates a Russian diplomat and hears he is performing in precisely the same way as his adversary in Moscow Central. In the last moments, after Smiley has forced Carla to defect by using KGB-style blackmail, a subordinate advises Smiley to be cool—"Be like Carla." In turn, Carla has become vulnerable because of his love for his daughter. In the view of at least one critic, this humanizing of Smiley's foe is a twist on Fleming. Smiley's quest was similar to Bond's battles with Blofeld as Smiley had magnified Carla into a larger-than-life adversary. For Smiley, Carla had been more monster than man, an icon that is demonstrated in the enlarged, blurry, and grainy copy of his passport photo in Smiley's office (Sauerberg 1984, 47, 202).

Beyond the Smiley television miniseries, Le Carré has remained a mainstay on both the large and small screen. Television projects included *The Perfect Spy*, a 1986 novel televised in 1987. This story was clearly the most personal for Le Carré, as it drew on his own relations with his domineering father, Ronnie Cornwell, who had engaged in swindles and was imprisoned for fraud. According to the author, this was one of the factors in his fascination with secrets ("John" 2003). In the lackluster film version of *The Little Drummer Girl* (1982), starring Diane Keaton, Klaus Kinski, and Yorgo Voyagis, Le Carré made a Hitchcockian cameo. *A Murder of Quality* (1962) was filmed for television in 1991.

Two Bonds took turns in Le Carré films: Sean Connery in *The Russia House* (book, 1989; film, 1990) and Pierce Brosnan in *The Tailor of Panama* (book, 1996; film, 2002). The former was considered a response to the end of the cold war, where a British publisher (Connery) is drawn into espionage by a Soviet woman (Michelle Pfeiffer). The latter, a low-key and underappreciated project costarring Geoffrey Rush, Jamie Lee Curtis, and Harold Pinter, has Brosnan working to set up a new MI6 network in Panama. Brosnan's character makes one statement emblematic of the period: "People don't want to know about the glorious past exploits of some shagged out old wino. They want the real stuff. Today's men. Tomorrow's, not yesterday's."

By the time of such projects, Le Carré knew it was time to retire Smiley in *The Secret Pilgrim* (1991). The author claimed he wanted to leave the world of Smiley's "Circus" and the cold war behind him because he felt the Middle East, the new center for international intrigue, was too removed from that conflict (Bold 1988, 130). Le Carré turned to drug smuggling in *The Night Manager* (1993), and former spies came to the end of the road in *Our Game* (1995). The Russian Mafia dominated *Single and Single* (1999), and *The Constant Gardener* (2000) was set in Africa, no important scene in the cold war. In 2004, Le Carré returned to the cold war in *Absolute Friends*, framing past history with stories about two agents unable to find a place for themselves without a secret world to give them identity.

Over the years, whenever a new espionage scandal broke, the most frequently cited novelist has remained John Le Carré for his pointing to what most think is the world's dirtiest business. For example, when the 2001 Robert Hanssen spy scandal broke, commentators noted the seamier realities of spycraft, especially the often unseemly morals of agents whose job it is to seduce and turn opposite numbers with sex, ego gratification, or greed into double agents. Such agents themselves are subject to the same pressures, and such morality plays provide the human realism if not professional accuracy of novelists such as Le Carré and his fellow 1960s alumni, Len Deighton.

Your job is an extension of mine. Your job is to provide success at any price. By means of bribes, by means of theft or by means of murder itself. Men like you are in the dark and the subconscious recesses of the nation's brain. You are a cipher—you are no more than the England with which history is written.

Minister to Harry Palmer in *Horse under Water*

Somewhere between Ian Fleming and John Le Carré was another novelist who mixed his deep interest in history, thrillers, and humor over three decades of successful and influential espionage novels. Len Deighton, who'd worked in the British National Service as a photographer attached to the Special Investigation Branch in World War II, debuted in literary circles with *The Ipcress File* in 1962. In subsequent novels featuring the same agent, the lead character remained anonymous, although the series became known as "the Harry Palmer" books when three of the novels became films starring Michael Caine. According to dust jackets for Ted Allbeury books, the novelist to begin his own spy novels in the 1970s was the model for Palmer.

Both the book and the 1965 film version of *The Ipcress File* introduced a new kind of antihero, a reluctant agent given the choice of prison or government work, a motif important in later film and television projects from *It Takes a Thief* to *Le Femme Nikita*. Palmer was a working-class hero pulled into the world of intrigue, responsible to people outside of his class and whom he did not trust. According to Lars Sauerberg, Palmer's character was miles apart from those of both Fleming and Le Carré, who both used gentlemen of one breed or another; Deighton used a spy with an ironic attitude about the world around him (1984, 65). Palmer didn't wish to operate like a gentleman and said he didn't like chess because he preferred games in which it was easier to cheat. Unlike Commander Bond of the British Royal Navy, Palmer was a sergeant in the army. He preferred tea to alcohol. He didn't report to an admiral but rather to Colonel Ross, who saw his agent as "insubordinate, insolent, and prone to criminal tendencies." Bond and Palmer shared one interest—gourmet food, although Palmer was as interested in cooking as eating. One secret meeting with his boss was in a grocery store, the one area in which he showed mastery. His one highbrow taste was for classical music, a devotion Bond never showed interest in.

The movie version of *The Ipcress File* had a wide influence on the spy milieu. The production team, while headed by Bond coproducer Harry Saltzman, consciously tried to create an "anti-Bond" approach to the genre to avoid overt imitation. For example, Palmer was no globe-trotter. Although he was captured and apparently tortured in Albania, the setting was actually a fake and Palmer never left the boroughs of Westminster and London. Such situations became a staple of the television series *Mission: Impossible*, whose creator, Bruce Geller, later wanted his television series to emulate the tone and cinematic approach of the movie (Britton 2004, 129). In particular, Geller liked director Sidney Furie's pioneer work in unusual camera placement, such as shots from under cars and through lampshades. Beyond looking experimental, these angles conveyed the clandestine, eavesdropping nature of the spy business.

The second 1963 Palmer book, *Horse under Water*, was never filmed. Its manuscript is of special note, as the British Office of the Navy asked to examine it to ensure that modern secrets weren't being revealed (McCormick 1977, 61). In 1965, Harry Saltzman turned to *Goldfinger* director Guy Hamilton to make *Funeral in Berlin* (book, 1964) the second Caine vehicle. The story and approach were as different from *Goldfinger* as Hamilton could produce. Unlike 007, Caine's Palmer has to sign expense vouchers and is mocked by an East German general for his British salary of 30 pounds a week. Palmer isn't happy about it, resentful that he has to spy on the weekend. He has to sign for a gun that he doesn't want, and refuses to kill in cold blood. Instead of getting gadgets from a cranky Q, he gets fake documents from a crusty forger that, naturally, he also has to sign for. When a beautiful girl picks him up, he's immediately suspicious of her because he doesn't feel he is the type to be so lucky. He is right—she is an Israeli agent seeking money from an ex-Nazi who'd stolen it during World War II. And, very unlike *Goldfinger*, the film's story line is a clever sandwich of two plots. In the beginning, Palmer is assigned to help a defector get out of East Berlin. After a series of twists and turns—including realizing that the defector was simply trying to trap the master of aiding escapees from Berlin—the film ends with an ex-Nazi trying to go in the opposite direction, getting into the forbidden sector of East Berlin so he can keep his ill-gotten gains. This twist echoed Graham Greene's *The Third Man*, where Orson Welles's Harry Lime continually escapes to the Russian sector of Vienna to avoid prosecution for his black market empire.

In 1967, former documentary director Ken Russell completed the Harry Palmer trilogy with *Billion Dollar Brain* based on the 1966 novel. Following popular trends, Bond connections were more overt in *Brain*, including John Barry's music, Ken Adams's sets, Peter Hunt's editing, and Maurice Binder's title sequences. Some critics felt this adventure was too un-American because the Russians were portrayed too sympathetically and the U.S. military was not. Well, that was part of the point, if the original novel is any guide. In the novel's early scenes, Palmer is an independent private investigator trying to distance himself from MI5 until he is again drafted by Colonel Ross. Palmer then infiltrates an American organization, "The Crusade for Freedom," which is allegedly trying to bring "freedom and Coke" to satellite countries behind the Iron Curtain. In the film version, the group's head, General Midwinter, represents how much times have changed since the 1950s. He is no screen villain out for his own gain. Instead, he is a devout, idealistic anti-Communist wanting to instigate a revolution in Latvia to atone for the "shameful" takeover of Hungary in 1956 when NATO stood by and did nothing. His scheme, planned by the billion-dollar computer that would "send the CIA and MI-5 into the stone age" is undone by one of his subordinates who lied about the number of operatives in Latvia. Like a good capitalist, he'd been telling the brain the general had three hundred nonexistent agents in the country but was pocketing their expenses himself. In a foreshadowing of the détente seen in the 007 films of the 1970s, Palmer is assisted by his chief's good-natured, laughing Russian opposite number who admits Midwinter would deserve medals during wartime, but is stupid and nuts in the era of the cold war.

Ironically, this film has been rarely seen after the 1960s because of one scene's use of the Beatles' song, "A Hard Day's Night." As rights to the song are somewhat expensive, neither video nor DVD releases of the movie are likely. Thus, bootleg versions command high prices on eBay. *Billion Dollar Brain* was the last of the film series until 1995, when Caine starred in two films showing the character becoming a private investigator in Moscow in *Bullet to Beijing* and *Midnight in St. Petersburg* (both 1995). The last of the Palmer novels, *Spy Story*, appeared in 1974. In 1986, it became a non–Harry Palmer film directed by Lindsey Shontoff starring Don Fellows, Michael C. Gwynn, and Nicholas Parsons in a mix of counter-espionage and nuclear submarine antics.

According to Ron Miller, Deighton's post-1960s work was more accomplished, partly because the writer "developed a wide network of insider contacts around the world," which resulted in the ongoing saga of Bernard Sampson who became the central figure in books written over a decade (Miller 1996, 181). In fact, Deighton is now perhaps best noted for the three trilogies and one "prequel" based around

British agent Sampson and the political and family conflicts during the cold war and its aftermath. Of special note are the first series, *Berlin Game* (1983), *Mexico Set* (1984), and *London Match* (1985), all later anthologized as *Game, Set, and Match*, which in turn became a thirteen-part PBS television miniseries in 1988. In both the books and the lavish television adaptation, Bernard Sampson (Ian Holm) is a disgraced British agent specializing in German affairs trapped in a menial desk job, while his wife, Fiona (Mel Martin), has moved up the ladder of espionage as a senior security officer (Miller 1996, 179). In the script, adapted by John Howlett, the unusual move into spying for the *Mystery!* series was designed to be a complex detective story in an era of cold war paranoia. *Game, Set, and Match* was intended to be a modern espionage drama with betrayal of friends and family "a required condition of employment, and the incentive to betray one's colleagues is sometimes too compelling" (Miller 1996, 179). Filmed on location in Berlin and Mexico, the project included a huge international cast with 3,000 extras and a budget of $8 million. The thirteen hours comprised the most ambitious espionage miniseries ever filmed.

    Game, Set, and Match, clearly fare for adult audiences seeking intellectual puzzles as well as action adventure, mirrored similar treatments of Le Carré novels, in that espionage was dealt with on moral grounds in ways untypical of most American ventures. The central character has felt betrayed for five years, believing his MI6 supervisors were bogged down with administrative affairs and unfamiliar with true field work. When Sampson is reactivated to find a double agent behind enemy lines, he has his own double mission—to find the mole and his own redemption (Miller 1996, 180). His story is something of a parable echoing the biblical Samson. Like Samson, the Cold Warrior has his own Delilah, his wife, Fiona, turning out to be the double. According to one critic, the series was "The *Waiting for Godot* of spy stories," as the themes of truth vs. illusion gave depth to the intertwining of politics, family drama, and Sampson's personal quest (Miller 1996, 180). While praised by critics, the ratings were a disaster for the network, as viewers shrank each week. The miniseries, sadly, was the last such long epic for *Mystery!* However, the trials of the Sampson family had just begun.

    In 1987, Deighton issued a prequel to the saga, *Winter: A Berlin*

Family (1899–1945). The second Sampson trilogy included *Spy Hook* (1988), *Spy Line* (1989), and *Spy Sinker* (1990). In the various threads in this series, Sampson thwarts a security leak, but is rewarded with a warrant for his arrest and forced to flee to Berlin. He learns that Fiona, a former Oxford graduate who understands the espionage game better than her male colleagues, is in fact a triple agent sent to be a mole under deep cover. While her husband finds consolation with a younger agent, both spouses wonder about another level of betrayal—that of being a wife and mother while doing her country's work over a period of years. Fiona is finally extricated from behind the Iron Curtain, but to do so, her sister is sacrificed, another tragic spin on the use of "innocents" in the covert world.

The last of the Sampson series, *Faith* (1994), *Hope* (1995) and *Charity* (1996) explored the impact of the end of the cold war on these agents. Each book recounts the same events from three different perspectives, and the theme in each is healing and reconciliation, not between governments, but with spies needing to find a road to trust themselves, their spouses, and the superiors who had treated them like disposable pawns in a game without true victors. As in Le Carré's books, Deighton's characters in the Sampson epic battle Communist plots usually set in East Germany where a culture of espionage draws in friends and family alike, all of whom live in a world unto themselves. Throughout the ongoing saga, their realms of power and influence seem downgraded into deadly games within a circle that have little to do with any political or social stratas uninvolved with secret methods, enigmatic files, or planting moles in each other's headquarters. As in the words of *Casino Royale*'s Sir James Bond, it's a world in which espionage replaced war. In Deighton's imagination, the secret world was a private jungle that was also an underground soap opera.

To date, the canon of twenty-six fiction and nonfiction Deighton books has spanned a wide range of arenas from his interest in cooking, World War II, espionage, and humor. Other spy thrillers by Deighton include *Yesterday's Spy* (1975) and *Twinkle, Twinkle, Little Spy* (1976), renamed as *Catch a Falling Spy* in the United States. Two of Deighton's four World War II novels, *SS-GB* (1978) and *City of Gold* (1993), employed espionage elements, since the plot of the former revolves around potentially embarrassing secret documents for the British, and *Gold* has spies working in Egypt.

> It happened before. You work out a good trick and you calculate the odds and they look O.K. I'll put it this way. They don't look actually lethal. So you gird up the loins and put the turn-screw on the nerves till they're tight as harp strings and you go in with at least the thought that if something goes wrong, then you end up spread-eagled across enemy terrain with a shot in the spine or a knife in the throat. It would have been your fault. It was simply of being a calculated risk that turned suddenly into a certainty. A dead certainty. . . . And then afterward, when you've got away with it, you look back and suddenly know that you were out of your mind even to think of going in at all.
>
> Adam Hall, *Quiller: Salamander*

One author frequently compared to Deighton, primarily for their shared use of an elliptical style, is Adam Hall, creator of a number of spy thrillers including *The Berlin Memorandum* (1965), *The Ninth Directive* (1966), and *The Striker Portfolio* (1969). These novels dealt with special agent Quiller, a human machine who "knows to the second how long a drug will take to fog his brain" and how he can move quicker when covered in sweat (Winks 1982, 54–55). Quiller's every movement is guided by his awareness of body chemistry, of friction and physics, and the speed of sound. Quiller's identity is determined only by his work, a man clearly detached and clinical. Quiller refers to himself as "The Organism" and blocks out all but his automatic responses when preparing for a mission. Quiller works for "The Bureau," a group so secret most of the British government doesn't know of its activities (Winks 1982, 71). In Quiller's own words, "The Bureau is a secret underground outfit that doesn't officially exist. They answer directly to the Prime Minister without going through the hysterical clowns in the Foreign Office. And one of the reasons for this is to give us the freedom to do things no one else is allowed to do. And I'll say no more" (Hall 1994, 3).

Hall's 1965 *The Berlin Memorandum* was a worldwide best seller. In the opinion of John Cawilti, the book was an example of the "Spy Goes Over" theme of the era, that is, a tale of an agent forced to first become the hunted behind enemy territory and then becoming the hunter (Cawilti and Rosenberg 1987, 86). In this case, Quiller is a spy looking to the past—tracking down neo-Nazis—and the future, in that he's a spy awaiting retirement, agreeing to do one last job. Typical of the decade, the main weapons used against Quiller are drugs used to disorient him and hopefully trick him into revealing information.

Distinguished author Harold Pinter scripted the film version, *The Quiller Memorandum* (1965), starring George Segal as Quiller, Senta Berger, Alec Guinness, George Saunders, and Max Von Sydow. The film earned high critical praise, including one review from the *London Daily Telegraph* that liked Pinter's "slightly surrealistic dialogue . . . [which was] nicely matched by director Michael Anderson's use of locations to make West Berlin seem at once substantial and fantastic" ("Quiller" 2004).

By 1992's *Quiller: Salamander*, Hall looked for fresh ways to explore his character, and in this tense drama had Quiller doing a mission not sanctioned by "The Bureau." The story has the intelligence officer—who steadfastly refuses to become an assassin for his agency—pulled into a suicidal attempt to stop the slaughter in Cambodia. But, like other spies in fictional dramas, he shoots the murderous general trying to take over the country when the mission becomes personal. When your girlfriend is killed, it's time to put principles aside. Hall's 1996 *Quiller: Balalaika* (first appearing in the United States in 2003) was the novelist's eighteenth Quiller book, and seemingly the last in the series.

BLOCKBUSTERS AND LITERARY EPICS

But many novels and films of the decade cannot be described fairly as "anti-Bond" as much as "un-Bond." Beyond the more famous novelists creating worlds far removed from 007 and those who saw him as the center of the spy universe in the 1960s, a number of significant writers and Hollywood projects could trace their roots to other facets of the genre. Characteristics included films based on best sellers employing ensemble casts of well-known box office draws. In such films, the enemies tended to be realistic representatives of a cold war still very much in the public eye.

For example, one of the most important novels of the decade was Richard Condon's *The Manchurian Candidate*, although the book was first published in 1950. For ten years, Condon had been unable to sell it to Hollywood until director John Frankenheimer and screenwriter George Axelrod snapped up the rights. In 1962, they created a landmark classic movie based closely on the book that warned about the ill uses of both science and politics. The film starred Lawrence Harvey as Raymond Shaw, a Korean War POW who had been brainwashed to assassinate a presidential candidate. Frank Sinatra, whose early desire to star in the project helped get the film off the ground, is the company commander who beats his own brainwashing to figure out the plot. Angela Lansbury is both Harvey's mother and the Soviet agent who controls him in order to put her senator husband, clearly modeled on Joseph McCarthy, in the White House. The film was nearly killed by United Artists who feared a movie about such assassins might pollute the air when President Kennedy scheduled a summit with Soviet secretary Nikita Kruschev in Geneva. According to Sinatra, the movie was saved when he told studio executives he had just met with Kennedy, then a personal friend, who was enthusiastic about the film. He wanted to know who would play the mother.

According to Frankenheimer's DVD commentary, research for the film included close study of the political convention where Kennedy had accepted his nomination, and Frankenheimer made a point of plugging the American Civil Liberties Union to underline the script's political bent. One aspect of the convention scenes was an overt "rip-off" from *Foreign Correspondent*. The director said he couldn't figure out a way to have Sinatra find Harvey inside the convention hall until he remembered how Joel McCrea had discovered the Nazis in the Hitchcock film. Just as McCrea had noticed that all the windmills had stopped except for the one powered by electricity, Sinatra noticed that all the convention lights had dimmed except for Harvey's hiding place. According to Frankenheimer, *Candidate* contained several firsts. While the McCarthy era had lost steam, the blacklist was still hovering over Hollywood so the attacks on the anti-Communist crowd was among the first to be filmed. Frank Sinatra was the first American star to have a karate fight on film. Ironically, the tale about an assassination plot against a U.S. president seemed prophetic when Kennedy later lost his life in Dallas (Strada and Troper 1997, 62).

While the movie went on to be known as a classic, novelist Richard Condon was never again to stir up as much interest in his spy books. He later issued *Winter Kills* (1974) and *The Whisper of the Axe* (1976).

The latter was involved with urban terrorism and an incestuous brother and sister working for the CIA, an echo of the same relationship between mother and son in *The Manchurian Candidate*. Like his most famous novel, *Whisper* used secret training camps in China and brainwashing. A lover of acronyms, Condon wrote that to get accuracy in his spy novels, he wrote Len Deighton or Charles McCarry (McCormick 1977, 50).

In July 2004, *The Manchurian Candidate* was adapted into a new vehicle for Denzel Washington and Meryl Streep. This time around, soldiers in the Gulf War are captured and implanted with controlling chips. In this version, Liev Schreiber plays a new Raymond Shaw, who becomes a congressman running for vice president twelve years after Desert Storm. In interviews, Washington made it clear that the film was intended to be very different from the original. He said he had never watched it to avoid being influenced by Sinatra's performance. To the surprise of those believing that no remake could match the power of the original, the 2004 version quickly earned high critical praise. Again, the film unintentionally mirrored contemporary history. The new Raymond Shaw runs for office basing his campaign on his war record, a situation identical to that of presidential candidate John Kerry that same year. Echoing concerns after the Kennedy assassination, the film's ending is full of ambiguities with no certain resolution.

Back in 1967, Frank Sinatra had returned to spycraft in *The Naked Runner* directed by Sidney J. Furie after the director's work on *The Ipcress File*. Costarring Peter Vaughn, the script was yet another story of an American businessman asked by British intelligence to do a mission for them in East Germany. Francis Clifford wrote the original novel of the same name in 1966 before producing two other spy books, *All Men Are Lonely* (1967) and *The Blind Eye* (1971) (McCormick 1977, 49).

Major star Gregory Peck distinguished *The Chairman* (1969), in which the Russians and Americans unite against the Chinese who have developed a miraculous food-growing enzyme giving them considerable clout in poverty stricken countries. The U.S. scientist and agent John Hathaway (Peck) doesn't know that a bomb had been implanted beneath his skin and that his true mission is to die when he meets the Chinese leader, Mao Tse-Tung. In this convoluted story, the Soviets save Hathaway (Strada and Troper 1997, 115). The

Chinese are foes yet again in director Henry Levin's *Kiss the Girls and Make Them Die* (1966) starring Beverly Adams, Dorothy Provine, Terry-Thomas, and Mike Connors in a story about a CIA agent chasing an industrialist who has agreed to sell the Chinese a means to sterilize men. According to Bill Koenig, because of some similarities, perhaps the film inspired many of the aspects of the 1979 Bond film, *Moonraker*. For example, the Dino DeLaurentis production had an American CIA agent (Conners) teamed with female British spy— Provine; *Moonraker* had Bond working with American operative, Holly Goodhead (Lois Chiles). The 1966 film's lavish budget and realistic settings in Rio de Janeiro were later praised by director Quentin Tarentino, who claimed the movie was among his favorites of the period.

While the Red Chinese occasionally appeared as adversaries during the 1960s, adventures set in the Far East remained as rare as World War II films that focused on encounters with the Japanese. Even rarer were films in which Asians, or any other minority, worked as heroes beyond supporting roles. The notable exception was scriptwriter and novelist Bill Ballinger's CIA operative Joaquim Hawks, who first appeared in the novel, *The Chinese Mask* (1965). The resourceful, strong, and handsome Hawks is half Spanish and half Nez Percé Indian, a linguist and smooth killer. Because of his looks, Hawks is able to pose as a member of various ethnic groups and operates mainly in Southeast Asia. In *The Chinese Mask*, for example, he plays a Chinese circus performer stalking scientists also playing in circus acts. Ballinger also cowrote the screenplay for *Operation CIA* (1966) starring the young Burt Reynolds as Mark Andrews operating in Saigon to thwart a plot to assassinate a U.S. ambassador. This movie was one of the first to deal with Vietnam as a setting. Hawks continued his adventures in four other books, ending with *The Spy in the Java Sea* (1966).

Other films of the decade fused stories of World War II valor, espionage, and the box office draw of all-star casts like *Counterfeit Traitor* (1962) based on actual Nazi spy Eric Ericson (William Holden). *Operation: Crossbow* (1965) centers on the methods used to defeat Hitler's V1 and V2 rockets. The film includes references to Hannah Reich, an actual test pilot who flew some of the first "flying bombs." George Peppard plays Lt. John Curtis in perhaps the best of the actor's

World War II film trilogy. Anthony Quayle, as the Nazi Bamford, plays against his usual type as the adversary out to stop Peppard. Other top-drawer names include Sophia Loren as Nora, the girl who dies early in the film, Trevor Howard, and Lilli Palmer. The film is noted for its elaborate underground German rocket base similar to Bond designer Ken Adam's sets. In 1967, *Triple Cross* starred Christopher Plummer as a former British safecracker turned spy for Nazis before being turned by British intelligence. Based on the exploits of Eddie Chapman, the script was adapted from his book, *The Eddie Chapman Story.*

A *Man from U.N.C.L.E.* alumni, David McCallum, tried for big-screen stardom in *The Mosquito Squadron* (1969). McCallum played a Canadian-born RAF pilot undertaking a crucial behind-the-lines mission to destroy Germany's ultimate weapon project (Davenport 2004, 237). Another effort with multiple star power was *Charade* (1963) starring Cary Grant, Audrey Hepburn, Walter Matthau, and James Coburn. The film was also distinguished by original Oscar-nominated music by Henry Mancini and Johnny Mercer with titles by Maurice Binder. Based on the story "The Unsuspecting Wife" by Marc Behm and Peter Stone, the stylish Paris-set comedy thriller was director Stanley Donen's overt nod to the influence of Alfred Hitchcock. The plot involves a young widow (Hepburn) on the run from crooks and double agents wanting money that her murdered husband might have stolen during World War II. Matthau is the CIA man, Coburn one of the thugs, and Grant the helpful if mysterious love interest.

Of course, Alfred Hitchcock contributed his own efforts to the boom he had done so much to shape. After completing the nonespionage 1964 film *Marnie* (starring Sean Connery), Hitchcock again looked to a Richard Hannay story, this time Buchan's *The Three Hostages* (1924). But as the plot depended on the baddie using hypnotism, the director abandoned the idea as being too hard to film, a decision he'd made earlier in shaping the script for the original *The Man Who Knew Too Much* (Truffaut and Scott 1967, 231). Instead, Hitchcock directed the lackluster *Torn Curtain* (1966), a story of American atomic scientist Michael Armstrong (Paul Newman) pretending to be a defector to regain a secret formula. Complications follow when the scientist's fiancee, Sarah Sherman (Julie Andrews), follows him to East Berlin when he's forced to participate in a murder. Hitchcock said he was inspired by the disappearance of two British diplomats, Guy Burgess and Donald Maclean, two members of Kim Philby's "Cambridge Spy Ring." Hitchcock claimed he wondered what Mrs. Burgess must have thought, and built the film from the woman's point of view (Truffaut and Scott 1967, 233).

Looking to his own past work, Hitchcock cut one scene in a factory where the lead reluctantly killed an enemy. The director felt this had been one failure in *Secret Agent*, in which the hero found his mission distasteful and the audience couldn't relate with this (Truffaut and Scott 1967, 235). For some, this move distinguished the film, because the professor was Hitchcock's first use of a hero taking on a mission by choice rather than by falling into adventure by chance (Wood 1989, 198). He is a man on a quest who must descend into symbolic levels of hell to fulfill his mission. From a feminist perspective, Sarah is the key to the script. "In some ways, *Torn Curtain* refers us back to *Notorious* and *North by Northwest*, in both of which monstrous demands were made on the heroine in the name of political necessity." In *Torn Curtain*, Armstrong's political actions and morality are questioned and it is Sarah's steadfastness and pulling for a more ordered life that gives the film its moral foundation. Neither the hero nor heroine are the innocents in danger—it is the bystanders who are potential victims in the wake of a quest that could endanger them all (Wood 1989, 204). But *Torn Curtain* was more of a disappointment to most observers, partly due to the use of big-name stars miscast in the roles.

Hitchcock's final spy effort was equally below par, the 1969 *Topaz* based on the novel by Leon Uris. At the time, the 1962 book had an unusual reputation. The fictional account led to speculations that the plot, involving a mole in French intelligence close to Charles De Gualle, might have been based in fact. An international scandal brewed and indeed a mole was found (McCormick 1977, 178). One scene in both novel and film, in which a French spy for the Soviets dies falling on a car, was based on fact (Wise 1992, 87). The much-awaited film was the most expensively produced movie of Hitchcock's career, although the cast was largely unknown beyond the American John Forsyth. A critical and audience bomb, Hitchcock later virtually disowned the film. Most of the problems resulted from a rushed script with a confusing ending. Sadly, what would have been the director's fifty-third film would have been his last spy effort called *The Short Night*. In 1978, an ailing Hitchcock wanted to base a film on the British double agent George Blake, and drafted the first scenes about his traitor escaping from prison before raping and murdering the woman who'd helped in the escape (Spoto 1983, 574). However, the project was abandoned before the director's death in April 1980.

One novelist who was a harbinger of things to come was Alistair MacLean, a writer first noted for naval and sea adventures with one eye clearly on future adaptations for the screen. His first spy offering was *The Last Frontier* (1959), about an unlikely agent blundering through Hungary. Shot on location, the book was filmed as *Secret Ways* (1961) starring Richard Widmark as a hard-boiled American penetrating Hungary to help refugees escape. More successful was MacLean's *Ice Station Zebra* (1963), in which a British secret service team races across the Arctic to rescue a capsule that has fallen from outer space with a top-secret reconnaissance camera. According to some critics, the plot was better for melodrama on the screen than for reading (McCormick 1977, 130). In 1968, director John Sturges's film version did earn a measure of success with a cast including Rock Hudson, Ernest Borgnine, Jim Brown, Lloyd Nolan, and television's *Secret Agent*, Patrick McGoohan. Similarly, *Where Eagles Dare* (1967) was a World War II adventure with paratroopers dropping behind enemy lines to rescue an American general. In 1968, the same year as the film release of *Ice Station Zebra*, MacLean wrote his own screenplay for *Eagles*. The result was considered a well-made, suspenseful vehicle for Clint Eastwood, Richard Burton, and Mary Ure (Connors and Craddock 1999). In 1975, MacLean went further back in time with his screenplay for *Breakheart Pass*, a nineteenth-century set story with Charles Bronson protecting a serum for immunizing settlers on a train. In the same year, MacLean's novel, *The Circus*, had the greatest high-wire artist in the world attempting to penetrate a fortress to obtain the secrets of antimatter and the mad scientist who'd learned how to control it.

Other films and novels worthy of passing mentions include *A Dandy in Aspic* (1968), in which a double agent is hired to kill himself in a hard-to-follow film based on the novel by Derek Marlow. Starring Tom Courtenay and Mia Farrow, the movie's first director was

Anthony Manne, who died midway through the shooting, so Lawrence Harvey finished the project. James Munroe, a pen name for James Mitchell, wrote two literary spy series. As Munroe, he had created the John Craig books in the 1960s, including the novel *The Man Who Sold Death* (1964). Under his own name, Mitchell penned one script for the UK series *Armchair Theatre*, called "A Magnum for Schneider." The story was made into the pilot episode for the British series *Callan* (1967–1973) starring Edward Woodward as a world-weary spy with a conscience. Once *Callan* went to series, Mitchell adapted his teleplay into the first of four novels called, among other titles, *Red File for Callan* (1969).

Another honorable mention must go to novelist Kurt Vonnegut, Jr. His 1961 *Mother Night* was the story of American artist-turned-agent Howard Campbell transmitting secret codes in pro-Nazi radio broadcasts. Using the actual case of Fascist sympathizer and poet Ezra Pound, who had become famous for his pro-Mussolini broadcasts during World War II, Vonnegut's tale explored the idea that Campbell's codes were known only to secret agencies. Thus, when the war ended, Campbell wasn't believed to have been a covert patriot. Worse, whatever good his hidden messages might have provided was seen to be outweighed by the damage of his propaganda (Melley 2000, 22).

END OF AN ERA

By the end of the 1960s, the presence of spies was still pervasive in popular culture, but espionage never again enjoyed its former place as a phenomena dominating publishing as well as movie and television production. The genre had been stretched to all extremes, and many subsequent efforts were more reworkings of old templates than fresh approaches in literature or film. This is not to say that the genre was nearly out of gas, rolling forward merely on fumes of old ideas. As the cold war lumbered on, seemingly without victories or a light at the end of the tunnel, attitudes about East and West dichotomies changed as more and more information was made public about actions from behind formerly closed doors. As the 1970s dawned, Watergate and the fall of Vietnam contributed to a spirit of cynicism that overshadowed both fact and fiction for decades afterward. Reds no longer seemed the primary adversary of Western values. As established in the fiction of Le Carré, Deighton, and the other writers compared to them, just who our enemies were was now an open question. For many, as stated in Walt Kelly's famous 1970 Pogo poster, "We have met the enemy and he is us."

The spy as dandy: Leslie Howard as the Baroness Orczy's nineteenth-century French spy, the Scarlet Pimpernel (1935). *Larry Edmunds Cinema and Theatre Bookshop.*

British director Alfred Hitchcock, the most important shaper of the spy movie genre. *MovieStore.com.*

Sexual duels with a touch of the kinky: Robert Donet and Madeline Carroll in Alfred Hitchcock's *The 39 Steps* (1935). *Larry Edmunds Cinema and Theatre Bookshop.*

While filming *Robin Hood* in 1937, swashbuckler Errol Flynn allegedly began his career as a Nazi spy. *MovieStore.com.*

Before reheating the cold war in the 1980s, actor Ronald Reagan was a secret agent looking for a defense shield in the film *Murder on the Air* (1940). *MovieStore.com.*

Flaunting sexuality while bowing to censorship: Cary Grant and Ingrid Bergman in Alfred Hitchcock's *Notorious* (1946). *The Remember When Shop.*

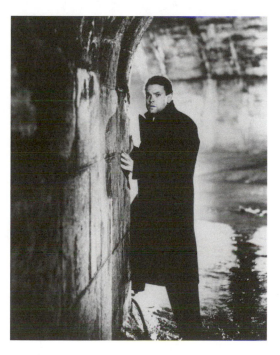

Going underground in the cold war: Orson Welles in Graham Greene's *The Third Man* (1949). *MovieStore.com.*

Spying on national landmarks: Cary Grant and Eva Maria Saint by Mt. Rushmore in Alfred Hitchcock's *North by Northwest* (1959). *The Remember When Shop.*

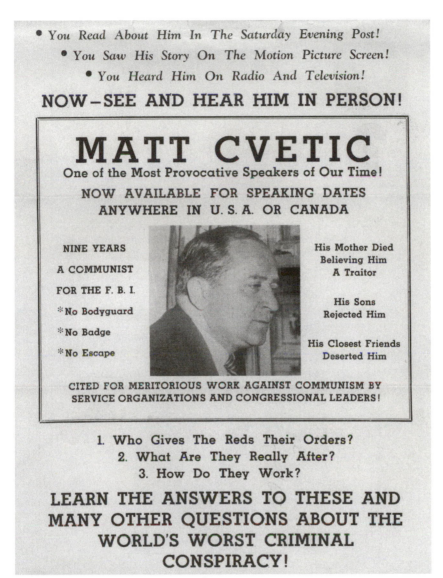

In the 1950s, Matt Cvetic capitalized on his undercover work in the film and radio series *I Was a Communist for the FBI*. He helped heat fears during the McCarthy era, making public appearances advertised on this flier. *Courtesy Matt Cvetic, Jr.*

Creating the spy music genre: The John Barry Seven included composer Barry (*center, holding trumpet*), who scored the musical legacy of the 007 films. Guitarist Vic Flick (*second in from right*) created the signature hook for the "James Bond Theme," the most famous pre-title music in spy movie history. *Courtesy Vic Flick.*

Former Reuters correspondent and British Naval Intelligence officer Ian Fleming created the world's most popular spy when he penned *Casino Royale*. Written after Fleming had retired from public service and taken up residence on the north coast of Jamaica, the book's hero, James Bond, became the ultimate symbol of dashing masculinity in a series of books and films released before and after the author's death in 1964. *Photofest*

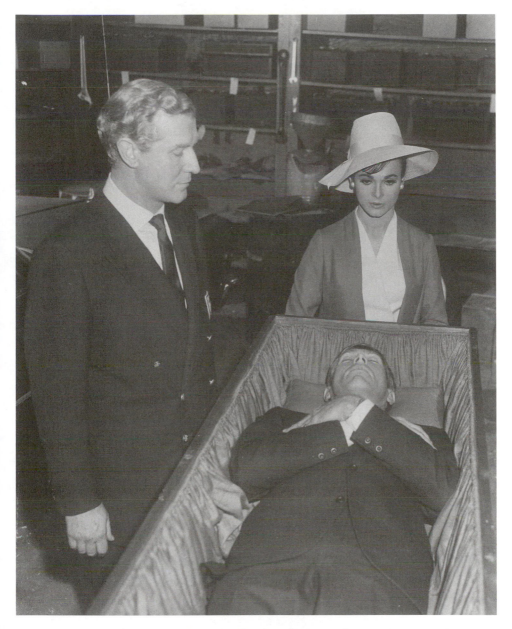

An American James Bond: James Coburn as Derek Flint in *Our Man Flint* (1965). *The Remember When Shop.*

In *Carry on Spying* (1964) Desmond Simpkins (Kenneth Williams) and James Bind (Charles Hawltry), seen here in drag, were the comedic answers to James Bond. *MovieStore.com.*

The "Rat Pack" Spies: Sammy Davis, Jr. and Peter Lawford in *Salt and Pepper* (1966). *The Remember When Shop.*

The first important "anti-Bond" film: Richard Burton and Claire Bloom in John Le Carré's *The Spy Who Came in from the Cold* (1966). *The Remember When Shop.*

The "human" 007 meets the Avengers: George Lazenby carrying Diana Rigg in *On Her Majesty's Secret Service* (1969). *The Remember When Shop.*

James Bond meets *Star Wars*: Roger Moore and Lois Chiles in *Moonraker* (1979). *The Remember When Shop.*

Updating *The 39 Steps*: Robert Redford and Faye Dunaway in James Grady's *Three Days of the Condor* (1975). *Larry Edmunds Cinema and Theatre Bookshop.*

Secret alumni from *Saturday Night Live*: Dan Aykroyd and Chevy Chase in *Spies Like Us* (1985). *The Remember When Shop.*

Len Deighton meets Frederick Forsythe: Michael Caine, the former Harry Palmer, in *The Fourth Protocol* (1987), based on Forsythe's novel. *The Remember When Shop.*

Looking for James Bond in the late 1980s? Check your local casino: Timothy Dalton in *License to Kill* (1989). *The Remember When Shop.*

Fact meets fiction: Actor Harrison Ford and producer Mark Neufeld discuss *Patriot Games* at CIA headquarters. Behind them is a statue of William "Wild Bill" Donovan, the creator of the OSS. *The Remember When Shop.*

An author on a sound stage: Tom Clancy on the set of *Hunt for Red October* (1990). *The Remember When Shop.*

A future governor and his celluloid wife: Arnold Schwarzenegger and Jamie Lee Curtis in *True Lies* (1994). *The Remember When Shop.*

Nicollette Sheridan and Leslie Nielsen in *Spy Hard* (1996), yet another parody of the already parodied. *The Remember When Shop.*

Secret agents versus aliens from other worlds: Will Smith and Tommy Lee Jones in *Men in Black* (1996). *The Remember When Shop.*

More stunts than dialogue: Tom Cruise in *Mission: Impossible 2* (2000). *The Remember When Shop.*

Prepubescent spy: Daryl Sabara in *Spy Kids* (2001). *The Remember When Shop.*

7

The Cold War Inside Out: "Whose Side Are You On?"

You're a regular desperate character, Mr. Thorpe. But then the press always prefers sensationalism. If you're wondering whether the charges bother me, let me say that it does not. Does not. Mr. Smith and I share a certain world view that permits us a number of presumptions. The first is that the enemy of my enemy is my friend.

E. Howard Hunt, *Berlin Ending*

By the 1970s, espionage fiction had splintered into a wide spectrum of approaches. On one hand, satirical television series like M*A*S*H portrayed the CIA as arrogant and comic bumblers like the double-talking Colonel Flagg (Edward Winter). On the other extreme, films like 1973's *Executive Action* (starring Burt Lancaster, Robert Ryan, and Will Geer) merged speculation, history, and fear about an agency the filmmakers felt was capable of setting up the Kennedy assassination. But clearly the tone of such projects was quite different from what had come before. Colonel Flagg was no likeable Max Smart, but a ruthless and sadistic conservative who practiced torture and wanted his prisoners kept alive so they would be healthy for their executions. The CIA in *Executive Action* was portrayed as a rogue agency out to maneuver American politics to achieve its own ends. U.N.C.L.E. and Control had been replaced by operatives and organizations more to be feared than trusted.

Behind the scenes, actual spy agencies were making secret progress in technology. In 1973, U.S. intelligence made an important break-through when it sent up its first satellite equipped to monitor microwave transmissions. Three years later, silicon chips made it possible for the next generation of satellites to spy in the sky and send down real-time photographic images. This changed the face of crisis management ever afterward (Richelson 1995, 337). By decade's end, satellite eavesdropping posts covered the planet from Arctic ice stations to posts hidden in Pacific island bunkers that once held secret Japanese forces during World War II.

At the same time, Congress began worrying about the seemingly unrestricted independence of U.S. agencies with such power and capability. Fears were fanned when news headlines continued to shake public confidence in secret actions. In 1973, President Richard Nixon used the CIA to interfere with elections in Chili, forcing a coup against freely elected president Salvador Allende. With echoes of *Mission: Impossible* coups, this extraordinary action tarnished the reputation of both president and agency, as Allende was no threat to American interests. As a result of such actions, congressional committees headed by Frank Church and Otis Pike held public hearings in 1975 that led to the Foreign Intelligence Surveillance Act establishing new guidelines. The Church Committee finally forced the FBI to cease inserting itself in political dissent and artistic expression because, during the anti-Vietnam War era, the bureau had acted very much like the national police feared in the first half of the century. Another important shift occurred in 1977, when Attorney General Griffen Bell began to prosecute spies rather than allow them to quietly resign as had been the practice under his predecessors. In 1979, a Muslim fundamentalist revolution toppled the CIA-backed Shah of Iran, a dramatic change in the course of Middle Eastern history that had important repercussions into the twenty-first century.

One case demonstrating new public attitudes involved the bombshell best seller, *The CIA and the Code of Intelligence* (1974) by Victor Marchetti. The long-delayed publication of this nonfiction work came to the public's attention after a long battle between the author, his publisher, and the CIA because it apparently revealed too much the agency didn't want known, especially regarding machinations within the Nixon and Ford administrations. Already unpopular with the CIA for his articles in *The Nation* claiming that the agency was too much involved in interfering with the affairs of other countries, Marchetti turned to novels to illustrate his points. *The Rope Dancer* (1971) was his fictional account of these matters (McCormick 1977, 131–32). With both journalism and storytelling, Marchetti and others wanted to distinguish between the myths and reality of a profession they felt was being too glamorized. For CIA insiders, the most reviled ex-agent to publish exposes was Philip Agee, whose *Inside the Agency: CIA Diaries* (1975) was but the first of his scathing attacks on his former employer. In 1978, he coedited *Dirty Work: The CIA in Western Europe*, followed two years later by *Dirty Work II: The CIA in Africa*. The number of such books prompted former CIA director William Colby to respond with his own *Honorable Men* (1978), something of a sequel to his predecessor Allen Dulles' 1963 *The Craft of Intelligence*. Both books were part memoirs, part defenses for their agency.

With such ongoing news headlines, the romance of Ian Fleming and his imitators began to lose their lead in fictional projects to be replaced by books and films emphasizing brutality, fears of home-grown conspiracies, and a continuing "credibility gap" between governments and their citizens. In a sense, these concerns joined in a thematic arc that had begun with John Le Carré and continued until the end of the cold war.

CARRYING ON ROMANCE

This is not to say that fantasy and spoof efforts disappeared from popular culture. In the 1970s, the Roger Moore 007 movies had strayed so far from the Ian Fleming plotlines, which were admittedly dated, that novelizations of the films began in 1977 with Christopher Wood's *The Spy Who Loved Me* and *James Bond and Moonraker* in 1979. The original *Moonraker*, first published in 1955 before Sputnik had been launched, and *The Spy Who Loved Me*, a unique first-person narrative from 1962, showed that characterizations and fantasies from earlier times didn't translate well for new generations. The original *Moonraker* plot by Sir Hugo Drax to drop a bomb on London and a tale of gangsters in the Canadian woods in *Spy* were too low-key for the era. EON Productions was forced to try a series of new scriptwriters to create stories that would reinvigorate the franchise after the lowest ebb in Bond history, the disappointing (in terms of box office receipts) duel between Roger Moore and Christopher Lee in 1974's *Man with the Golden Gun* (Gergely 2004).

Further, the old battles between Her Majesty's Secret Service and Russia's SMERSH didn't work in the era of detente. According to James Chapman, as the series progressed, the visual spectacles were more important than any cold war references (Lindner 2003, 92). At the close of the film version of *The Spy Who Loved Me*, for example, KGB chief General Gogol (Walter Gotell) is a warmly smiling rival, not an automaton of a vicious cold war state. The megalomaniac of the film, Stromberg (Curt Jergens), laughs when he observes 007 with KGB agent Triple-X (Barbara Bach): "Well, well, well, a Russian agent in love with an English agent. Détente indeed." According to 007 expert Lee Pfeiffer, Bond producers had the future in mind when scripting such scenes:

The character of Gogol was shrewdly crafted to be charismatic and somewhat sympathetic. He was never made a complete villain because even during the height of the Cold War, Broccoli and Saltzman foresaw the day when they might be able to show the Bond films behind the Iron Curtain, thus they didn't want to totally offend the Soviets. That's why in *Octopussy*, Gogol is helping MI6 catch the renegade terrorist Soviet general.[1]

Future Russian enemies of 007 would be old-guard diehards or rogue elephants out to recapture the glories of the past.

During the 1970s, while the debut of each new 007 film was now an international ritual, James Bond became more a representative of the decade rather than an arbiter of popular culture. *Moonraker*, in particular, owed its framework to the science fiction vogue established by *Star Wars* and *Close Encounters of the Third Kind*. In addition, according to Jeff Smith, by the time of *The Spy Who Loved Me*, women weren't being exploited as much as the Women's Liberation Movement in the Moore films (Lindner 2003, 127). Still, Bond contributed new figures to the spy pantheon, notably Richard Kiel's "Jaws," a clear nod to the Stephen Spielburg thriller, *Jaws*. Commercial success also included musical hits, most notably Paul McCartney's 1973 "Live and Let Die," which earned a rare Oscar nomination for a Bond film. Moore's films enjoyed more chart hits than his predecessors or successors, including Carly Simon's "Nobody

Does it Better" for *The Spy Who Loved Me* (1977), Sheena Easton's "For Your Eyes Only" (1981), and Duran Duran's "A View to a Kill" (1989), the last major chart success for a Bond song.

I cast around for a hero who cut a different mold, one who wasn't a secret agent, police detective, or a private investigator. Someone with rough edges yet a degree of style who felt equally at ease entertaining a gorgeous woman in a gourmet restaurant or downing a beer with the boys at the local saloon. A congenial kind of guy with a tinge of mystery about him. Instead of a gambling casino or the streets of New York, his territory became the sea. His challenge—the unknown. Out of the fantasy, Dirk Pitt.

Clive Cussler, *Pacific Vortex*

While Roger Moore's 007 cast a smaller shadow than Sean Connery, Bond still influenced both literature and television in the 1970s. For example, in 1973, Clive Cussler created his main character, Major Dirk Pitt, the troubleshooting security service officer for the National Underwater Marine Agency. According to Cussler's publisher, the adventures were partially based on the author's own experiences seeking gold mines in the Southwest, looking for missing aircraft in the Rockies, and leading expeditions underwater to find sunken Revolutionary War and Civil War battleships.

While the author maintained that his books weren't intended as part of any secret agent canon, Cussler's first Pitt novel, 1973's *Mediterranean Caper*, was a model of the clichés to which such post-Fleming books had fallen prey. For example, Pitt seduces a girl by slapping her to knock sense into her, escapes from a torture maze, battles a mammoth muscle-bound giant impervious to pain, uncovers a duplicitous policeman, learns the baddie is an ex-Nazi who stole a shipping magnate's identity, and that the girl is an agent from drug enforcement. The evil German had cleverly used hidden submarines attached to cargo ships to smuggle narcotics, steal sunken gold, transport criminals and, for good measure, is engaged in white slavery.

Throughout this series, as in *Pacific Vortex* (1983), Cussler played with innovative technology like artificial gills that allow pirates to steal ships and submarines commanded by megalomaniacs hiding in island hideaways waiting for East and West to obliterate each other. Submarines and battles in secret caverns, of course, were staples in spy fiction long before 007 and would continue to be an evergreen setting in such books as Tom Clancy's *Hunt for Red October*. Such cliches, and continuing characters including buddy Albert Giordino, appeared in other Cussler novels such as *Raise the Titanic* (1976), *Deep Six* (1984), and *Cyclops* (1986).

By 2004's eighteenth Pitt novel, *Black Wind* (co-written with his son, Dirk Cussler), Cussler had spun off three franchises and brought in a fictional new generation into his Pitt novels—Dirk Pitt, Jr., of course—as well as bringing his own son, Dirk, into the family business. Perhaps taking himself a bit too seriously, Cussler wrote a concordance to his Pitt novels in 1998 (*Clive Cussler and Dirk Pitt Revealed*). With a bit of wish-fulfillment, Cussler made himself a character in Black Wind.

"I am not, after all," reflected LaRue, "a thief bound by regulations, the rigid core of criminal justice. My calling is a higher one. My goal is not the corpus of a man but the contents of his brain . . . [a man like me] is not a mercenary agent. He's of a higher plane."

E. Howard Hunt, *Berlin Ending*

While many books and films of the era were seen as dramatized fears from the liberal Left, conservative writers added their own nods to Bond with very different voices. One unusual pairing would be the intellectual fiction of William F. Buckley, Jr. alongside the prolific efforts of Buckley's former CIA supervisor in Mexico, E. Howard Hunt. Hunt, with twenty years in the CIA, became known for his assistance in the ill-fated Bay of Pigs invasion and the equally infamous performance of the "Plumbers Unit" that sparked the Watergate affairs. A former war correspondent and winner of a Guggenheim prize for creative writing, Hunt wrote forty-three novels under various pseudonyms, including Gordon Davis, John Baxter, Robert Dietrich, and David St. John (East 1983, 153). Apparently, the CIA supported these series beginning in 1961, believing they would be good propaganda for the American agency in response to the British James Bond, especially as the publisher, New American Library, also published the Fleming novels. Like W. Somerset Maugham before him, Hunt's role as a spy writer became his cover while he continued his intelligence work. According to Donald McCormick, none of these efforts were praised for either content or style (1977, 103). For some critics, Hunt was more important in fact than fiction, and they assert that the most noted Hunt books were his two autobiographical works, *Give Us This Day* (1973) and *Undercover* (1974). For these reviewers, Hunt joined former FBI agent G. Gordon Liddy in cultural consciousness when they became figures spotlighted during the Watergate investigations.

However, such claims may be letting distaste for Hunt's association with Watergate override what he actually contributed to spy fiction. The number of his books alone should indicate that Hunt was more than a spy pretending to be a writer. Much of his fiction, such as 1973's *Berlin Ending*, stands up against many other novels of the period and retains readability long after publication. In a story told from multiple perspectives and avoiding clichés, the plot revolves around Communist attempts to get a West German the Nobel Peace Prize and for him to become secretary general of the U.N. For much of the book, readers could easily see the influence of Hitchcock, as a young couple in love spend most of their time on the run. But in the final moments, there is no happy ending. The hero walks away in disgust when the girl turns coward and refuses to testify against her stepfather. Because of her weakness, the mission fails. In a rare moment of realism, the Communists win.

Another novel of note was *The Gaza Intercept* (1981) because it was both somewhat prophetic and a document of the early Reagan years. Alternating between third- and first-person narratives, the story is partly about reckless advertising executive Jay Black, who becomes involved with a half-Arab, half-Jewish agent whose loyalties are questionable. The plot centers on an Arab terrorist cell that steals a neutron bomb that they plan to ignite over Tel Aviv. (At the time, the "neutron weapon" was widely discussed, as it reputedly spread radiation that killed humans but did not destroy buildings or land.) However, circumstances in 1981 were quite different than actual attacks after the cold war ended. In this fictional account, it was clear that the Israelis would have responded with atomic bombs on Baghdad, Tripoli, Cairo, and Damascus. The United States and Soviet

Union would have become involved because, in that era, the USSR was aligned with various Arab states. Thus, the conflicts in the Middle East were then seen as something of a proxy war between the "Super Powers."

And if you have a Cold War, you don't want to get hot. You are going to need to know what are the enemy's resources, number one, and that is relatively easy. And then you are going to need to know, number two, and that is relatively hard, what are the enemy's intentions.

William Buckley, *Tucker's Last Stand*

William Buckley's first fictional spy effort was *Saving the Queen* (1975), which introduced his hero, Blackford Oakes. In this implausible yarn, the CIA agent beds Queen Caroline of England. Set during the 1950s, the Oakes series continued with *Stained Glass* (1978), in which the part engineer—part spy is forced to assassinate a leading anti-Communist West German political figure pushing for reunification of the two Germanys. Despite Buckley's often light, humorous touch, the book implies that history might have been changed if the West had been more aggressive before the Berlin Wall was erected. Oakes tries to alter the outcome, believing Stalin wouldn't follow through with military threats if the Western powers refused to submit to covert blackmail. Poking fun at the "Red Scare" era, Buckley has Oakes spotting Joseph McCarthy in a movie theater, where he impishly gives him a secret note saying "Investigate Allen Dulles." Oakes reappears in *Who's on First?* (1980), another "what if" story. In this case, Oakes tries to help America launch the first orbiting satellite in a futile attempt to beat the Russians before they send Sputnik into space. The agent puts humanity above his mission, not telling Washington that the Soviets are capturing an essential device because this news would lead to certain death for an honorable Russian scientist. In the end, Oakes leaves the agency and sees this man's life was worth the sacrifice, a tangible accomplishment of his career. In 1990, Buckley brought Oakes into the 1960s as a supporting character in *Tucker's Last Stand*. In this Vietnam-set excursion, Buckley explores the covert events leading up to the expansion of the war in 1964.

———————

The world of espionage was the region of the mad in which men who could not write or paint or sculpt created distorted works out of the flesh of living persons and said, believed, that the result was art. It was like watching the inmates of an asylum dob an army of stick figures onto an enormous canvas using buckets of blood for paint.

Charles McCarry, *The Last Supper*

However, Buckley and Hunt were not alone in championing conservative viewpoints. While known for his journalism, nonfiction books, and nonspy novels, American Charles McCarry has drawn on both his reporting background and his 1958 to 1967 CIA experience to create a series of suspenseful espionage novels, many of which featured second-generation CIA agent and poet, Paul Christopher. Christopher was introduced in *The Miernik Dossier* (1973), a story actually told in the form of a dossier including reports, intercepted letters, written communication, and bugged telephone conversations ("Charles" 2002). In Christopher's second outing, *The Tears of Autumn* (1975), McCarry offered an unusual twist on the Kennedy assassination. A specialist in Vietnamese affairs, Christopher discovered a link between the killings of Ngo Dinh Diem and Ngo Dinh Nhu in Saigon and Kennedy's subsequent death. The assassination is portrayed as a revenge killing—blood for blood ("Charles" 2002). Once Christopher realizes that prominent members of the administration were inadvertently responsible for Kennedy's death, he is forbidden to continue his investigation. He resigns, only to become hunted by both the assassins and his own government.

In *The Secret Lovers* (1977), Christopher witnesses the killing of a Russian courier who is carrying a potentially damaging manuscript for Moscow. The Americans ponder whether to publish the files or wait until the death of a Russian leader. During the twists and turns, Christopher tries to hold his unraveling marriage together. *The Last Supper* (1983) was as much about Christopher's father, Hubbard, and family connections through various wars. One episode contained nods to both *The Third Man* and actual espionage history when Paul Christopher operates out of a secret headquarters hidden in Vienna sewers. The base has to be destroyed when the Russians invade. It turns out that the Reds had known about the underground base, a circumstance echoing that of the "Berlin Tunnel" in the 1950s. It had been thought to be a premier German operation before it was revealed that British traitor George Blake had blown the secrecy from the beginning of the project. Apparently, Christopher's last mission was *Second Sight* (1991), which played on the retired agent theme. The elder spy fights against penetrators into the CIA while getting to know his long-lost daughter, Zarah, who was raised by a band of Jewish nomads.

Our Better Angels (1979) was a non-Christopher novel that foresaw many themes of future fact and fancy. In a mix of historical anachronisms and speculation, Arab terrorists blow up five planes simultaneously before plotting to destroy Jerusalem and Tel Aviv. A discredited CIA is disbanded in favor of a stripped-down Foreign Intelligence Service. Twenty-two years before McCarry's ideas became commonplace, security at airports is so tight that terrorists are forced to hide plastic explosives inside their thighs, which can be ignited by batteries inside wristwatches.

During the 1980s, McCarry found his spy work compared to, and often in the shadow of, then newcomer Tom Clancy. Both writers were noted for realistic details, vivid storytelling, and clearly conservative views. McCarry's right-wing connections were apparent when he coauthored two books with Reagan administration members Donald T. Regan, *For the Record* (1988) and Alexander M. Haig, Jr., *Inner Circles: How America Changed the World* (1992). A man of broad interests, McCarry has long been associated with the National Geographic Society, for which he has written both books and articles.

In the Devero theory, those who could order another to plant a bomb in a food hall and gloat over the resulting images, all had one thing in common. They possessed a fearsome capacity for hatred. This was the genetic given. The hatred came first. The target could come later and usually did. The motive also came second to the capacity to hate. It might be the Bolshevik Revolution, National Liberation, or a thousand variants thereof. . . . But the hatred came first. Then the cause. Then the target. Then the methods. And finally, the self-justification. And Lenin's dupes always swallowed it.

Frederick Forsythe, *The Avenger*

However, the most influential writer of the 1970s in terms of techniques and depth was Frederick Forsythe, the novelist Tom Clancy later cited as one of his favorite authors. In particular, Forsythe's *The Day of the Jackal* (1971), an instantaneous success, marked a new development in the spy story. The novel brought together espionage, counter-espionage, and political assassination told in such detail and realism that some critics saw the book as almost a documentary spy thriller with events and characters based on real-life events. Admitting he didn't have the imagination to "spin a character out of the air," the author said he built his style on journalistic experience (McCormick 1977, 78).

In his debut novel, Forsythe based his story on the French group calling itself the OAS (Organization Armee Secret), which consisted of ex-military officers turned criminals and terrorists who opposed French president Charles De Gaulle ("Jackal" 1998). In the early 1960s, the group was finally destroyed by the military wing of the French Secret Service (SDECE, or Service de Documentation Exterieure et de Contre-Espionage). In fact, the OAS had failed in an attempt to assassinate De Gualle. Forsythe's premise was to explore what might have happened had they hired a professional killer to do their work ("Jackal" 1998).

Director Fred Zinneman's 1973 *The Day of the Jackal*, with a screenplay by Kenneth Ross, starred Edward Fox as the Jackal, supported by an international cast and location shoots throughout England, France, and Italy. The killer, a cipher, a man of disguise and deception, is tracked by Michel Lonsdale as Detective Claude Lebel, who has to work outside of legal constraints, and a French cabinet secretly hoping for the Jackal's success. The film was, and is, praised by critics who see it as a rare example of a film faithfully adhering to the story, spirit, and suspense of the original book ("Jackal" 1998).

Forsythe's next effort, *The Odessa File* (1972), took his journalistic interest into a logical place. The writer made his spy a reporter, based on his own experiences in Eastern Europe. In the growing circle of books about Arab-Israeli conflicts, Forsythe fused ex-Nazis with a German journalist's search for a secret group of former SS officers who have hidden a gold treasure. The 1974 film version starred Jon Voight, Maximilian Schell, Maria Schell, and Derek Jacobi. (Robert Ludlum's 1989 *The Holcroft Covenant* was also based on the *Odessa* story, with hidden Nazi funds and a generation of neo-Nazis plotting to start a Fourth Reich.) Also in 1974, Forsythe's next novel, *Dogs of War*, appeared, dealing with a group of professional mercenaries hired to overthrow the newly established government of a West African nation. The 1981 film version starred Christopher Walken, Tom Berringer, and Colin Blakely. In 1987, before becoming James Bond, Pierce Brosnan played an elite Russian agent sent out to blow up a British nuclear plant in Forsythe's *The Fourth Protocol*. In the movie, the sophisticated, savvy, and amoral KGB agent meets his match in Michael Caine's John Preston, who battles his own bureaucracy and Brosnan with the help of a squad of commandos.

Reportedly against the wishes of Forsythe and Fred Zinnemann, a new version of *The Day of the Jackal* was produced in 1997. The new producers agreed to the shortened title *The Jackal*, and featured Bruce Willis as the assassin ("Jackal" 1998). In this version, the plot about a refined killer bringing a sophisticated rifle into France was dropped in favor of a cannonlike Gatling gun mounted on a truck for maximum pyrotechnics. The FBI sends agent Carter Preston (Sidney Poitier) after Willis, but the respectful relationship between hunter and prey from the original project is dropped in favor of a macho squabble equivalent to a schoolyard brawl ("Jackal" 1998). Two non-Forsythe characters enter the picture: Richard Gere as imprisoned IRA soldier Declan Mulqueen and Valentina Koslova (Diane Venora), a Russian intelligence agent.

It was probably mere coincidence that 1997 was also the year Forsythe announced his retirement from writing, but readers were delighted when *The Avenger* appeared in 2003, a novel clearly inspired by the tragedy of 9/11. However, while the novel has much to recommend it, Forsythe now seemed in the shadow of his disciple, Tom Clancy. The story is an accumulation of clichés rather than an example of literary innovation. *The Avenger* centers on a private quest by a Vietnam vet to revenge the death of an innocent American killed during the Bosnian conflict. Like other such books of the period, Forsythe reached back to events in World War II and Vietnam. He crafted grim passages, including an American unit performing literally the dirtiest undercover job in history—seeking the Viet Cong in booby-trapped unlit tunnels where no special weapons can help. Much of the story shows how the vet makes connections and contacts with experts in various fields that allow him to become almost a comic book vigilante with a secret identity drawing on personal resources built over the years. Part III of the book returns Forsythe to his specialty, having his hero stalk, study, and finally trap his prey in Central America. Unknowingly, he is upsetting a CIA machination to use the killer to take out Osama Bin Laden. The book's last sentence states the tragedy clearly—the assassin is arrested on September 10, 2001.

I have tried in my novels to show that people employed in espionage or in intelligence work have private lives, and that their work affects their lives. . . . I believe that all wars have sad endings for both losers and winners, and that those who are concerned with espionage and counterespionage tend to have sad endings even in peacetime.
Ted Allbeury, *St. James Guide to Crime and Mystery Writers*

In 1972, English novelist Ted Allbeury debuted with his spy novel, *A Choice of Enemies*. While praised for his realism by drawing from his experiences in the British Intelligence Corps as a lieutenant colonel from 1939 to 1947, Allbeury claimed he was inspired to write his first thriller after the kidnapping of his four-year-old daughter in 1970, which resulted in her disappearance for several years ("Ted" 1996). Written at the age of fifty-four, his first book was to let her know "that I cared and tried to find her" ("Theodore" 2003).

A Choice of Enemies was clearly influenced by tragic events and serves as a model of all Allbeury's work. In the novel, British spy Nicholas Bailey defects to Poland after learning that his missing daughter is there under the control of Berger, a Belgian double agent. Like Len Deighton's Harry Palmer, who was reported to be based on Allbeury, Bailey is a "working-class" spy who feels unconnected to his Oxford-educated controllers. Believing that personal loyalties are more important than national interests, Bailey still makes an attempt to thwart Berger's plans, but he is forced to leave his daughter in Poland under the protection of an American agent.

In *Choice* and later novels including *Snowball* (1974), *Moscow Quadrille* (1976), and *Shadow of Shadows* (1981), ruthlessness, suicide, murder, and a willingness to torture is a characteristic of agents on both sides of the cold war. In many plots, connections between allegiances from World War II complicate motivations for these agents long after the end of the conflict. For example, Allbeury's 1990 *Time without Shadows* was essentially a reworking of his 1978 *The Lantern Network*, which explores characters who have operated in the French Resistance during World War II, and the aftermath of these relationships and actions when humans are under forced occupation. Complications often make motivations murky, as when the French have to forge uneasy alliances between those who simply want independence and those hoping for a Communist state after the war. Both groups are uncertain how to deal with their English helpers.

Often compared to John Le Carré, Allbeury's cold war books feature the "subordinate agent, operating in the no-man's-land between the superpowers, as much exposed to betrayal by his masters as by his colleagues" ("Theodore" 2003). Cynical endings typify novels such as *The Only Good German* (1976), *The Alpha List* (1979), and *The Secret Whispers* (1981). Still, Allbeury was credited with heroes dubbed "feeling man spies" as he disliked "undue dwelling on hardware, organization, and method." Rather, his intent was to look at the character beneath the actions, as in perhaps his best novel, *Deep Purple* (1989), in which a British agent allows a Russian spy to escape because the traitor's motives seem more honorable than the agent's higher-ups. As one Russian defector notes in the novel, facts have little meaning—interpretation and opinion are what matter in the secret world. In 1996, Allbeury claimed, "It is reckoned that it is better to use men who feel some doubt about the morality of what they are doing. This, naturally, has some disadvantages in operational terms, but it also has the advantage of avoiding excessive use of power. I have tried to get this over in my books" ("Ted" 1996). One example of this thinking was expressed in the author's note to *Rules of the Game* (1988). Allbeury claimed the book's inspiration came from his days after World War II, when his job was to interrogate Germans to determine who should be prosecuted for war crimes and who should be allowed to go and begin their private lives. He had to create his own plans to make these judgement calls and said his novel was built around the idea that agents must make their best decisions outside of more restrictive formal codes.

While some critics saw a lessening of the anguished tone in his later books, his 1990 *A Time without Shadows* was still seen to be full of bitterness and mistrust ("Theodore" 2003). Described as a novelist that has yet to get his due, Allbeury continues to earn critical warmth for his thirty-five books to date and has been called "the spy writer's spy writer," although this term is arguably more a publicist's phrase than consensus among critics. His *The Other Side of Silence* (1981) is considered by some to be his finest book, yet another exploration of the British traitor Kim Philby. It "presents layer by layer the inquiry of a naïve young SIS employee into the reasons for Philby's betrayal" ("Ted" 1996).

Allbeury wrote two novels under the pen name of Patrick Kelly and two more as Richard Butler. The Butler books, *Where All the Girls Are Sweeter* (1975) and *Italian Assets* (1976), center on luxury boat salesman Max Farne. Both involve Farne in descriptive seacoast adventures drawing him back into World War II intrigues. Allbeury's 1984 *No Place to Hide* was adapted into director Robert Young's low-rated film, *Hostage* (1992). In the story, Agent John Rennie (Sam Neill) has a crisis of conscience after a mission in Argentina and tries to begin life over with a new lover (Talisa Soto). As usual, the agency has other ideas.

THREE DAYS OF THE CONDOR

Another landmark spy adventure of the 1970s, director Sydney Pollack's *Three Days of the Condor* (1975), featured Robert Redford as an enthusiastic, if naïve, CIA researcher. Based on the James Grady novel, *Six Days of the Condor* (1974), the story is typical of the 1970s in that the hero flees his own agency rather than any international or independent adversary. The novel has been seen as a Buchanesque synthesis of moral allegory, social commentary, and fantastic scrapes (Cawilti and Rosenberg 1987, 86). In both the film and novel the hero is at first a man full of trust, unable to conform to security directives. A lover of comic strips, his job is to read adventure literature and journals to find new ideas and uncover possible leaks. Inadvertently, he stumbles across a conspiracy and finds himself on the run in an obvious homage to themes from Alfred Hitchcock. Another Hitchcockian twist is Redford's pulling an even more reluctant innocent, Faye Dunaway, into his chase, the two becoming partners after Redford convinces the fearful Dunaway about the truth of his circumstances. In many ways, the film's style still marks it as a product of its era, but it also foreshadowed the future. In the end, the audience learns that the "CIA within the CIA" is linked to Middle Eastern oil.

In Grady's follow-up novel, *Shadow of the Condor* (1975), he continued his device of using an agent looking at fiction to find clues, again an interesting flashback to actual circumstances when the Soviets looked at novels to study Western propaganda (McCormick 1977, 88). Praised over the years as a novelist with a mastery of Washington intrigue, Grady drew from his experiences as a scriptwriter, senate aid, and reporter to base his stories in the capitol that he portrays as being full of cynical power. And he occasionally pointed to the future. In his tenth novel, *Thunder* (1994), senate aid/CIA agent John Lang appears before a congressional hearing, where one conservative senator asks about the meaning of the end of the cold war, the new role of the CIA, and if the agency will now deal with terrorists as the present enemy. This was ten years before 9/11 and the years when such hearings became daily news.

Everything we do cuts both ways.

Marathon Man

Another new direction could be seen in such novels as William Goldman's 1971 *Marathon Man*, from which Goldman adapted his own screenplay for the 1976 film. According to John Cawilti, both the novel and the film version represented a new trend in spy fiction, that of a secret agent turned vigilante. In such stories, heroes must act on their own when their organizations refuse to provide justice and retribution in the name of secrecy or agendas they view as more important (1987, 181).

The dark, tense film starred Dustin Hoffman as a graduate student preparing for an Olympic marathon. He's haunted by memories of his father, who was unfairly hounded into drink and suicide by congressional hearings during the McCarthy era. Roy Scheider plays Hoffman's secret agent brother, Doc, working for a unit called the "Division," which takes on jobs "in the gap between what the FBI can't do and what the CIA won't." After Doc's murder, Hoffman is chased and tortured by a Nazi fugitive (Laurence Olivier) who, in the end, leaves behind a trail of destruction simply to ensure that he can safely collect diamonds from a bank without being robbed.

Costarring Marthe Keller and directed by John Schlesinger, the film is remembered for its clever series of accidents and a notable torture scene in Olivier's dentist chair. The film won 1976's Golden Globe for best supporting actor (Olivier), who was also nominated for an Academy Award.

All other characters and organizations in this book lack any basis in reality—although some of them do not realize that.

Trevanian, Dedication, *Shibumi*

A more controversial debut came with the novels of Trevanian (pen name for Dr. Rodney Whitaker), the creator of Johnny Hemlock. Portrayed by Clint Eastwood in the 1975 film version of *The Eiger Sanction* (book, 1972), Hemlock was a cynical, greedy art professor and reluctant assassin for C-2, headed by the albino, Dragon. Dragon gives orders from a protective headquarters that keeps him free from germs and direct sunlight. In the books, Hemlock was seen by John Cawilti as representing an unhappy vogue for brutality. Trevanian, in Cawilti's view, wrote with a "genuine relish for inflicting physical pain" with much squirting of blood, sadistic deaths, and can best be seen in the emblem of a dentist's chair (Cawilti and Rosenberg 1987, 202).

Critic Donald McCormick also noted that Trevanian tended to be shocking and brutal, but with obvious sick humor. For him, *The Eiger Sanction* was full of sex and sophistication surrounding Johnny Hemlock, the mountaineer, art historian, collector of rare paintings, and assassin. The humor can be seen in character names like Felicity Arse and Randi Knickers, and in scenes such as when an inept CIA agent collects a stick of bubblegum from a contact and swallows it to keep the enemy from gaining a microdot on the gum. However, the foreign agents rip his stomach open to get the gum in what McCormick called "horror humor" (1977, 172).

Perhaps one window into the enigmatic personality of Trevanian is the lengthy footnote he provided in 1979's *Shibumi*. He begins by claiming that he won't describe graphic incidents because in the process of converting *The Eiger Sanction* "into a vapid film, a fine young climber was killed." In a later book, the author detailed a method for stealing paintings from any well-guarded museum: "Shortly after . . . three paintings were stolen in Milan by the exact method described, and two of these were irreparably mutilated" (Trevanian 1979, 135). After claiming that "simple social responsibility" dictated he should avoid "exact descriptions of tactics and events," the footnote added these thoughts, which undercut any real fears of fact following fiction: "In a similar vein, the author shall keep certain advanced sexual techniques in partial shadow, as they might be dangerous, and would certainly be painful, to the neophyte" (1979, 136).

For years, mystery and speculation circulated around the author, who avoided publicity of any kind. Trevanian's identity was a closely guarded secret, and rumors suggested that Robert Ludlum was using the pseudonym. Trevanian allegedly refused to offer his novels to any publisher who had published a book by a Watergate conspirator, and that he absolutely refused to take an advance up front. He also seemed to be particularly interested in the Basque people and their political situation.[2] Even after the Texas-born novelist's name was revealed, he refused to grant interviews, so little remains known about the creative approaches or intentions of Dr. Whitaker.

> She had always been fascinated by people who lived outside the ordered social world, criminals, Bohemians, anarchists, prostitutes and tramps. They seemed so free. Of course, they might not be free to order champagne or fly to New York or send their children to university. She was not so naïve as to overlook the restrictions of being an outcast. But people such as Harry never had to do anything just because they were ordered to. . . . She dreamed of being a guerilla fighter, living in the hills wearing trousers and carrying a rifle, stealing gold and sleeping under the stars. . . . She hadn't met people like that or if she had met them, she didn't recognize them for what they were.
>
> Ken Follett, *Night over Water*

Another novelist debuting in spy fiction was Kenneth Follett, whose first spy books included *The Shake Out* (1975), *The Bear Raid* (1976), and the highly regarded *Triple* (1979). Such books dealt with the then neglected subject of industrial espionage as a result of the author's desire not to go where others had already been and to create something fresh. According to Donald McCormick, Follett's character, Piers Roper, was the only industrial spy in fiction during that era. Roper, a high-powered marketing executive, took posts with a series of companies simply to steal their secrets. In these early books, Follett explored why such a man would betray his background to be a snoop (McCormick 1977, 77).

Follett was another writer who enjoyed seeing his books turned into media projects. His 1978 novel *Eye of the Needle* was made into a 1981 film starring Donald Sutherland and Robert MacKenna. The story involved a German spy shipwrecked on a remote English island. Lonely and violent, the Nazi (Sutherland) becomes involved with Kate Melligan and reconsiders his role in the war. *Needle* was typical of most of Follett's adventures set during World War II, some of which were adapted into television miniseries. One was *The Key to Rebecca* (1985) starring Cliff Robertson and Robert Culp with a script by Sam Rolfe.

In subsequent decades, Follett wrote a series of popular thrillers, but only a handful dealt with espionage. In *Lie Down with Lions* (1985), an idealistic female socialist finds herself in a love triangle between an American CIA agent and her husband, a KGB doctor betraying Afghan rebels in their war with the Soviets. Follett's *Explorer I* (2000) was set in the 1950s and focused on Americans trying to quickly respond to the launch of Sputnik. Follett's 2001 novel, *The Jack Daws*, featured five women showing three sides of adversaries (Allies, Nazi, occupied French) as sympathetic patriots. His 2002 best seller, *Hornet Flight*, was another fictionalized World War II adventure in which an eighteen-year-old Dane discovers a secret Nazi radar installation near his home. With the aid of his brother's girlfriend, a spy for the Danish Resistance, the young man travels across the North Sea to warn the Allies.

FROM WORLD WAR II TO THE IRA: JACK HIGGINS

But the outstanding World War II effort of the decade came from writer Jack Higgins (pseudonym for Harry Patterson), who had served two years as a noncommissioned officer (NCO) in the Royal House of Guards on the East German border during the cold war. He published the first of his sixty-two adventure novels in 1959, but came to popular acclaim when at the age of forty, he wrote his World War II drama, *The Eagle Has Landed* (1975). One of the eight Higgins novels to be filmed, *Eagle* had the distinction of becoming a highly regarded movie directed by John Sturges in 1976 with an all-star cast including Michael Caine, Donald Sutherland, Robert Duvall, Donald Pleasence, Anthony Quayle, Treat Williams, and Larry Hagman.

But Higgins was to become known for more than his historical spies. Raised in Belfast in a family with a political background, Higgins frequently experienced the worst aspects of Irish troubles during his youth ("Unofficial" 2004). The backdrop of Irish/English conflicts, especially with IRA terrorists, led to an extremely popular series of books with a continuing cast of characters working on both sides of the conflict. Sean Dillon, Higgins's whiskey-swilling top agent, begins his career as an IRA assassin, nearly blowing up the prime minister. Eventually pardoned for past sins, Dillon joins a secret team called "Group 4" headed by Brigadier Charles Ferguson with his personal assistant from Scotland Yard's special branch, Hannah Bernstein. Frequently criticized as being characters who relish drinking, smoking, and brutality, Higgins's group is often assisted by CIA agent, Blake Johnson. To date, these characters, along with many trustworthy but rough-edged IRA veterans, have been featured in formulaic books, including *Thunderpoint* (1993), *Edge of Danger* (2002), and *Midnight Runner* (2003), among others. Two films starred Rob Lowe as Dillon, *On Dangerous Ground* (1995) and *Midnight Man* (1995), the latter based on the 1992 book *Eye of the Storm*. *The Windsor Protocol* (1992) starred Kyle MacLachlan as Dillon going after yet more Nazis hoping for a Fourth Reich.

During the months he had peeled away the layers of Jason Bourne, one theme kept repeating itself. Change, change, change. Bourne was a practitioner of change. They called him "The Chameleon," a man who could melt into different surroundings with ease. . . . Effortlessly, with a minimum of artifice David Webb would trust the chameleon within him, free fall, go where Jason Bourne directed.

Robert Ludlum, *The Bourne Supremacy*

In the view of many, the most popular and influential new author to debut in spy fiction during the decade was Robert Ludlum. Among his early critically praised novels was *The Matlock Paper* (1974) in which the agency tries to sacrifice an innocent college professor in the name of national security. Other books of the era included *The Osterman Weekend* (1977, film 1983) and *The Scarlatti Inheritance* (1977). Over the course of his career, Ludlum wrote twenty-one novels, each a *New York Times* best seller. To date, there are more than 210 million of his books in print, and they have been translated into thirty-two languages. He is most noted for the landmark Jason Bourne series—*The Bourne Identity* (1980), *The Bourne Supremacy* (1986), and the contrived finale, *The Bourne Ultimatum* (1990).

This saga involves David Webb, who is at first a highly trained operative who had once been code-named "Delta" in Vietnam. Based on this experience, Webb is sent to Europe to create the mythological assassin Jason Bourne and track down the killer, Carlos "The Jackal." Headquartered in Paris and disguised as a priest, Carlos is sending out an army of old men beholden to him to kill and act as his couriers. After suffering amnesia, Webb seeks to determine the truth about himself in *The Bourne Identity*, where he is aided by French economist Maria. For a time, Bourne fears that he is the Jackal himself until he discovers that he is an agent for the Treadstone group, who think his amnesia is in fact a cover for Webb turning on them. In the end, Carlos is stopped (but not killed) and Treadstone has to atone for their attempts to kill Webb.

In *The Bourne Supremacy*, Webb and Maria are married and trying to build a new life away from the government that had betrayed them. However, in Hong Kong, a group wanting to instigate an incident that would allow Red China to seize the city has its own Jason Bourne, an imposter trying to kill prominent Chinese officials. Feeling that only the original Jason Bourne can stop him, the U.S. government forces Webb to return into the field by seizing Maria as a hostage. Shifting between his various identities—Webb, Bourne, Delta, and "The Chameleon"—the reluctant agent succeeds in catching his namesake and blocking the coup. Five years later, the Jackal returns in *The Bourne Ultimatum* in order to secure his reputation as the number one assassin before his death. An aging Bourne, now a father, is forced to protect his family while still trying to balance the divisions of his multiple personalities and reaching inside himself to use skills he had tried to forget (see discussion of Bourne films in chapter 9).

> But something happened. As Cons-Op was changing, so was Brendan Scofield. The more vital those highly specialized defections were considered, the quicker the violence escalated. Very quickly, Scofield eclipsed his commando training. He spent five months in Central America going through the most rigorous survival techniques, offensive and defensive. He mastered scores of codes and ciphers. He was as proficient as any cryptographer in NSA. When he returned to Europe and became "The Expert," there was no turning back.
>
> Robert Ludlum, *The Matarese Circle*

A writer who adapted quickly to changes in political circumstances, Ludlum coined the years after the fall of the Berlin Wall the "Cold Peace," which gave old stories new depth in the last years of the twentieth century. For example, Ludlum's own *Materese Countdown* (1997) focused on old foes reactivated in "board room terrorism," that is, power brokers less interested in political power than international economic collusion flaunting antitrust laws. In such stories, old agents like Ludlum's Brandon Scofield were forced out of retirement to be mentors to younger agents like Cameron Price, as well as to learn new computer-based skills undreamed of in the cold war. On a deeper level, the senior Scofield has nightmares about what he had once been forced to do in Consular Operations, a group that included strategic cooperation with agents from other countries.

Scofield had a career marked by brutality and bloodshed and was, in many ways, a character clearly owing much to his literary forebears. In the 2002 *The Jansen Directive*, for example, Ludlum brought an old device from the 1930s into the new century—blowpipes. In this case, modern technology had created miniature-looking insects with poison to confuse those attacked by Ludlum's strike force. As in countless other projects, the protagonist was skilled in infiltration and extraction based on military training. While many British officers of the Clubland era had traced their experience to work in India, Ludlum's Paul Jansen had served in Vietnam, learning how to read maps, blueprints, and how to judge air currents when parachuting. Agents like

Jansen knew that their own body smells would betray them as meat-eaters and that they would stand out in cultures of vegetarians. Like many agents on the run, Paul Jansen had to outmaneuver snipers while outfoxing angry mothers armed with pepper spray. In short, John Buchan would be able to see his influence on Ludlum.

During the 1990s, Ludlum began his trade paperback series based on the "Covert-One" top-secret team of political and technical experts fighting corruption and conspiracy at the highest levels. Like spies typical of the 1960s, these specialists had no family encumbrances, their lives were their own, and their credentials were impeccable. None knew each other, but all had computer notebooks to contact headquarters. The first book in the series, *The Hades Factor* (cowritten with Gayle Lynds) introduced Col. Jonathan Smith. *The Cassandra Compact* (written with Philip Shelby) and *The Paris Option* (with Gayle Lynds) were followed by *The Altman Code*, which was the apparent end of the series, when Ludlum passed away in March 2001. According to the official Robert Ludlum Web site hosted by St. Martin's Press, other books are in their files and the coauthors have future books to add to the series.

A few other novelists debuting in the 1970s are worthy of honorable mentions, including Evelyn Anthony, who created *The Tamarind Seed* (1971), filmed in 1973 and starring Omar Sharif and Julie Andrews. In this novel and other spy books, Anthony featured unmarried women engaged in spycraft (McCormick 1977, 26). Reversing the usual pattern of a writer becoming a Hollywood insider, Wilson McCarthy was a former Hollywood producer for Warner Brothers and MGM before writing thrillers such as *The Fourth Man* in 1972 and *The Detail* (1974) (McCormick 1977, 122). John Howlett's *The Christmas Spy* (1975), in Donald McCormick's opinion, introduced a new kind of spy, Railway Joe, an agent in his mid-forties employed by an unnamed security organization. Joe is a "sad man" of the postwar era whose idealism has eroded. He's lost faith after once clear missions had become chess games in international politics (McCormick 1977, 102).

HARSHNESS IN HOLLYWOOD

Like the new trends in fiction, the 1970s was a decade of disillusionment and violence on the large screen. While the cold war was in earnest, World War II movies like *Eye of the Needle* still appeared, although the vogue for combat films during the Vietnam era tended to explore current events and not those of the generation before. One look back was *Brass Target* (1978), based on Frederick Nolan's 1978 book of the same name. The casting tried to capitalize on two ex-television spies. Robert Vaughn (*The Man from U.N.C.L.E.*) was an American colonel and Patrick McGoohan (*The Prisoner*) was head of the OSS. Together they conspired to steal Nazi gold. George Kennedy played Gen. George Patton, who uncovered their plot and whom they tried to kill (Davenport 2004, 45).

Cold war themes were evident in films such as *The Kremlin Letter* (1973), a box office disappointment despite the all-star cast of Orson Welles, Max Von Sydow, Bibi Anderson, Barbara Perkins, George Saunders, and Richard Boone under the guidance of noted director John Huston. Described by critics as harsh, muddled, and cynical, the twist was an attempt to have the Russians and Americans working together against the Chinese (Strada and Troper 1997, 143). However, the plot to recover a letter written by a Western spymaster, duped into promising to help Russia in blocking China's nuclear plans, turns out to be a mere ploy by one Russian to discredit one of his peers (Gorman 1998, 131). The film has no real heroes, as the agents are killers, perverts, and tortured specialists who run drugs, kidnap children, and rape and murder the defenseless. In the view of one critic, the letter is essentially a Hitchcockian McGuffin, a "False Grail," as the true quest turns out to be one agent's need to recover his humanity (Gorman 1998, 133). Director Don Siegel's 1974 *The Black Windmill* also earned mixed reviews. Michael Caine returned in a film spy story about and English agent caught between his government and gun runners when his son is kidnapped and his supervisors won't help.

In Charles Bronson's *Telephon* (1977), an ex-KGB loose cannon wants to blow up U.S. cities whose first letters would spell out his name. He plans to use deep-cover agents who had been hypnotized and drugged years before. To foil the rogue KGB madman, the KGB send Bronson, a spy with a photographic memory, along with his CIA partner, Barbara (Lee Remick). In this reversal of standard male-female roles, the two take on the psychopathic killer, learn that their agencies plan to kill them to keep the old Telephon network secret, and go off together in the final reel having outfoxed everyone in the triangle of murderous intent. Thus, *Telephon* allows the independent agent to overcome three levels of contemporary conspiracies and get the girl as well. The film was based on the 1975 book by Walter Wager, normally an author of OSS stories. Another novel to be filmed was Robert Rostand's *The Killer Elite* (1974), which became a bloody United Artists film directed by Sam Peckinpah. It starred James Caan and Robert Duvall as two professional assassins who were once friends but end up tracking each other.

Other cold war efforts included *Nightflight from Moscow* (1973) starring Yul Brenner as an arrogant defector who turns out to be a Soviet plant. In *Russian Roulette* (1975), George Segal plays a Canadian policeman drawn into espionage, in this case a scheme to assassinate Soviet leader Alexei Kosygin. While the plot was fictional, the story was based on an actual attempt on Kosygin's life by refugees who had fled to Canada (Strada and Troper 1997, 173). In the same vein, *The Cassandra Crossing* (1976) tried for box office success drawing on another all-star cast, in this case Sophia Loren, Richard Harris, Ava Gardner, Burt Lancaster, and Martin Sheen. Filmed in France and Italy, the story focuses on a terrorist carrying a plague on a transcontinental luxury train.

More significantly, producer Robert Evans and director John Frankenheimer's *Black Sunday* is regarded as one of the best "disaster films" popular during this period. Bond costar Robert Shaw battles crazed ex-Vietnam veteran Bruce Dern and members of the "Black September" Palestinian terrorists plotting to attack Americans attending the Super Bowl. This film, and related projects of the decade, gave a new emphasis and direction to stories involving Israeli agents. Prior to the actual September 5, 1972, "Black September" attack at the Munich Olympics by PLO terrorists, most Jewish spies looked for lost Nazi treasures or sought revenge for deaths during the Holocaust. While such plots continued into the twenty-first century, a new subgenre developed with Israeli agents now seeking vengeance for Palestinian terrorism.

But not all projects were exercises in tough-minded updatings of G-men or, as it were, KGB-men. In 1974, S*P*Y*S tried to capitalize on the success of the film version of M*A*S*H by sharing the same costars, Donald Sutherland and Elliott Gould. In this forgettable farce, the two former doctors become bumbling CIA agents, botching a defection that annoys both sides of the political spectrum, not to mention critics and audiences. Some movie offerings in 1977 included the light spoof *No. 1 of the Secret Service*, starring Geoffrey Keen and Sue Lloyd. Ending the decade on a very light note, former *New Avenger* Gareth Hunt starred in the lackluster Bond imitation, *License to Love and Kill* (1979). In the same year, *The In-Laws* starred *Columbo* lead Peter Falk and Alan Arkin. In this comedy, Falk claims to be a CIA agent, while Arkin plays a dentist. Both set out to foil a South American dictator's counterfeiting scheme. Described as convoluted but likable, the concept was trotted out in the 2003 remake with Michael Douglas as the CIA agent and Albert Brooks as his partner.

SUPERSPIES IN THE SKY (AND WONDER WOMEN)

Of all the venues to try new spy projects, only one can safely be described as the nadir of the genre during the 1970s. Television wasn't a breeding ground for memorable secret agents. One dominant theme of the decade had been prefigured in the British 1968 series *The Champions*, in which Stuart Damon, William Gaunt, and Alexandra Bastedo were secret agents endowed with superpowers of ESP, telekinesis, and enhanced physical strength. The comic book spy genre began in earnest with astronaut spy Steve Austin (Lee Majors) in *The Six Million Dollar Man* (ABC, 1974–1978). Like the series' spin-off, *The Bionic Woman* (ABC, NBC, 1976–1978) and Lynda Carter's *Wonder Woman* (ABC, CBS, 1976–1979), the technological wizardry of the Bond pictures were made part of the spy's anatomy as they battled aliens, mutants, and even diabolical roller-derby queens. When David McCallum's 1975 *Invisible Man*, NBC's first attempt at a transparent spy, didn't work, the network tried again with *The Gemini Man* (1976) starring Ben Murphy.

Even when such agents weren't supercharged in themselves, shows like Robert Conrad's *A Man Called Sloane* (NBC, 1979–1980), *U.N.C.L.E.* creator Sam Rolfe's *Delphi Bureau* (ABC, 1972–1973), and NBC's *Search* (1973) featured forgettable characters noted for gimmicks and gadgets, repetitive scripts, and ordinary adversaries. Only one theme of most of these series was shared with literary and film projects: from Steve Austin to David McCallum's invisible man, television spies were no longer agents joining government service by choice; having a superpower was an obligation that entrapped super-heroes in games they couldn't leave. Typical of the decade, champions of law and order would prefer simpler lives.

THE TRANSITIONAL DECADE

To sum up the 1970s in the spy genre, clearly fiction readers gained more than watchers of either small or large screens. The pickings from Hollywood were thin, but both old and new novelists ensured that espionage remained a viable genre in hardcover and paperback. One theme dominated the decade more than any other—the good guys were usually pawns trapped in a shadowy realm of uncertainty, and the goals they fought for were typically personal and not to secure values represented by any government or entity. When battles were won, they were but skirmishes within the context of a war that seemed impossible to win or even define. In a sense, the decade was a transition between times of heroes. The 1960s had its share of Bondian defenders of the West alongside satires and nonsense playing on escapism and cold war dualities that were becoming increasingly blurred. In the 1970s, writers like Jack Higgins and Robert Ludlum, whose best work was arguably yet to come, were not alone in creating antiheroes, brutal men often out for vengeance or vindication in a climate of bureaucratic indifference. In the 1980s, heroes returned with a vengeance, but such agents were rarely stamped in the mold of earlier light diversions. Instead, agents played by Sylvester Stallone, Arnold Schwarzenegger, and the like were rock-ribbed and unquestioning of their missions. However, carrying on themes of the 1970s, such missions rarely came from superiors but were instead reactions to them.

8

From the "Evil Empire" to "The Great Satan": Spying in the Reagan Years

In my time, Peter Quillim, I've seen Whitehall skirts go up and come down again. I've listened to all the excellent arguments for doing nothing, and reaped the consequent frightful harvest. I've watched people hop up and down and call it progress. I've seen good men go to the wall, and the idiots get promoted with a dazzling regularity. All I'm left with is me. And thirty years of Cold War without the options.
Alec Guinness as George Smiley in *Smiley's People*

When William Casey became head of the CIA in 1981, he knew one important mission was to restore morale and effectiveness of an agency reduced in scope after the congressional reactions to misdeeds of the 1970s. Strangely, while Americans wished to restrain a feared "shadow government," most insiders considered the CIA more like a convalescing patient on a table (Persico 1990, 75). The agency's initials were sometimes seen to stand for "Caught in the Act." In addition, insiders were extremely unhappy when James Bamford published *Puzzle Palace* in 1983, the first in-depth look into the formally ultra-secret National Security Agency (NSA). The public was now aware of an NSA that few had heard of before.

Before this book, the CIA was still the organization Americans knew well and it had no reputation for obvious successes. The most visible occurred in 1980, when Tony Mendez, head of the disguises branch of the CIA's Technical Support Division (TSD), provided fake identification for six Americans who had been hiding in the Canadian embassy after students took over the American embassy during the revolution in Iran (Hitz 2004, 134–35). Mendes, with the help of Oscar-winning special effects wizard John Chambers, succeeded at documenting the six as members of a commercial film crew.[1] During the turbulent months of the Iran hostage crisis, the American government was happy to tout this coup as one small bit of good news as one president left office and a new era began.

The media dubbed 1985 "The Year of the Spy" when a series of news stories seemed to blend into one long espionage soap opera. To begin with, two Russians added new twists to the concept of defection. Gitaly Yurchenko apparently fled to the West only to turn around and protest that the CIA had captured him against his will, a claim believed by no one. KGB operative Oleg Gordievsky defected and then redefected by walking away from his protectors and back into a Russian embassy. At first, some thought he was either a plant or new kind of strange deception, but the briefings he gave the CIA resulted in the arrests of NSA spy Robert Pelton and CIA traitor Edward Howard. In separate actions, the John A. Walker spy ring was broken, and Jonathan Pollard was discovered to be an Israeli spy against the United States (Richelson 1995, 390). Despite advocates claiming that Pollard spied for a "friendly ally" and such espionage wasn't the same as working for an enemy, such underhanded "cooperation" was something the U.S. government didn't want to encourage. As of this writing, Pollard remains in jail (Hitz 2004, 151). (The Walker story was dramatized in the three-hour miniseries, A Family of Spies, which starred Powers Booth and Lesley Ann Warren in 1989. The series was nominated for two Golden Globes, including best miniseries.)

In 1985, a total of eleven spies were captured and tried. One got away. Edward Lee Howard evaded the FBI and escaped to Russia despite constant surveillance. Reportedly, he died in Russia in 2002 (Hitz 2004, 119). In February 1994, it was learned that 1985 had also been the year America's most deadly double agent, Aldrich Ames, began his sellout of his country's secrets leading to the deaths of ten American agents. In the 1980s, defectors, moles, and traitors no longer seemed to be motivated by ideology. Ironically, real-world spies followed the course set by fictional spies, who had long been battling the forces of greed and ego, more so than East/West philosophic differences. In each case, money, spite, or revenge prompted disgruntled citizens to turn on their homelands.

While all this was going on, the 1980s were dominated by the leadership of U.S. president Ronald Reagan, who reheated the cold war with speeches branding Russia as "the evil empire." He sought massive buildups in military spending, most notably his SDI (Strategic Defense Initiative) dubbed "Star Wars." Some analysts wondered if the president was trying to recycle a 1940 movie script in which Reagan had played a double agent in quest of a weapon similar to his new defense shield (Strada and Troper 1997, 178; see discussion in chapter 3). Simultaneously, Reagan's White House ordered the CIA to create the "Contra" movement in Nicaragua, which greatly, and illegally, expanded on the mission that Congress had earlier approved. In 1985, Congress outlawed such efforts after hearing reports of civilian casualties due to mining in Nicaraguan harbors. However, Col. Oliver North became a household name when Americans learned the president had bypassed the CIA to fund his so-called Freedom Fighters on his own terms. Subsequent revelations led to the Iran-Contra investigations. However, many secrets perished when former CIA director William Casey died in 1987 while congressional probes were under way.

In 1989, the CIA fought its last cold war battles in Afghanistan, where anti-Russian rebels were given "Stinger" missiles to bring down Soviet helicopters. The new Afghan government, led by the Taliban, wasn't grateful and instead joined the chorus of fundamentalist Islamic forces branding the United States "The Great Satan," setting up the terrorist activities that led to the 2001 World Trade Center attack and the following war in Afghanistan, where the first American casualty was a CIA officer. This example of blowback became a revelation that the CIA, in the 1980s, had followed presidential marching orders without much awareness of what could result. This was the agency that didn't even foresee the end of the cold war, learning of the fall of the Berlin Wall at the same time as CNN viewers. Blowback in the 1980s also included terrorist bombings of CIA headquarters in Beirut, Lebanon. In addition, the agency was derided for its hypocrisy when the cold war and the war on drugs collided. For example, unsavory dictators like Panama's Manuel Noriega earned CIA support to fight Communism even as he pedaled drugs across borders. Noriega wouldn't be the only CIA-backed leader to later feel the wrath of changing American policy. Before the administration of the first

George Bush, Iraq's Saddam Hussein was reportedly only off the CIA's payroll during the Carter years. The FBI, too, was found to have engaged in questionable practices thought outlawed. In 2001, according to CBS News, while Robert Hanssen was spying for the Russians, he was also spying on innocent American citizens for the FBI in an operation called "Active Measures." Particularly during the Reagan years, it was learned, the FBI was still targeting antinuke groups that the agency feared were easy targets for Soviet propaganda.

Still, times changed dramatically in both fact and fiction during the 1980s. Like no other era since World War II and its aftermath, the 1980s began with old enemies still center stage only to be quickly replaced by new adversaries. By the end of the decade, as 1950s and 1960s literature and films had brought back Nazis after their war had been lost, post–cold war projects featured unhappy Soviet generals and rogue KGB agents seeking ways to restore their homeland to superpower status or, at least, find means for their own place under the new sun.

RONALD REAGAN'S HOLLYWOOD

During the 1980s, more than thirty films featured Russians portrayed in Reagan's terms, that is, evil and unworthy of détente or character development. Responding to this perceived "cultural orgy of Russian bashing tantamount to 'war-orgraphy,' " in 1986, the Soviet Writers Union protested the spate of anti-Russian Hollywood films, including *Rocky IV* (1985), *Red Dawn* (1984), and *Invasion U.S.A.* (1985) (Strada and Troper 1997, i). *Invasion U.S.A.*, for example, cast Chuck Norris as reluctant ex-CIA agent Matt Hunter fighting terrorists with violent vigilante vigor. Norris, who coauthored the screenplay, preferred monosyllabic lines for his character and nothing more than sadistic ruthlessness for the Russian agents disguised as policemen killing innocent Americans (Strada and Troper 1997, 179).

Another action film mainstay, Clint Eastwood took a turn in undercover work in *Firefox* (1982). The former Western star played yet another reluctant hero drawn out of retirement to save the United States from Russian radar technology that would give the Reds first strike capability. Eastwood's Michael Gant, a Vietnam veteran, is a top pilot who speaks Russian but suffers from postwar flashbacks. He has to pretend to be a businessman behind enemy lines, hook up with dissident Russian Jews, and sneak out the Soviet jet and fly it to the West while under air attack, in between memories of his Vietnam days. In short, as some reviewers noted, a James Bond film without girls.

In the same tough-guy mold, Steven Seagal starred in quasi-spy stories like *Above the Law* (1988), *Under Siege* (1992), *Under Siege II* (1995), and *Under Siege III* (2004), in which he played Casey Ryback. For his earlier films, Seagal was noted for ego-drenched press releases and interviews where he dropped cryptic hints that he had past connections to the CIA. After investigative reporters disproved these claims, Seagal showed that he had other talents, including producing a number of his own films (Maltin 1994, 804). He served as a martial arts instructor for a number of movies including Sean Connery's 1983 Bond return, *Never Say Never Again*, although Seagal wasn't credited for his work.

Similarly, the Rambo series showcasing Sylvester Stallone, notably *First Blood Part II* (1985), showed that independent agents had to go beyond what was asked for or expected by their country. In this case, Johnny Rambo is asked to document the existence of soldiers Missing in Action (MIA) still in Vietnam. But Rambo goes against orders to break the prisoners free. In the same thematic mold, *Red King, White Knight* (1989) featured an American agent saving Soviet leader Mikhail Gorbachev from an assassination plot, a story preceding headlines. Unlike the actual events in which the KGB participated in a bungled coup to oust the reformer, the *Red King* bad guys were sophisticated, with complicated schemes. The CIA's "white knight" (Tom Skerritt) goes off on his last mission to save Gorbachev, only to learn that the CIA wants to keep the cold war alive. As in previous films and books, the agency has placed their own agent on a hit list.

"Remember," she said, "You're da amateur. Der da professionals. Use dat position. Turn your liability into an asset. De amateur does the unexpected, not because he's clever or experienced, but because he doesn't know any better. Do the unexpected rapidly, obviously, as if confused. Den stop and wait. A confrontation is often da last thing surveillance wants. But if he does want it, you might as well know it. Shoot."
Robert Ludlum, *The Holcroft Covenant*

But, with fewer special effects and more reliance on spy literature, quality spy projects also appeared in the Reagan decade. In 1981,

Charles Jarrott directed the above-average *The Amateur*, based on Robert Littell's novel of the same name. Littell had already gained a reputation for spies in black-humor novels like *The Defection of A. J. Lewinter* (1973), *Mother Russia* (1978), and *The Debriefing* (1979). But *The Amateur* had no pretense for comedy. In both book and film, CIA cipher expert Charlie Hiller (John Savage) decides he wants to be a field agent after his girlfriend is killed by terrorists. To get the information and training he requires, Hiller blackmails the agency, as no one seems interested in avenging the death. While the agency seeks the file Hiller has hidden, the agent goes behind enemy lines in Czechoslovakia where he meets up with a CIA contact (Marthe Keller). She is also motivated by revenge, in her case, for the death of her husband at the hands of the Czech secret police. Vengeance is the central theme of this taut drama as the couple discuss how this mission is personal and not part of their usually dispassionate duties. This emotional dimension is juxtaposed against the backdrop of the CIA seeking to kill Hiller to keep him from learning the truth about the death of his girlfriend and to avenge the embarrassment of the blackmail.

In the end, Hiller learns that the murder was part of an agency setup to give the terrorist, also employed by the agency, credentials in the enemy camp. While critical and audience response was mixed, *The Amateur* enjoyed a distinctive European flavor with believable accents and motivations. While slow paced, the film carried over some of Littell's philosophical thinking, as Hiller and the captain of the secret police (Christopher Plummer) explore the themes of truth and ciphers because both are interested in the controversy of whether or not Francis Bacon wrote Shakespeare's plays. Because of this common ground, Hiller and his new love are allowed to leave the country alive.

Ironically, this literary motif connected *The Amateur* with the history of the OSS. During World War II, William F. Friedman was a profit-motivated geneticist from Cornell who had been hired by a wealthy eccentric to crack the "Shakespeare code." Among some spy buffs, the question remains of special interest because it involves another playwright, Christopher Marlowe, a secret agent to Queen Elizabeth I. Beyond this connection, both the film and novel owed much to previous espionage efforts. According to Robin Winks, "*The*

Amateur takes up where Richard Hannay left off, in the modern world" (1982, 55). This old theme was expressed by Plummer in the film when his character tells Savage in the final moments that the only reason his mission was a success is because he is an amateur—a professional would never have made it. The story is a well-done re-working of the innocent involved in espionage, as all involved were characters with dark intentions. The finale seems to say that what matters are missions with purpose and human depth, not assignments calculated for covert accomplishments. Littell went on to issue other novels, including the clever *The Sisters* (1986), in which two sisters trick the KGB into revealing one of their sleepers so the women can get him to help in a crime. *The Once and Future Spy* (1990) inter-twines the past and present when a historian discovers a CIA leak. Littell's interest in espionage history was best realized in *The Company: A Novel of the CIA* (2002), a book discussed in chapter 9.

Other praised films included *The Falcon and the Snowman* (1985), which earned critical acclaim for its treatment of a true story about two young men, Dalton Lee and Christopher Boyce, who had tried to sell secrets to the Russians in 1977. In the movie, Boyce (Timothy Hutton) is the son of a former FBI agent and is disillusioned by the Vietnam War. After further disillusionment when he learns the CIA is meddling with the internal affairs of Australia, he contacts friend Dalton Lee (Sean Penn), a drug dealer, to help him with his scheme before the pair are caught and convicted.

Cold war themes were also evident in 1983's *The Jigsaw Man*, star-ring Michael Caine and Laurence Olivier, in which a British-Russian double-agent is sent to England to retrieve a list of Soviet agents he had left behind years before. Caine also helped distinguish *The Holcroft Covenant* (1985) in which he and Anthony Andrews were part of a superlative cast in an intelligent script based on the Robert Ludlum novel.

No Way Out (1987) stars Kevin Costner as Tom Farrell, a naval of-ficer working in the Pentagon. He discovers that his girlfriend, Susan (Sean Young), is having an affair with her State Department boss be-fore he kills her to keep the secret. Seeking revenge, Costner gets help from ruthless Will Patton, who "cleans" the murder site and throws the investigators onto the trail of a fictitious KGB mole. This movie is a remake of a film noir classic, *The Big Clock* (1948), which stars

Ray Milland and Maureen O'Sullivan in a similar story without the espionage trappings. *The House on Carroll St.* (1988) was another project linked to the past. Set in the early 1950s, the film cast Kelly McGillis, who teams up with FBI agent Jeff Daniels to uncover a plot similar to the Julius and Ethel Rosenberg case (Barson and Heller 2001, 89).

Some films dealt with non-cold war themes, focusing on the brewing conflict in the Middle East. John Shea and Eli Wallach starred in the excellent 1987 BBC TV movie *The Impossible Spy*, a fact-based drama about Israeli agent, Elie Cohen, an originally reluctant spy who helped Israel win the Six Day War against Syria in 1967. If the film is close to accurate, Cohen was an agent unlike many of his fictional colleagues. Rather than wishing to leave the secret life, he stayed on too long against the advice of his supervisor and was hung for his espionage. Israeli actor Topol starred in and provided voice-overs for *House on Garibaldi St.* (1979), a fact-based history of how Jewish agents found and captured former Nazi Adoph Eichmann in Argentina in 1959.

However, some films dealt with espionage with a light touch, beginning with the 1980 *Hopscotch*, centered on a disheveled CIA agent, Miles Kendig (Walter Matthau). After being demoted to clerical duties, Kendig decides to write his memoirs and seeks out old flame Isabelle Von Schmidt (Glenda Jackson). While based on the more serious 1974 novel by Brian Garfield, the casting of Matthau lightened the tone into a witty chase yarn with the CIA and KGB pursuing ex-agents to keep their secrets (*Movie Guide* 1998). Earlier, Garfield had published *Deep Cover* (1973), a speculation about Russians taking over an American base (McCormick 1977, 85).

One possible indication that the Red-bashing trend had outworn its welcome was *Red Heat* (1988), in which future California governor Arnold Schwarzenegger plays a Soviet cop tracking drug smugglers to Chicago. In an effort to encourage cooperation between Hollywood and the Russian government, *Heat* was the first production allowed to film scenes in Red Square (Barson and Heller 2001, 89). Other efforts were critically panned, including *Little Nikita* (1988), which featured newcomer River Phoenix alongside acting veteran Sidney Poitier. In but one example of a growing trend for cross-generational stories, Phoenix discovers that his parents are Soviet sleeper agents.

Two peculiar spoofs blending satires of various genres were deliberately bad. In 1984, *Top Secret* starred Val Kilmer as singer Nick Rivers in a parody of World War II spy dramas, cold war spy dramas, and, for good measure, 1960s rock 'n' roll movies. The tone of the film was set by the theme song, which was a Beach Boys takeoff with lyrics about the joys of skeet shooting on surfboards. *Top Secret* was followed by *Young Nurses in Love* (1987), a strange spoof of both hospital and spy movies also in the mold of the *Airplane* and *Spy Hard* series. A KGB agent (Jean Marrow) is sent to steal a priceless American treasure— sperm that the Americans keep in a guarded vault. Suffering from a "sperm gap," the Russians need a spurt to boost their genetic engineering. The agent is warned that, in order to succeed, she might well have to make the greatest of sacrifices for the Motherland—her virginity. In 1985, *Saturday Night Live* veterans Chevy Chase and Dan Aykroyd teamed in *Spies Like Us*, a comedy in the mold of the earlier Bing Crosby–Bob Hope "Road" pictures. In the story, the two meet while taking entrance exams for the CIA. Caught cheating, they are of course suitable candidates for a secret mission. Pursued by the Russians, the pair almost spark World War III (Connors and Craddock 1999).

The man fumbled with a briefcase and Bond saw a hypodermic being made ready. He made a slight threatening move toward the syringe bearer whose partner immediately performed a small magic act with an automatic pistol. One moment, his hand was empty. The next it was full of gun. The one-eyed muzzle of which pointed steadily at Bond.

John Gardner, *No Deals, Mr. Bond*

In the 1980s, James Bond was again an important reflection of the times. *For Your Eyes Only* (1981) saw a shift to more realistic spy adventure when former scriptwriter Richard Maibaum returned, replacing the more fantastic Christopher Wood in an attempt to move away from the over-the-top parody aspects. Moore's send-off, *A View to a Kill* (1985), clearly showed that the series had become anachronistic, with 007 receiving the Order of Lenin from his former KGB archenemies. The two Timothy Dalton Bond efforts, *The Living Daylights* (1987) and *License to Kill* (1989), were clearly designed to show a change in the franchise's direction. Dalton's 007 became a brooding secret agent known more for acting than stunts. He now dealt with realistic arms merchants and with Sanchez the drug smuggler, who ruled an underground empire from Chile to Alaska. Like other films of the era, in *License to Kill*, 007 quits the Secret Service to revenge a friend when politicians and his superiors choose to do nothing about Sanchez.

In 1968, Glidrose Productions had planned to release a series of James Bond continuation novels with a number of writers using the pseudonym Robert Markum. However, after Ian Fleming's widow issued very public complaints about Kingsley Amis's *Colonel Sun*, the project was dropped until after her death. The new writer to take up the mantle was former Bond parodist John Gardner. His *License Renewed* appeared in 1981, the same year Roger Moore's 007 came down to earth in the less-fanciful *For Your Eyes Only*. For fifteen years, Gardner kept the literary flame alive with *For Special Services* (1982), *Icebreaker* (1983), *Scorpius* (1988), and *Cold* (1996), among others. Gardner's tenure began with the understanding that his books could reflect contemporary events and changes in technology, but 007 himself was frozen in time, just as in the films.

Ironically, James Bond nearly appeared in a play in 1986. According to future Bond novelist Raymond Benson, he approached Glidrose Productions with the idea of putting *Casino Royale* on the stage, as it was the only Fleming book not controlled by EON Productions. "I wrote the play in 2–3 months and then held a staged reading of it in New York City in February 1986, using professional actors. The reading went very well" (Cox 2004). While paying Benson for his work, Glidrose shelved the project saying that a James Bond play wouldn't work. "The films had Bond in a monopoly and there was no way a play could compete" (Cox 2004).

SPIES ON TELEVISION

One popular vogue for secret agents during the Reagan era was in collectibles and nostalgia for baby boomers wishing to reconnect with heroes of the past. For television spies, this trend began in 1977, when Patrick Macnee reprised his role as John Steed in *The New Avengers* and Roger Moore look-alike Ian Ogilvy starred in *The Return of the*

Saint. In 1979, James West (Robert Conrad) and Artemus Gordon (Ross Martin) returned in *The Wild Wild West Revisited* and *More Wild Wild West* (1980).

But matters escalated in the 1980s on the small screen when the men from U.N.C.L.E. reunited in a 1983 television movie which also returned actor George Lazenby to a brief cameo as 007. As a result, 1983 was the year that all three screen Bonds up to that time (with Roger Moore's *Octopussy* and Sean Connery's *Never Say Never Again*) played the role simultaneously. Five years later, Peter Graves again took up the mantle of Jim Phelps in a hastily revamped *Mission: Impossible* and Simon Dutton again tried to give *The Saint* new life in syndication.

But series more representative of the times revolved around new themes of more down-to-earth domestic lives and concerns about the cost of spying on its participants. In particular, the very popular *The Equalizer* (CBS, 1985–1989) starred Edward Woodward as an agent who breaks away from the covert world to both atone for his past and to reconnect with a son he barely knew. According to scriptwriter and special effects designer Robert Short, "*The Equalizer* was originally created for [ex-Bond] George Lazenby by [producer Michael] Sloan because he always liked George which is why he appears in the *Return of the Man From U.N.C.L.E.* The *Equalizer* character was supposed to be a retired James Bond, wink wink. The network wanted someone more well known and Woodward was brought in to star."[2] Another mix of realism and romance, and romance in this case with a double meaning, was *Scarecrow and Mrs. King* (CBS, 1983–1987). Scarecrow was Bruce Boxleitner and Kate Jackson played Amanda King, an ordinary housewife pulled into the covert world. In the spirit of the times, these two tried to balance saving their country with worries about babysitters and soccer games, concerns far removed from the issues of 007 and his generation. Like other shows of the decade, there was little globe-trotting, as Scarecrow and his future bride did most of their work in Washington, D.C. In a sense, the 1990–1991 *Undercover* (ABC), starring Anthony John Denison and Linda Purl, was a series bridging *Scarecrow* and the 2001–2003 *The Agency*. In such series, romance disappeared. Married couples didn't lead glamorous lives, but instead tried to ground themselves in family responsibilities in between missions of life and death. For the most part, as in *The Equalizer*, the family tended to lose.

However, fantasy and humor didn't vanish completely. From 1986 to 1988, CBS's *Adderly* starred Winston Rekert as an agent of E.C.H.O., an organization established to deal with rogue agents disenfranchised after the fall of the Berlin Wall who became private criminals. Less humorous with decided nods to the new interest in special effects was *Airwolf* (CBS, 1985–1986), in which a tortured Vietnam vet (Jan-Michael Vincent) did secret missions with his supercharged helicopter. Most fantastic of all was *The A-Team* (NBC, 1983–1986), in which a team of misfits—including one icon of the decade, Mr. T—turned *Mission: Impossible* upside down when the former Napoleon Solo (Robert Vaughn) joined the cast as General Stockwell and put them in the vise of many agents of the era—work for me or go to jail.

> Isolation, solitude, secret plotting. A novel is a secret a writer may keep for years before he lets it out of his room. Writers in hiding, writers in prison. Sometimes their secrets turn out to be dangerous to the state machine. For most writers in the West of course this danger is extremely remote. The cells we live in are strictly personal constructions.
>
> Let's change the room slightly and imagine another kind of apartness. The outsider who builds a plot around his desperation. A self-watcher, a lonely young man, living in a fiction he hasn't bothered to put down on paper. But this doesn't mean he is unorganized, he organizes everything. This is how he keeps from disappearing. His head is filled with dangerous secrets, and he may finally devise a way to come out of his room. He invents a false name, orders a gun through the mail, then looks around for someone famous he can shoot.
>
> Don DeLillo, *The Word, the Image, and the Gun*

For darker themes, as always, literature led the way. Novels by Len Deighton, John Le Carré, and Robert Ludlum remained at the heart of paperback sales, but other writers made important contributions as well. One interesting case was the work of Don DeLillo, although, in the strictest sense of the term, he was not a writer of spy fiction. However, the important prize-winning writer, known for exploring themes of menace and meaning, violence and paranoia, did touch on cultural reactions to events that many associate with the covert world.

For example, his *Running Dog* (1978), an imaginative tale about a use-less quest to find a secret pornographic film of Adolf Hitler, was partly a statement about the inquisitive nature of Americans who uncover things they no longer care about once the secrets are discovered. The meaning of terrorism was dealt with in *The Names* (1982), set in Greece and the Middle East, and *Mao II* (1991), which was a winner of the PEN/Faulkner Award. In the latter psychological drama, DeLillo claimed that the powerful exercise and retain their control in secret, which forces the powerless to act in more dramatic ways.

This concern was a continuation of themes expressed in DeLillo's most overt nod to espionage, *Libra* (1988), a novel on the life of Lee Harvey Oswald. The book is told from the point of view of Nicholas Branch, a retired senior CIA analyst who has been hired to write the secret history of the Kennedy assassination. According to Branch, dis-graced and overzealous CIA agents hatched a plan to undo the di-saster of the Bay of Pigs by staging an assassination attempt on President Kennedy. With a carefully manufactured trail leading to Fidel Castro, they hoped to provoke the United States into a full-scale second invasion of Cuba. Two agents think they're planning a surgi-cal miss; a third intends to make the murder real and finds his gun-man in the cipher, Lee Harvey Oswald. In this account, Oswald is a man who, in both fact and fiction, eludes easy description (Towers 1988, 6).

After reading parts of the Warren Commission Report and visiting sites where Oswald lived, DeLillo's fictional biography and thoughts on the aftermath of the murders in Dallas resulted in the author's con-clusions that the killing led to Americans living in a culture of na-tional paranoia from which we have not recovered. He claims that his novels, ultimately unresolveable, could not have been written in the world before the Kennedy assassination. In later interviews, DeLillo stated that *Libra* was a story without end because new theo-ries, new suspects, and new documents appear that keep conspiracy fears alive (Gardner and Nel 2003). On another level, DeLillo's in-tellectual fiction can be seen as the other side of books in the John Buchan tradition, where independent agents are drawn into defend-ing their homeland. The dark side of covert loners, the terrorists and assassins in DeLillo's works, choose a secret life that empowers them in ways writers of fiction no longer have as a means to address social grievances. The writer's last use of intrigue, to date, was 1997's *Underworld*, in which J. Edgar Hoover is a principal character.

> Obviously, most people perceive themselves to be "regular" people, and they're more likely to identify with a normal person than with Batman or Julius Caesar. So, you take an ordinary sort of guy and drop him into a serious situation. It's the same technique Hitchcock used, though he always seemed to use Cary Grant or Jimmy Stewart as his "regular guy."
>
> Tom Clancy to Katie Struckel, 2001

However, all the rules changed—in literature, the large screen, and television—with the rise of novelist Tom Clancy. Quickly dubbed the creator of "techno-thrillers" (a term Clancy disavows), the Clancy franchise centered on the ten Jack Ryan novels that developed his hero from marine to stockbroker to history professor to CIA analyst to CIA director to vice president to president of the United States. Ryan may have been compared to James Bond both within and outside of the books themselves, but this character was fresh and new on a variety of levels. Jack Patrick Ryan reflected Clancy's own deeply conservative perspectives, especially his fondness and support of military thinking and purpose. Ryan's realm was that of international geopolitics, and the stories within stories were told from multiple points of view revealing in-depth looks into terrorists, dictators, politicians, and the heads of state, who typically got tongue lashings from Ryan when their moral compasses went off direction.

Throughout his career, Clancy has repeatedly claimed that his much-discussed use of technological terminology was merely a means to provide verisimilitude to his stories. One critic boiled down Clancy's vocabulary as "a bewildering mixture of spook-speak, military tough talk and bureaucratic buzzwords" (Anderson 2003, C4). He often says the success of Jack Ryan is that he is an ordinary man caught up in extraordinary situations, a theme adopted from the films of Alfred Hitchcock. In 2001, Clancy observed, "I would go so far as to say that the way I tell my stories largely results from a 90-minute show I once saw on PBS about Hitchcock and his films. Suspense is achieved by information control. What you know. What the reader knows. What the characters know. You balance that properly, and you can really get the reader wound up" (Struckel 2001, 20). Without question, Clancy benefited in his stories by research and help from intelligence insiders to whom he paid tribute in character names. For example, his friend John Martin, a Justice Department lawyer, helped provide legal detail in a number of books and became Robert Martin in *Executive Orders*.

It all began in the early 1980s when Clancy ran his own independent insurance agency while writing his first novel, *Hunt for Red October*.[3] A member of the U.S. Naval Institute, Clancy submitted the manuscript to their press, which published *Hunt* in October 1984. Soon after, an editor with the *Washington Times* got White House insiders to read the book and one was given to President Reagan (Struckel 2001, 80). Not surprisingly, as John F. Kennedy had enjoyed Ian Fleming, Reagan in turn praised *Hunt*. Later, CIA director William Casey, no fan of spy novels, read Clancy's *Red Storm Rising* (1986), one of the novelist's most overt cold war propaganda efforts. *Cardinal of the Kremlin* (1988) echoed the same themes, including the virtuous American intelligence community and military battling morally questionable politicians and journalists, not to mention the KGB and Muslim terrorists.

The Ryan film series, beginning with director John McTiernan's *Hunt for Red October* (1990), has seen mixed responses from audiences and Clancy alike. For many viewers, Alec Baldwin's version of Jack Ryan, a young analyst trying to determine the intentions of Soviet skipper Marko Ramius (Sean Connery), was outshined by ex-Bond Connery on the large screen. On at least one level, this was by design. Five years after the book's publication, Hollywood had sensed a shift in tone and looked to Gorbachev's reforms for their direction (Strada and Troper 1997, 191). In the film, Connery's submarine commander has chosen to defect to preserve the balance of power, while Ryan, a CIA analyst, finds his job is to persuade his American bosses not to overreact to what they perceive, and he reads the Russian's actions perfectly. According to John Belton, the film's use of the Russian defection is juxtaposed against the backdrop of the political and military repercussions on both sides of the cold war. In the final scenes, the defecting Russian and Jack Ryan collaborate and evade destruction from within (a KGB saboteur) and without (an overzealous

Soviet submarine commander). The film, in Belton's opinion, suggests a promise of healthy revolution in the Soviet Union, the peaceful co-existence between East and West, and a shift in Hollywood, as a Russian is the dominant hero in the film (Belton 1994, 254). Publicity for the film came from unexpected sources. Just as the media blitz began, Soviet government newspaper *Izvestia* reported that a real-life mutiny had taken place on a Soviet antisub destroyer off Sweden in 1975, inspiring Clancy's best seller. The mix of headlines with Hollywood hype led one reviewer to muse, "Overnight the cold-war thriller has become a historical genre" (Broeske 1990, A7).

Beginning with director Philip Noyce's *Patriot Games* (1992), Clancy's well-publicized feud with Paramount Productions began. For one thing, Clancy thought that actor Harrison Ford was too old for the part, and the novelist bitterly complained about the screenplay having little to do with his book. He didn't like Paramount reshooting the ending for a more dramatic duel between Ryan and vengeful terrorist Sean Miller (Sean Bean), a member of the fictional IRA splinter group, the Ulster Liberation Army (Galbraith 1992, 2). Audiences, however, liked the Ford version of Ryan, a mature hero concerned with family matters as he protected his pregnant wife, his daughter, and their waterfront home from terrorists. Still, Ford's 1994 return in *Clear and Present Danger* was uneven in audience response as Ryan battled Colombian drug cartels, outsmarted Oval Office conspirators, and told off the president of the United States. The original 1990 novel was one of Clancy's more layered and complex outings, forcing screenwriters to streamline the original plot into a workable script. Again, Clancy was unhappy that his conservative values weren't reflected in the film.

In *Sum of All Fears* (2002), the younger Ben Affleck took over the role, tracking neo-Nazi terrorists who are planning to detonate a nuclear bomb at the Super Bowl. Although Ryan is deputy director of the CIA in Clancy's 1991 book, in the movie he's back to being a neophyte CIA analyst whose specialty is Russian political history. However, times had changed after 9/11; according to Affleck, "The cautionary elements that Clancy cared very much about, chief among them terrorism, nuclear proliferation and the security of nuclear resources, will be discussed and dealt with. . . . [The movie] reflects a new reality that we all have had to come to accept" (Gerston 2002,

37). While Clancy again grumbled that the film wasn't the same as his book, he sat with director Phil Alden Robinson to share his commentary for the DVD version and grudgingly admitted that it was a good piece of work.

The books, however, followed a different chronology. Two related novels without Ryan were *Without Remorse* (1993) and *Rainbow Six* (1998), the latter an adventure that was marketed in tandem with a new video game. Both centered on a former supporting character, John Kelly/Clark, who was first a vengeful undercover operative before becoming head of an elite antiterrorist unit. Their single action, to date, was knocking off ecoterrorists in a clear literary stab at environmentalists. In *Debt of Honor* (1994), Clancy left the cold war behind and staged an economic war with Japan that ended in what was to become one of the most discussed scenes in literature—the crashing of a plane by a Japanese pilot into the Capitol. When the book first appeared, it was an imaginative tale that elevated Jack Ryan to the presidency. Of course, the book's conclusion wasn't seen in post–9/11 terms, nor was it described as a cautionary warning in 1994. One typical review by John Lehman, mentioning the then current debate over term limits, expressed contemporary wish fulfillment: "Clancy carries out a fantasy I have dreamed about for years, one that involves a very large plane and a kamikaze pilot: 'The entire east face of the building's southern half was smashed to gravel which shot westward—but the real damage took a second or two longer, barely time for the roof to start falling in on the nine hundred people in the chamber'" (Lehman 1994, A7).

The follow-up book, *Executive Orders* (1996), has Ryan suddenly forced to participate in the political realm he has avoided, having to comfort a nation while rebuilding the presidency, Congress, and the Supreme Court, all destroyed at the end of *Debt of Honor*. Apparently, the last President Ryan book, *The Bear and the Dragon* (2000), had Ryan facing brewing trouble in Russia and China and a global struggle for Siberian oil. Publicity for the book was a clear statement of Clancy's place in the publishing world. Simultaneously, the book appeared as an audio book, in a large-print edition, as numerous book club editions, and a signed limited edition at $150. Several weeks prior to publication, the book was ranked No. 1 on Amazon.com, and Barnes and Noble.com countered with its "Tom Clancy Superstore."

By the time of the critically panned *Red Rabbit* (2002), Clancy had nowhere to go with a spy in the White House. So he returned to 1981, when Ronald Reagan, Margaret Thatcher, and Pope John Paul II were all new to office. The story was based on an actual attempt on the pope's life in 1981, almost certainly planned by the KGB. To most readers' distress, Ryan was only marginally involved in the story line to bring a Russian defector, the Red Rabbit, over to the West to stop the plot. Similarly, in *The Teeth of the Tiger* (2003), Jack Ryan was off-stage as an ex-president writing his memoirs. Instead, his son, Jack Ryan, Jr., is the new face in action adventure. According to reviewer Patrick Anderson, the tale trivializes the issue of terrorism, while seemingly trying to have the younger Ryan come into his own and out of his father's shadow (2003, C4).

Partly because of his difficulties with Paramount, Clancy turned to television by deliberately designing new projects with the small screen in mind. In 1995 with collaborator Steve Piescenik, Clancy created a new four-hour miniseries for ABC, *Tom Clancy's Ops Center*, which yielded a highly successful stream of new novels based on the concept. Scaling down his scope from the Ryan books, *Ops Center* focused on international dilemmas that mirrored domestic difficulties for his highly specialized team of crisis management analysts and agents. Again for ABC, in 1998, Clancy and Piescenik created another four-hour miniseries, *Net Force*, a specialized stand-alone FBI unit organized to combat online espionage and terrorism. This project again launched a new franchise for Clancy, dealing with Alex Michaels, the chief of the group set in the year 2010. The science-fictional flavor of the series brought together many elements more associated with romantic than realistic espionage. Like *Ops Center*, *Net Force* became a new vehicle for a series of novels that featured spy adventure, romantic twists and turns, and the home lives of both agents and their teenage offspring. Despite Clancy's stated goodwill for the ABC productions, his next franchise, the *Power Play* books, wasn't launched by either film or television. In 2004, yet another concept, "Tom Clancy's Splintered Cells," debuted first as a computer console game. In December of that year, the first of the "Splintered Cells" books appeared written by former Bond novelist Raymond Benson using the pseudonym David Michaels. Clearly, the name Tom Clancy will keep appearing above movie and book titles, even if the originator has little to do with the products involved.

THE RETURN OF HEROES

In the 1980s, bigger was better in both literature and film. The days of pulp paperbacks of less than two hundred pages were gone in favor of hefty epics that couldn't be digested in a single airline flight. Films competed to outdo those that came before them in star power, spectacle, and box office receipts. The most obvious thematic change in such projects was that, while a suspicion of government and intelligence agencies was now taken for granted, spies of the Reagan era were rarely mere pawns in the "Great Game." More likely, Jack Ryan or Johnny Rambo saw a job to do and moved heaven and earth to accomplish it, despite obstacles from friends and foes alike. More often than not, revenge was the central motive in both books and films, and vengeance usually came against the wishes of governments with other ideas in mind.

The beginning of the decade had seen spies still locked in the cold war with the renewed anti-Communist rhetoric spearheaded by the Reagan administration. Then, suddenly, it was over. Almost overnight, old fears evaporated with new questions. What did the breakup of the "Evil Empire" mean? What was the new role, if any, of agencies formed specifically to battle the old Red menace? For half a century, a war seemingly without end had dominated geopolitics in general and espionage in particular. It would not be clear for ten more years that another conflict had already begun, which was equally unlikely to be resolved in a foreseeable future. When the 1990s dawned, the Western powers seemed to have won a great victory over a discredited economical and political house of cards. But a new learning curve had just begun that didn't come into the general public's focus until the fall of 2001.

9

Big-Screen Pyrotechnics and Eyes in the Sky: Spies in a Technological World

Once in intelligence work, one cannot bring oneself to desert it. A spy is like an alcoholic. One espionage act and then another until he is irretrievably hooked on spying.

Dr. Hermann Friedrich to an OSS officer in 1946 Shanghai, quoted in Higham, *Errol Flynn*

"Why did you go running back when they called?"
"Too much unfinished business. I've never known anyone who left the secret world with all his affairs in order. We all leave behind bits of loose threads. Old operations, old enemies, they pull at you like memories of old lovers."

Daniel Silva, *Kill Master*

Even before September 11, 2001, a debate over the uses of new technology and espionage was a concern within the real-world intelligence community. By 1998, the central debate was whether the emphasis should be "toys vs. boys," that is, should technology supercede the place of agents in the field (Bamford 2001, 476)?

This interest in "toys" in both fact and fiction seemed appropriate on a number of levels. In the post–cold war era, the intelligence services of many nations monitored the manufacturing, sales, and purchases of advanced weaponry by countries such as Pakistan, Korea, Iran, and Iraq. At the time, satellite reconnaissance capabilities seemingly made the task easier (Richelson 1995, 417). As the new millennium approached, drawing from old science-fictional stories, the

National Security Agency (NSA) was working on computers integrating biological entities, including bacteria used to build transistors. Such machines were planned to be able to reproduce themselves, combining electronic components with DNA (Bamford 2001, 613). New technology even allowed spies to have their own supersecret television channels. The NSA had its own spy talk shows aired throughout its community and had its own CNN-like news network tailored for spies (Bamford 2001, 511). As Frederick Hitz put it, Will Smith's *Enemy of the State* (1998) was set in a world of computer hackers where stealing financial information and manipulating data are all taken for granted (2004, 136). Once, agents of U.N.C.L.E. stood in hallways lined with new computers on all sides; less than forty years later, such computers filled acres of land in supersecret cities on America's East Coast. The role of the hero, it might seem, had shrunk in such surroundings.

Despite all this, with unintentional irony, U.S. attorney general John Ashcroft told the Senate Judiciary Committee on September 25, 2001, that the new war on terrorism was being fought with "antique weapons." Technology was one matter, how it was being used was another, but even more important was who could use it and when. New wizardry couldn't do the job alone, and many commentators noted that we still need "boys" of both genders. Digital incriptions and fiberoptic cables defy electronic surveillance. The actions of terrorist groups often don't lend themselves to sophisticated eavesdropping. For example, according to a CBS 2001 report, ELF (Ecological Liberation Front), a phantom organization with its members not even known to its founder, made at least five terrorist attacks without a single electronic trace. On September 11, 2001, counterterrorist experts like Jeffrey Beatty claimed that the teams who destroyed the World Trade Center and damaged the Pentagon used "Low tech, high concept" techniques that turned commercial planes into bombs. As many later noted, the nineteen terrorists might have been primitive technologically, but were well-organized, sophisticated agents who were masters of espionage tradecraft.

Clearly, "boys" of many capabilities were needed in the field as well as behind computer screens. Jeffrey Richelson was not alone in writing that humans must provide documents, technical samples, and on-site reporting. He wrote that secret agents must be able to determine motivations, capabilities, and tensions, and make judgment calls. Many mind-sets and opinions must determine how to use needed information (Richelson 1995, 429). As former president Bill Clinton observed on the David Letterman show in August 2004, intelligence has never been a science but instead relies on judgment calls. From another angle, the lack of such agents was seen as a case of history repeating itself. For example, cryptologists were breaking Japanese codes before Pearl Harbor, but the messages that might have given Washington foreknowledge of the coming attack weren't broken until September 1945, after the war was over. The government lacked the staff to handle all the traffic that had come in (Persico 2003, 10). Fifty-six years later, who was listening to threats and who was able to prevent enemy action? Where were all the "boys"? It's one thing to install metal detectors in airports, but without qualified operators, guns still get through.

From the other side of the debate, however, human involvement had led to a history of seeming misdeeds and fumbles that had given the community of espionage a reputation it struggled to overcome. Only occasionally did it appear that the defenders of democracy had palpable successes. During the 1990s, the FBI arrested spies Aldrich Ames, Harold Nicholson, Earl Pitts, and Robert Lifka, among others. According to Frederick Hitz, intelligence agencies had performed credibly in alerting policymakers about leaks in Russia's nuclear stockpile and containing the spread of Soviet power into Angola, Afghanistan, and Central America (2004, 167). Some successes simply needed time to be revealed. In April 2004, former national security advisor Sandy Berger told CNN anchor Wolf Blitzer that there had been a spike in terrorist alerts around the month of the millennium, and he had gained more wiretaps during that month than any time in history. Despite many "millennia fears," no terrorist plans came to fruition.

No matter how many successes could be marked, however, each accomplishment seemed like cutting off only one head of a Hydra. For many experts, one important turning point occurred in July 2000, when PLO leader Yasser Arafat rejected out of hand Israeli prime minister Ehud Barak's concessions at the Camp David discussions brokered by President Clinton. This seeming last chance at Middle East peace initiatives resulted in the al-Aqsa intifada beginning in

September 2000. One year later, this war of cultures spread into America. At the turn of the century, fear of saboteurs and mad bombers had become more a part of American culture than during the Red Scares of the 1920s and 1950s. Once, the television series *The Prisoner* showed electronic observers in statues and trees as a cautionary fable about the dangers of a "Big Brother" government. Now, Americans demanded just such watchers, as public safety seemed to outweigh civil liberties. During the 1950s and 1960s, civil defense signs and air raid drills were commonplace in America's schools. Half a century later, bags and baggage were searched at airports and public events as the government issued various levels of color-coded alerts. Both toys and boys were seemingly needed in every American town. Culture had indeed changed.

WELCOME BACK, 007

Hollywood also had questions to deal with regarding technological advances. The question often seemed to be whether cutting-edge special effects and spectacle should replace other aspects of drama such as character development or plotlines worthy of the pumped-up animation or digital machines. Such had been the case with Bond films, as when producer Michael Wilson described the creation of 1983's *Octopussy*. In DVD commentary for the special edition, Wilson discussed flying around the world to find exotic settings that 007 hadn't visited. Then scriptwriters cobbled a story together to incorporate these set pieces in the minimal plot. Similarly, according to DVD commentary by the participants in crafting *Mission: Impossible 2* (2000), director Jack Woo had created the action sequences before the scriptwriters were brought in, so the plot was built around the motorcycle, helicopter, and car chases.

According to Martin Willis, the new emphasis on overheated technology had much to do with the return of James Bond in the person of Pierce Brosnan. Willis claimed that the Bond series had always portrayed a 007 who had an ambivalent relationship with technology. This is shown in the popular "Q scenes," when Bond first demonstrates mastery over the gadgets before famously showing disrespect for them by destroying them (Lindner 2003, 159). One notable example is the scene in *Tomorrow Never Dies* (1997), when Bond's supercharged BMW crashes into a car rental where Q sees his work demolished. Such moments show that Bond will not be outdone by technology; other scenes demonstrate that those who misuse it will be hoisted on their own petard. A case in point from the same film is the death of Jonathan Price's Elliott Carter, who is drilled by his own machine (Lindner 2003, 159).[1]

Of course, more had changed than fantastic machines and devices. According to Michael Strada, Bond wasn't alone in Hollywood's search for new enemies to fill the void left by the end of the cold war. Producers found "Japanese underworld figures to kick around in *Black Rain* (1992), IRA terrorists to condemn in *Patriot Games* (1993), greedy Colombian drug dealers to loathe in *Clear and Present Danger* (1994), and rogue Arab states to despise in *The American President* (1995)" (Strada and Troper 1997, 197). In the 1990s, Russia was most often seen as a fragmented society ruled by Mafia-like gangs, as in Pierce Brosnan's first Bond opus, *GoldenEye* (1995), in which the threats now came from and were targeted onto computer technology and energy resources. In the opening moments, the film connects to the past with a pretitle sequence set before the breakup of the Soviet Empire. But as the new theme, sung by contemporary songstress Tina Turner, fills the speakers, the title sequence and later scenes in the film show broken, toppled statues in Moscow clearly demonstrating that times have changed. But such shifts aren't limited to Russia. In *GoldenEye*, actress Judi Dench is introduced as the new M, who sees Bond as an anachronistic, chauvinist, cold war dinosaur; in turn, Bond sees his new boss as a "bean-counter." An accountant has replaced the old M, who stood for England's imperial past with trophies and mementos of the naval empire decorating his office (Lindner 2003, 227). At the same time, the new Miss Moneypenny (Samantha Bond) is less pliant than her predecessor (Lois Maxwell), telling Bond that his flirtatious comments border on sexual harassment and he needs to back up his words.

As it had always been in the Bond universe, 007's exploits were typically based on speculations built on either topical or potential world events. *Tomorrow Never Dies* reflected changes also seen in post–cold war John Le Carré novels in which the writer "replaced his cast of spies with corporate villains, supplanting those who'd acted lawfully in the name of national security and ideology with those acting in the name of profit and position, the latter capable of much greater damage" (Hoffman 2001, 238). The opening sequence of *The World Is Not Enough* (1999) has Brosnan falling off London's Millennium Dome, a reflection of that year's worries about terrorist attacks during the first days of the new century. The film shows the retreat of Soviet power in its former provinces, placing the distribution of oil in jeopardy when patriotic ethnic groups seek independence by gaining their power from natural resources, not fantastic technologies (Britton 2004, 222). In *Die Another Day* (2002), 007 battles North Korean bad guys intent on making their country a new superpower in the international community. At the same time that the film earned its box office bonanza, North Korea in fact initiated an international crisis by reactivating its nuclear arms program and was dubbed part of George W. Bush's "Axis of Evil" in the new president's 2002 State of the Union address.

But Bond, in the guise of Pierce Brosnan, was a character with a long tradition built on past models. Brosnan frequently admitted that he looked back to *Goldfinger* for his inspiration to play Bond. As Timothy Dalton had stated that his version of 007 was based on the character in the Fleming books, Brosnan claimed that Sean Connery was the model he worked from. Without question, Connery continued to cast a wide shadow in the 1990s. For another example of his presence, in the 1996 cult classic *Trainspotting*, Scottish junkies saw Connery as a cultural hero, and frequently mentioned his Bond films. In the end credits, one character recited all the titles to Connery's 007 movies. Such homages, in one form or another, were evident in many films of the period.

———

I married Rambo.

Jamie Lee Curtis in *True Lies*

One above-average Bondian blend of action adventure, comedy, and big-budget special effects was director James Cameron's 1994 *True Lies*. According to *U.N.C.L.E.* expert Bill Koenig, Cameron was a fan of the 1960s series, and the movie was his homage to it. Some aspects of *U.N.C.L.E.* seem obvious. Special agent Harry Tasker (Arnold Schwarzenegger) works for the ultrasecret, heavily technological Omega Sector, headed by eye patch–wearing Charlton Heston. (As Cameron was also a fan of Marvel Comics, perhaps the eye patch was a nod to Nick Fury, head of S.H.I.E.L.D.) The film also had a slice of *I Led Three Lives*. Tasker's wife, Helen (Jamie Lee Curtis), thinks her husband is a boring computer salesman. While he's infiltrating the "Crimson Jihad," she's being pursued by a car salesman pretending to be a secret agent. Trying to teach her a lesson, Harry inadvertently pulls her into his dangerous world, where she proves almost as adept in deceit as the fifteen-year veteran. By film's end, they're more of an undercover team like *Scarecrow and Mrs. King*.

Ten years later, another commercial success built on contemporary matters was actor Vin Diesel's 2003 *XXX*, a film geared for a young demographic, eighteen-year-olds being the high end of the intended audience. Diesel's Zandor Cage was another twist on the reluctant criminal being coerced into espionage because the NSA was losing all its trained agents to a new foe, Anarchy 999. Cage's most recent public outrage had been destroying the car of a senator who annoyed the hero because of his attempts to censor video games. Still, in one spymaster's opinion, he was "The best and brightest of the bottom of the barrel," just the sort of guy to go after foes like himself—"dangerous, dirty, tattooed, uncivilized"—not to mention bald in the new vogue for shaved-headed heroes and just as anarchic as the bad guys. "If you want to send someone to save the world," Cage tells his new boss, "make sure they like it the way it is." Such heroes do save the world, but to do so they invest a lot of screen time demolishing everything in sight along the way. Well, even such new heavyweights have to make nods to the past. Only in *XXX* would modern viewers be likely to hear strains of the old "Third Man Theme." In addition, probably unintentionally, Anarchy 999 is but a high-tech throwback to the first foes of literary and film villains of the twentieth century, the anarchists found in the books of Joseph Conrad and the films of Alfred Hitchcock.

However, the most overt nods to the past, particularly the 1960s, came in a number of parodies beginning with comic actor Leslie Nielsen's bumbling secret agent WD 40 in *Spy Hard* (1996), an ineffectual *Mad* magazine–inspired attempt to lampoon the already lampooned. The film had its moments, as when Nielsen ordered Samonelli and Russo "on the rocks, stirred, not beaten, with a twist of lemon in chilled glasses, not frozen, with two of those curly little straws." Television spies were clearly in Spy Hard's sights, including the obligatory parody of the Mission: Impossible self-destruct messages.

Spy Hard was followed by Mike Myers's Austin Powers: International Man of Mystery (1997), The Spy Who Shagged Me (1999), and Goldmember (2002). All of these parodies were pastiches of spy film motifs, Bond in particular, with the humor depending on viewers knowing the references to situations from both television and film spies (Lindner 2003, 78). In the first of the series, Powers is transported from the 1960s to the present, connecting generations with the music of Burt Bacharach and Powers's "Swinging London" sexual attitudes in a clash of cultures (Lindner 2003, 164). Goldmember made another overt connection to the era, casting the "Harry Palmer" of the 1960s, Michael Caine, as the younger Powers's spymaster father.

The market for recycling such parody is apparently a bottomless pit. The title for Men in Black (1996) came from an actual NSA team of commandos who dress in black paramilitary uniforms and wear special headgear equipped with potent weapons. Film director Barry Sonnenfeld cast Will Smith and Tommy Lee Jones as MIB agents of a shadow organization merging the NSA, CIA, and Immigration and Naturalization Services. In some reviews, the film was seen as using deadpan humor to parody cold war melodramas like The Hunt for Red October and Crimson Tide where secret agents fought against apocalyptic nuclear war (Bamford 2001, 35). With the MIB taking on aliens of every stripe, it can also be viewed as a parody of The X-Files and the spy-fi series that rose to prominence in the 1990s. Other such attempts included Bill Murray as The Man Who Knew Too Little (1997), about a video store salesman who thinks he's in a live-action play when he falls into an espionage plot. He's very courageous because he thinks it's all street theater. Earning far less interest was Rowan Atkinson playing the droll, understated, gadget-hating, and inept Johnny English (2002). In this attempt to use both physical and "spectacle comedy," English battles John Malkovich, who is trying to seize the British crown. The British audience liked this would-be hero far more than Americans, and it did have its laughs. English's slogan was "Jesus is coming. Look busy." Comedians were certainly busy. Even as Johnny English came to DVD, the soundtrack to yet another comedy, *Wilson Chance*, with music by Bond guitarist Vic Flick, appeared months before the new Canadian spy bumbled his way into theaters.

Not all nods to previous fictional spies were intentionally comic. To no one's credit, the producers of *Men in Black* liked Will Smith enough to cast him as James West in the 1998 adaptation of the television series, *The Wild Wild West*. Like that year's similar reworking of *The Avengers*, audiences and critics blasted the exploitation of old titles to capitalize on fan bases who resented Hollywood's mucking up of successful formulas. Hollywood didn't care. When the first *Mission: Impossible* vehicle for Tom Cruise was released in 1996, fans and members of the original cast complained when the character of Jim Phelps, first played by Peter Graves, was turned into a villain and killed off. Producers responded with another *MI* film in 2000, and made plans for a third in 2005. When producer Betty Thomas bought the rights to *I Spy* and released her version in 2002, many were surprised that she didn't offer the usual cameo roles to Robert Culp and Bill Cosby, the original stars of the series. *TV Guide* speculated in March 2002 that no one involved with the remake thought the fan appeal was worth the trouble of dealing with either Culp or Cosby (Britton 2004, 91). The baby boomers, once the target for James Bond and the generation he inspired, were no longer in Hollywood's sights. No wonder that, when Embers Productions announced in 2004 that they had purchased the rights to *The Man from U.N.C.L.E.* for a feature film remake, the first supporters of the series cringed more than cheered.

SPYING IN PAIRS

What Hollywood did care about was the box office, and any formula that worked once or twice was worth repeating ad naseum. Bickering buddies, as in *I Spy*, was one such formula, and the wizened mentor with a rebellious newcomer, as in *The Recruit* (2003), was another. In this case, the actor who played the CIA mentor, Al Pacino, was praised by critics, but his student, Colin Farrell, and the movie around them, was not. Another "odd couple" pairing was *Company Business* (1991). Directed by *Star Trek*'s Nicholas Meyer, the story reworked the reluctant spy theme with Gene Hackman playing the retired CIA operative. In that film, times have changed. Hackman's boss admits that the agency now performs a lot of work with the KGB. The agent swap Hackman is supposed to oversee should be simple and a good public relations ploy for the CIA, which needs some good press. Becoming friends with the Russian agent that Hackman's character is delivering, the two become friends and agree that "desk jockeys" don't have the professional knowledge of field agents. Of course, there's more to the story than either have been told. In this case, they're bait dangled by CIA hard-liners wishing to reheat the cold war. Like previous such pairings, the two outwit their various departments and go on to live lives outside the duplicitous world of secret agents.

In the suspenseful made-for-television movie *Intrigue* (1990), Scott Glenn and Robert Loggia play two reunited old friends when Glen's character, an American defector to the KGB, learns he's dying and wants to come home. Loggia decides to help his buddy by smuggling him out of Russia. In 1991, Harry Anderson and Ed Begley, Jr. play crackpot CIA agents in the comedy, *Spies, Lies, and Naked Thighs*. They look for a deadly assassin who's the ex-wife of one of her trackers. Another such effort, in the eyes of reviewer Steve Simmels, was the film *Bad Company* (2002), a "by-the-numbers buddy thriller" with Anthony Hopkins and Chris Rock imitating Eddie Murphy (2003, 98). Of course, some duos were less buddies than bantering potential lovers. *The Spy Within* (1994) featured a call girl spy (Teresa Russell) and an explosives expert (Scott Glenn) on the run.

When a pair won't do, double them. Elya Baskin, Danielle DuClos, and Jason Kristofer are three of the four high school friends who concocted bogus military plans using futuristic toys for blueprints in *Spy Trap* (1992). Their problem is that they decide to sell the plans to the Russians. It isn't long before the unhappy Reds, along with the CIA, are chasing them. Four wisecracking whiz kids not enough? In *Sneakers* (1992), five questionable computer hackers work for an equally questionable government agency. The savvy group is played by Robert Redford, Sidney Poitier, River Phoenix, Dan Aykroyd, and Ben Kingsley.[2]

Another old ploy was duels between equally matched opponents. For example, in 1993's *In the Line of Fire*, Clint Eastwood stars as Harry Corrigan, an aging Secret Service agent haunted by his failure to protect President Kennedy in Dallas. John Malkovich plays an assassin working on Eastwood's failure in a duel reminiscent of *Day of the*

Jackal. Speaking of Carlos "The Jackal," the old foe in novels by Frederick Forsythe and Robert Ludlum pops up again in the guise of Aidan Quinn in *The Assignment* (1997). This time around, Carlos battles CIA agent Jack Shaw (Donald Sutherland) and a Mossad agent (Ben Kingsley), who thinks he got the Jackal, but it's a double agent sent to draw Carlos out. Similarly, *Shadow Conspiracy* (1997) features Charlie Sheen as a presidential assistant tracked by a hired killer also out to knock off his boss. In the tense drama, Sheen enjoys all the cliches—a female reporter helping him on the run, a presidential chief of staff thinking he can run the country better than elected officials, and every variety of murder, all of which pile up as clues. Another expert killer was Tom Berenger in *Sniper* (1993), in which Berenger played a military sharpshooter and assassin for a U.S. intelligence agency. He tended to lose partners in the jungle.

Jake Foley was an ordinary guy until a freak accident transformed him into the world's first computer enhanced man. Millions of microscopic computers interface with his biochemistry and make him stronger and faster and able to see and hear farther than normal men. They give him the power to control technology with his brain. Jake Foley, America's secret weapon. He takes on missions no ordinary agent can perform. He is the ultimate human upgrade.

Preamble to *Jake 2.0*

Without the budgets for such explosion-fests, television's secret agent dramas seemed absorbed into the new vogue for science-fictional adventures with a clear cynical tone. The trendsetting show was *The X-Files* (Fox, 1993–2002), in which David Duchovny and Gillian Anderson dealt with conspiracies within their own government, not to mention threatening aliens. Other spy-fi series with themes dealing with technological issues included *VR5* (Fox, 1995), in which a young student has access to a virtual world the government wants to use for its own purposes. UPN's *Seven Days* (1998–2001) focused on a secret unit of the NSA that must decide, each week, whether or not a world-changing event is worthy of sending a "crononaut" (Jonathan LaPaglia) back in time to alter history. Merging many of these themes was yet another incarnation of *The*

Invisible Man (Sci Fi Channel, 2000–2002), in which Vincent Ventresca is again a reluctant agent forced to work for a government he mistrusts in hopes of finally gaining a cure for a power that is more curse than blessing. The technology that allows him to be invisible also drives him insane, which forces the former criminal to do the bidding of "The Agency" to get the counteragent drugs that keep him mentally stable.

One series, *The Secret Adventures of Jules Verne* (Sci Fi Channel, 1999–2001), was something of a mixed message. In reality, the well-done show was the first all-digital production for television with elaborate special effects set in the nineteenth century. But the stories dealt with a mysterious League of Darkness led by a half-man, half-machine wishing to use then-new wizardry to fight democracy. Such devices continued in such shows as the UPN series *Jake 2.0* (2003), in which Jake Foley (Christopher Gorham) was an NSA technician with a low-security ranking until he was caught in a shootout in a secret lab. In an accident, he was infected with millions of nanites in his blood that gave him superhuman abilities. While short-lived, it seems doubtful that Jake will be the last such hero. Everything old becomes new again in such endeavors. For example, *Jake 2.0* reached back to one of its inspirations, the 1970s *Six Million Dollar Man*. In one December 2003 episode, former Steve Austin, actor Lee Majors, guest-starred as another type of superspy—a literal double with two bodies.

Put away the book. My people are earning a living. They're street stuff . . . It's a comedy. Everybody is paying for information. The British, the French, the West Germans, the Soviets. We happen to be paying the most. So our job is the easiest. Take a subway and go over to East Berlin to Café Warsaw. That's the place where they all hang out. Agents, informers, contact men, cut-outs, couriers, principals, even Russian and American case officers. . . . West Berlin may be a spy market but East Berlin is a bigger joke. Everybody is doubled and tripled. You can't even remember if they're supposed to be yours or theirs.

Norman Mailer, *Harlot's Ghost*

However, drawing from old motifs was but one aspect of the 1990s trend for exploring the history of espionage. A number of researchers poured over the bonanza of declassified KGB documents and decripted the Vevona files and pumped out a series of books revealing much about the Russian side of the cold war equation. In addition, after the KGB disbanded in 1991, a number of ex-agents negotiated book deals of their stories, along with sales of formerly secret documents, to make ready cash. Such was fodder for new novels and films, as well as evidence for solving old mysteries. For example, doubts about the guilt of traitors Julius and Ethel Rosenberg were finally laid to rest. In addition, from the beginning of spy literature, noted authors like Joseph Conrad, W. Somerset Maugham, and Graham Greene had written stories with espionage themes and settings while being known for many other books outside of the genre. By the 1990s, the history of modern espionage seemed worthy of a major epic explored by a major author, and Norman Mailer's best-selling twenty-seventh book, *Harlot's Ghost* (1991), was just that.

Covering the history of the CIA from its inception to 1963, *Harlot's Ghost* is told in the first person by fictional agent Harry Hubbard, the son of a former OSS operative who remains in the higher echelons of the CIA. Harry seems predestined for spycraft. As a child, he draws pictures of underground cities. He was groomed from a young age by both his father and his godfather, high-ranking intelligence officer Hugh Montague, code-named "Harlot." The world of men with secret lives gave Mailer a number of levels to explore, including the psychological and religious. For example, Hubbard keeps the secrets of his life by using microfilm and a special reader to look over his written memories. For Mailer, spycraft was a metaphor for personal relationships, such as when Hubbard equates jamming Soviet radio broadcasts with repressing writing about his marriage to Kitteridge, the widow to Harlot with whom Hubbard has carried on a long-term affair via secret correspondence.

From the beginning of his training through his early years as an agent, Hubbard reflected on his changing identity in a climate of mistrust and paranoia. For example, during his first assignment in Berlin, he spends all his time protecting the truth about one of his early blunders from a supervisor focused on internal investigations. Assigned to a station in Uruguay—a setting far from the center of the cold war—

Hubbard learns about spying and diplomacy from his supervisor, E. Howard Hunt. Far from a life of dangerous action, Hubbard observes Hunt enjoying life with government officials. In Uruguay, the games were largely of agents watching each other's embassies and playing tricks on each other simply to confuse observers wondering who was sleeping with who. There were games in the "Clubland" tradition—chess and polo—but the great game was sex, with operatives on both sides trading partners described as priestesses, prostitutes, and transsexuals.

Religious allusions are a continual motif in the story, beginning with descriptions of Hubbard's father as a cross between "a deacon and a swashbuckler." In a realistic world populated by the likes of Allen Dulles, Fidel Castro, and William Casey, men seek alternate selves as an honorable way of life. The agency is portrayed as "America's church," both holding the country's secrets and bearing its values. Misdeeds within the CIA are evaluated as either venial or mortal sins.

In the second half of the novel, Hubbard is based in Miami and becomes involved with the Kennedy administration's obsession with Cuba. More a privileged recorder of high-level sexual shenanigans and interdepartmental turf wars than secret agent, Hubbard recounts the history of the Bay of Pigs invasion and the subsequent Cuban Missile Crisis from various points of view, including correspondence and alleged wiretap transcripts of historical figures from Kennedy to Frank Sinatra. Along the way, insightful observations pepper the multitrack narrative. For example, Hubbard reports that, for him, intelligence can be defined as "whose will is stamped on which facts." Hubbard liked spy novels as, in life, plots were never complete. Written over seven years, with more than 1,295 pages including a lengthy bibliography and notes, perhaps the most surprising words end the book—"To be continued."

Harlot's Ghost can be seen as one representative of the most important literary shift in the 1990s. Tom Clancy had made the device of multiple story lines in any work almost mandatory; after the breakup of the Soviet Union, this style widened to bring history into complex stories. On one level, such books acted as evaluations of the cold war, allowing experienced agents to look back over their careers to unearth the meaning of their lives. On another, the idea of multigenerational story lines allowed both serious fiction and Hollywood blockbusters to exploit the device of seasoned mentors bringing new generations into the covert world. One highly praised novel with these themes was Robert Littell's best-selling *The Company: A Novel of the CIA* (2002). Dramatizing events from the formation of the agency after World War II to the foiled coup to oust Soviet leader Mikhail Gorbachev in 1991, Littell traced the history of the cold war by looking into the professional and private lives of three generations of agents on both sides of the Iron Curtain. Choosing watershed moments from each decade, Littell brought the careers of actual operatives and directors from Allen Dulles, James Angleton, Richard Helms, and William Casey into his fictionalization of the covert world. Littell's own characters were given credibility by the author's use of historic details from vacuum tube radios to watches that needed winding before the advent of new technologies. Readers saw the history of defectors and moles in Berlin, failed covert activities in Hungary in 1956 and Cuba in 1961, and the political jousting between elected policymakers and the intelligence community in the 1970s and 1980s. Graphic scenes of torture and assassinations, office debates over ends and means, and battlefield love affairs exhibited past behaviors while pointing to the future in scenes in Afghanistan and drop-dead exchanges between Robert Hanssen and his Russian handlers. In each section, the torch was passed from generation to generation, and with each change of characters a sense of purpose, history, and destiny made it clear that the novelist saw the CIA as a force to be proud of and necessary in the ongoing battles between the good guys and those with less-honorable intent.

One notable film entry into the history of espionage was director Tony Scott's 2001 *Spy Game* starring Robert Redford and Brad Pitt. According to Scott's commentary for the DVD release of the film, his research for the project included a visit to CIA headquarters to both establish a believable look for this recurring setting in *Spy Game* and to see what the faces of real agents looked like. One producer, he noted, claimed the real CIA looked more like "a car convention in Texas" than a Hollywood spectacular. But Scott decided to cast many of his characters based on how closely they resembled the faces he'd seen in Langley.

Scott's efforts for realism included showing the various time periods told in flashbacks by filming different eras in the style of the times. The Vietnam sequences were edited to look black and white with a green tint, and 1980s Berlin was filmed with the enhanced colors characteristic of the era. Scott pointed to the father-son relationship of the Redford-Pitt characters as the central theme of the movie, and described the impact of 9/11 on the content and context of *Spy Game*. Early screenings before the attack on America were positive, but after 9/11, along with many other projects, Hollywood worried about images in action films. In particular, *Spy Game's* climactic moment involved a suicide bomber bringing down a building in Beirut. Universal Studios at first suggested cutting the scene, but Scott worked to make the scene "less operatic" and more linear. Screenings ten days after 9/11 showed an audience response even more favorable than before, although Scott speculated for a few seconds that audiences would be out of the movie, thinking about its parallels to recent events. For a brief time, Universal held off release of the film, but Hollywood saw that audiences were quickly rebounding from the images of the Trade Towers collapse.

Control allowed himself to savor the miserly pleasure that comes to political insiders, secretive scientists, art thieves, enterprising journalists, and professional spies. The sense of early, exclusive possession of valuable information.

William Saffire, *Sleeper Spy*

Another example of the new scope in espionage fiction can be seen in *New York Times* columnist William Saffire's 1995 novel, *Sleeper Spy*. Combining his interest in world politics, espionage, and journalism, this complex post–cold war novel deals with a Soviet "sleeper" agent activated because he has access to hidden financial funds. In the well-crafted plot, the media plays a central role. Despite his reputation for serious reporting, experienced print journalist Irving Fine is forced by his agent to pair with a young female television newscaster to investigate the story. Their agenda is to discover the sleeper and have the publishing and broadcast rights for the expose. Their strategy is to set up a bogus financial wizard posing as the sleeper to draw the Russian out of hiding. But, in Russia, other schemes are afoot. After the breakup of the Soviet Union, two groups of intelligence operatives also seek the sleeper. One, comprised of old KGB agents in cahoots with the Russian Mafia want the money to restore the old order. The new Russian government wants it to save an economy in peril. Both groups focus on their own journalist, a female news personality who doesn't know she's the sleeper's daughter. And no one knows that the imposter is, in fact, the true sleeper.

Throughout the novel, Saffire makes overt nods to his predecessors in spy fiction, especially in his character's frequent references to Frederick Forsythe's *The Odessa File*, which had been about a search for Nazi gold after World War II, a similar circumstance to the modern retelling of a new treasure hunt. The dueling American reporters are extremely evocative of the earlier sparrings in Hitchcock's *The 39 Steps*, a film referred to in Saffire's updating. New twists include a head of the CIA whose mission is to downsize the agency and strip it of all counterintelligence activity. The most important double agent isn't working inside the CIA or KGB but within the Federal Reserve so that he can give the sleeper inside information on economic decisions. Saffire had previously published *Homage to E. Philip Oppenheim and James Jesus Angleton*, and his support for the latter came through in the novel. While Angleton had long been mocked for his paranoia, Saffire pointedly noted that Aldrich Ames and other CIA moles appeared after Angleton's tenure at the agency.

SERIOUS SPIES IN HOLLYWOOD

In a cynical age, one ongoing theme from the late 1960s returned, that of the villain being the organizations that are supposedly protecting civilians. One prime example was *La Femme Nikita*, first filmed as a highly regarded, R-rated French film directed by Luc Besson and starring Anne Parillaud in 1991. In this version, Nikita kills a policeman by shooting him in the face at point-blank range while in a drug-induced state. She was then forced by "Section One" to become an assassin assigned to take out a terrorist. For the director, Nikita was a representative of anyone who does not like or cannot change the life they are given, but is given a second chance. A Warner Brothers Hollywood remake, *Point of No Return*, starring Brigitte Fonda, was released in 1993, also R-rated. Critical reception to this incarnation wasn't kind because Hollywood's version both toned down the grittiness of the original and essentially remade it shot-for-shot without subtitles (Britton 2004, 225). In 1996, Peta Wilson became the character for television for the USA network. The concept was changed somewhat, as Nikita is "falsely accused of a hideous crime" she didn't commit. Thus, she is an innocent civilian forced to become a killer to get out of jail. According to a commentary for the DVD release of the first season, producer Joel Surnow claimed that he had the earlier series, *The Prisoner*, in mind; the agent in that series, Number Six, also wanted out of the covert world, but questionable forces refused to permit him to leave.

Other films of the era were equally serious with their use of espionage to probe human dramas. While not part of the spy genre per se, director Ron Howard's exploration of mathematician John Nash's schizophrenia in *A Beautiful Mind* (2002) focused on his delusions that he was an undercover operative for the CIA. Going even further back in time, a rare reexamination of World War II themes was *Windtalkers* (2002), a look at the exploitation of Navajo Indians using their language as a code to defeat the Japanese. Previously, playwright Hugh Whitemore's *Breaking the Code* (1997), a British play adapted for television, examined the plight of Alan Turing (Derek Jacobi), the mathematical genius recruited by the British government during World War II to decipher the Germans' "Enigma Code." In literature, some projects also went back in time without attempting to explore multiple generations. In 2002, John Altman's *A Game of Spies* was a Nazi adventure with a German "sleeper" spy, Eva Bernhardt, recruited and seduced by a British operative. A sequel to *A Gathering of Spies* (2000), Gestapo agent Hagan chases Eva as she tries to reveal the German plans to invade France.

However, writers reached much further back in time to create espionage yarns, most such books using spies as mere devices in literary costume dramas in the spirit of the Baroness Orczy and Dennis Wheatley. For example, in 2000, Fiona Buckley's *To Ruin a Queen* went back to Wales in 1564 to tell a story of a spy for Queen Elizabeth I, Ursala Blanchard, searching for evidence of treason in France. Candace Robb went even further back into history with *A Spy for the Redeemer* (1999), another Welsh-based tale set in the fourteenth century in which a murder investigation led to involvement with a rebel movement.

It had been six months since he had been pulled from retirement and given a simple mission. Rebuild morale in an intelligence service badly damaged by a series of highly-publicized operational blunders and personnel scandals. Restore the esprit d'corps that had characterized the office in the old days. Shamron had managed to stem the bleeding. There had been no more humiliations . . . But there had been no stunning successes either. Shamron knew better than anyone that the office had not earned its fearsome reputation by playing it safe. In the old days, it had stolen MIGs, planted spies in the palaces of its friends and its enemies, reigned terror on those who dared to terrorize the people of Israel . . . he wanted to leave behind an office that could reach out and strike at will, an office that could make the other services of the world shake their heads in wonder.

Daniel Silva, *Kill Artist*

Still, while history was the dominant theme of the era, there were novelists, as in days of yore, speculating about the future. Patrick Robertson's 2001 novel, *The Shark Mutiny*, was set in 2007, anticipating a secret alliance between China and Iran to control the oil flow in the Middle East. And not all new entries in the spy genre dealt with Western intelligence agencies. As the Israeli/Palestinian conflict moved center stage in geopolitics, it seemed appropriate that a Jewish secret agent dealing with terrorists should become important in fiction. Daniel Silva's Gabriel Allon was just that, a reluctant killer for Israeli intelligence. He was an art restorer who'd seen his wife and child blown up by PLO terrorists, which made all his missions personal, especially when stalking those involved in his family's murder. This focus on the personal resulted from the novelist's belief that spy thrillers should be primarily told from a single point of view, that too many novels were too complicated by the Clancy-inspired layered approach.

Before beginning the Allon series with *The Kill Artist* (2000), best sellers included *The Unlikely Spy* (1995), *The Mark of the Assassin* (1998), and *The Marching Season* (1999). The second Allon book, *The*

English Assassin (2002), was quickly followed by *The Confessor* (2003), in which Allon battles a secret conspiracy within the Vatican trying to keep hidden revelations about the church's silence during the Holocaust. Based on extensive research, the book explores the church's support of Nazis when both groups opposed Communism and the idea that Jews might get their own homeland.

The Confessor's success was partially due to the topicality of the issue, as the role of the Vatican during World War II was a widely discussed matter in the early years of the twenty-first century. Other concepts owed their framework to past efforts, as in the role of French spy Jacqueline in *The Kill Artist*. While in love with Allon, she has an affair with a Palestinian agent, strongly echoing the relationships in Hitchcock's *Notorious*. However, the backdrop of Middle Eastern history, intrigue inside Jewish and Arab organizations, and the tragedies afflicting both sides of the conflict give Silva's thrillers a canvas quite different from Soviet/Western duels. While his principal characters are members of the secret Israeli "Office," Arabs aren't simple hate-filled mad bombers. In *The Kill Artist*, for example, Allon bungles his mission to catch an assassin in order to save Jacqueline. The killer, out to murder Yasser Arafat to block the peace process, instead backs out of his quest when Arafat convinces him that Palestinians shouldn't be killing each other. Praised by many critics as a new force in espionage fiction, Silva benefits from contacts with a number of news correspondents, most notably his wife, NBC *Today Show* reporter Jamie Gangel.

RETURN OF JASON BOURNE

Other creative minds saw the past as but a touchstone from which to create their own fresh approaches. One quality project was director Doug Liman's 2002 version of *The Bourne Identity*, one of the best recent entries in the genre. While Robert Ludlum purists blasted the film, former independent producer Liman took on the project for love of the book and gained support from Ludlum, taking five years to make the Matt Damon vehicle a reality. In his DVD commentary for the film, Liman admits that he had to modernize the story, pointing to the fact that microfilm is no longer in use in libraries. He kept the premise of Ludlum's book, that of a secret agent with amnesia, but added many details based on his knowledge of the Iran-Contra affairs of the Reagan administration. He claims that his father had worked in the NSA and felt that realism depended on establishing a bureaucracy to make the conspiracy credible for new audiences.

While Ludlum supporters still claim that the 1988 television miniseries starring Richard Chamberlain was truer to the novel, despite some complaints that Chamberlain was too old for the part, Liman must be credited with a screenplay emphasizing character development and drama first, action second. While the director doesn't like the term "thinking-man's spy," he stresses that the fights in the film were character driven, as Damon's Jason Bourne has to discover his skills even though he doesn't know where they come from. To demonstrate mind over fists, Damon tears a map off a wall and consults it before a getaway. In promotions for the film, Damon pointed to this as an example of the quality of the script—most secret agents just jump in a car and race off as if they know where they're going. Filmed in seven countries, including Hungary, Italy, and France, the attention to detail gave the film's series of settings a level of realism unneeded in other blockbusters where explosions and allegedly witty dialogue are the point. But, of course, connections to past masters remain obvious. Bourne and Maria (Adewale Akinnuoye-Adbeje) are but the newest pair in the tradition of *The 39 Steps*, a reluctant couple pulled into matters far removed from ordinary life.

In various interviews publicizing the 2004 The *Bourne Supremacy*, Damon claimed there had been no plans for a sequel after the release of the first Bourne film. However, he liked the script for the follow-up, saying that the first movie was a story of "Who am I?" and the second, "How did all this begin?" Shot in Moscow, Berlin, and Italy, *Supremacy* had nothing to do with the Ludlum book beyond the title and lead character. However, critics still praised it as one of the best action adventure releases of the summer. In this version, Bourne seeks to find out why his wife, Maria, was killed while the CIA tracked him down, believing he'd killed two agents in Berlin. In the end, Bourne and the agency alike learn that he'd been framed and Bourne discovers the origins of his clandestine identity. The door is clearly open for another sequel. Earning $53 million its first weekend, the film was said to be the highest-grossing spy film ever in its first week. Beyond creating a new spy series, *The Bourne Identity* became something of a benchmark in new espionage projects. In his commentary for the DVD release of *Spartan* (2003), actor Val Kilmer said *Spartan's* fight scenes were like those in the earlier movie, which made them credible and appropriate in realistic films. The highly praised, if underwatched *Spartan* deserves special recognition for writer-director David Mamet's script and the thoughtful character portrayals by the cast in this story of a president's daughter kidnapped and sent into white slavery. In the tense drama, as Kilmer put it, "nameless agents in nameless organizations" are called on to do the nation's business and are often on their own, knowing that their missions are unsanctioned and their orders are necessarily oblique and not clearly marked out. This theme was underlined in the unspecified situations, such as in the fact it's never stated that the missing girl is the president's daughter but only inferred in the discussion over her missing Secret Service protection and the cover-up that results. In this cynical look at policymakers, the president is willing to allow a murder victim to stand in for his lost daughter to ensure that the press won't find out he had pulled the protective detail to hide his private amours. In turn, the daughter doesn't want to be rescued, fearing what might happen on her return.

The values in the film, in Kilmer's terms, are carried by the "nameless agents" who are efficient, poised, mentally and physically tough, and who expect to die in service to their country. Such people are admirable and operate, at least in the film, in ways necessary to achieve results. For example, while the agents are ruthless and have no qualms about torture, Kilmer liked the script's lack of profanity, "a hallmark of an embarrassing film." True, the story includes obligatory scenes, as when the younger disciple has information that his experienced mentor doesn't. But, in Kilmer's view, the movie shows what spies must act like in today's world, often out in the cold, whether they play by the book or act in ways both illegal and not officially sanctioned. The message of the film beneath the action is that we must not trust what we see on television news. Television no longer reflects culture—it is culture.

NEW AGE OF TERRORISM

Despite the quality of films like *The Bourne Identity*, *Spy Game*, and *Spartan*, it has become clear that Hollywood has little interest in realism or even using espionage to examine the human condition in wider terms. The demand for spectacle and special effects was one matter; another was that studios and producers wanted to appeal to a younger audience not interested in asking questions involving moral or political issues. Escapism, pure and simple, was what viewers wanted in summer blockbusters and holiday diversions.

On a deeper level, in both reality and fiction, the changes in international geopolitics were now casting the intelligence community into a state of some confusion. In fact, the FBI, which was frequently criticized by the CIA for not being especially capable when dealing with espionage, found its responsibilities expanding. In the 1990s, domestic terrorism came to the fore, notably with the Oklahoma City bombing, the cases of Eric Rudolf and Ted Kaczynski—the so-called Unabomber—and the deadly encounters with the Montana group, the "Freemen." There was new interest in China, as with leaks from the nuclear facility in Los Alamos, as well as allegations that China was funneling campaign contributions to the Democratic Party.

At the same time, law enforcement had to deal with the new global nature of crime, a case of fact following what fiction had been exploring for decades. In the 1990s, the FBI opened forty-four overseas offices from Moscow to Panama City. At the end of the cold war, the FBI began cooperating with old enemies in Moscow and began training agents in former Eastern bloc countries such as Poland and Czechoslovakia. It investigated the terrorist bombings at embassies in Kenya and Tanzania in 1998, the attack on the USS *Cole* in 2000, and the first attack on the World Trade Center in 1993. In addition, PLO terrorists had once been considered as small cells of destructive gangs operating in Europe, North Africa, and the Middle East. Suddenly, America itself was a battleground. The growing war on terrorism was now a worldwide struggle between cultures and the battlegrounds were no longer between operatives of nations playing by a certain set of rules. How do agents of Western democracies penetrate Arab "splinter cells" when a requirement for membership is committing a crime to establish dirty bona fides? Necessity is one matter, public demands are another. In the November 2004 *Atlantic Monthly*, two reports pointed to two shifts in international thinking. One discussed the trend for "forensic theology," a tool to diagnose which Islamic clerics should be considered threats and which not. In a separate report, one observer noted that business representatives were becoming better able to gather intelligence in parts of the world where the U.S. government had lost credibility. Clearly, the old games of blackmailing defectors, bugging embassies, and debating Western-Eastern cultural divides were giving way to a generation with different ideology.

To further complicate the stew, the FBI, CIA, and NSA were no longer working alone. By the 1990s, thirteen separate American intelligence agencies were working at home and abroad and one clear problem was a lack of coordination between them. In England, representatives of the Secret Intelligence Service (MI6, foreign), the Security Service (MI5, domestic), the Government Communications Headquarters (satellites), and the Special Branch of Scotland Yard met weekly to share information to avoid duplication and waste. American intelligence had nothing comparable. No one, it became clear, had a focused picture of what the covert world should be doing.

Perhaps, with all this, scriptwriters found the new world order overwhelming and hard to simplify into stories easily resolved in a matinee or even DVDs with extended playing times. Few novelists could engage in prophecies, as they had in previous decades. From another angle, old questions had been explored time and time again and new approaches were harder to come by. Fiction, films, and television had all looked into the morality of when ends justify the means, when personal sacrifices are worthy of the wider good, and what roles, if any, shadow governments should play in democracies. What were the new questions in an era of uncertainty? In less than one hundred years, the radio dialogue shared by film director Cecil B. DeMille and ex-spy Major Charles Russell during the 1937 broadcast of *The 39 Steps* now seemed a discussion from a more innocent era. No longer could spies be simply categorized as patriotic or mercenary, good or bad, ours or theirs. Perhaps, in popular culture, we were exhausted with old worries and could not grasp precisely what the new ones were. The future of espionage, therefore, was just as murky as its past.

Conclusion—More Fact than Fiction: Espionage after 9/11

> In the years of the Cold War there was danger, there was the danger that an enormous cataclysm might take place, affecting virtually every-one on the planet. . . . The danger is different now. The danger is much more specific. The world isn't going to be destroyed, but you don't feel safe anymore in your plane or train or office or auditorium.
>
> Don DeLillo to Gabe Pell, *Daily Princetonian*[1]

> "Dramatic, isn't it?" he asked.
> "You didn't say that happened the other day?"
> "The week before last."
> "Impossible," said Ashenden. "Why, we've been putting that inci-dent on the stage for 60 years! We've written it in a thousand novels. You mean to say that life has only just caught up with us? . . . If you can't do better than that in the Secret Service," said Ashenden, "I'm afraid that as a source of inspiration to the writer of fiction, it's a wash-out. Really can't write that story much longer."
>
> W. Somerset Maugham, *Ashenden*

In March 2004, former 007 novelist Raymond Benson looked back over his tenure as the latest official literary inheritor of Ian Fleming's mantle. In an interview with John Cox, Benson recalled that at the beginning of his contract in 1995, important questions had been raised about the continuation of an aging secret agent in commercial literature. Should the novels remain set in the cold war and James Bond frozen in time? "In the end," Benson said, "it was decided that we should stay in sync with the films and keep Bond updated. I was also told that I should do my best to blend elements of the original literary Bond with elements of the more widely known cinematic Bond. Thus, there had to be more action than what was in Fleming's books, more gadgetry, a little more humor" (Cox 2004).

With these directives in mind, between 1996 and 2002, Benson helped shape the new milieu for 007 with six original novels and the novelizations for *Tomorrow Never Dies*, *The World Is Not Enough*, and *Die Another Day*. Widening Bond's reach in print stories, Benson's three short stories included his first for *Playboy*, "Blast from the Past" (1997), the first use of Bond's dead son, James Suzuki. Benson's second story, "Midsummer Night's Doom" (1999), was a joke commissioned by *Playboy* magazine for their thirty-fifth anniversary issue. Bringing together two icons of popular culture, James Bond and Hugh Hefner meet at a party in the Playboy mansion. In the same year, *TV Guide* commissioned a Benson story dealing with television, "Live at Five," for a special Bond issue (November 13, 1999). Connections to the real world included the story taking place in 1985, so Bond could deal with a Russian defector. The Bond girl, real Chicago news personality Janet Davies, had to get permission from her station owner to have a fictional romance with 007 (Cox 2004). So, at the turn of the century, no one had better claim than Benson to ponder the future of James Bond and his ilk.

The literary Bond, in Benson's view, was in some trouble. In the Cox interview, Benson noted that his contract had ended when the literary estate decided to promote Ian Fleming's original works more during the fiftieth anniversary year of 2003, hence the reissues by Penguin in the United Kingdom and the United States. On top of that, Benson perceived an "apathy toward Bond novels on the retail side of the publishing business." While the publishers were happy with the sales of his continuation novels, Benson noted, "the problem is that very few non-Bond fans seek out the books and buy them. They serve a niche market. The *Star Wars* and *Star Trek* books do better than Bond novels because there's a much bigger fan base for those franchises. Another reason could be that people are so indoctrinated by the films that the books may seem like footnotes. Since the filmmakers don't bother to film John Gardner's or my books, book retailers can't expect them to move in great numbers" (Cox 2004). As to any future writer of Bond stories, Benson believed 007 belonged in the cold war just as Sherlock Holmes was of the Victorian era. While filmmakers wouldn't be likely to return Bond to the time that produced him, perhaps new books would.

Benson's notes point to changes in the spy genre as a whole in the new century. In particular, the importance of Hollywood influencing fiction rather than the other way around was a sign of new directions. Novelizations of blockbusters, for one matter, had reversed the process of novel to film. Hollywood even became part of the literary back lot. For example, in 2001, Benson's James Bond spent as much time on movie lots as Pierce Brosnan. In that year's *Never Dream of Dying*, 007 defeats his new enemy, the blind leader of a SPECTRE-like organization called "the Union." Along the way, Bond encounters evil movie producers trapped in lawsuits. Bad guys include special-effects wizards who are criminal explosives experts, creating a film that Bond himself described as "an odd mixture of period swash-buckler costuming and space-age slickness . . . all sorts of mayhem erupted including exploding grenades, fist fights, gunfire, and a hair-raising leap onto a gambling boat" (Benson 2001, 159). Much of the offscreen devastation took place on soundstages and film locations. Bond's love interest, not surprisingly, was a sexy leading lady. The dastardly plot turned out to be the Union's plan to blow up celebrities at the Cannes film festival as a terrorist act because deaths of entertainers would hurt the West more than any political assassination.

However, like the literary 007, where to go with the cinematic Bond was also in question. Ironically, Benson's memories shared in the Cox interview were posted online in the same month that a variety of articles and television interviews speculated about the future of Pierce Brosnan and his James Bond. During the March 10, 2004, edition of the American Movie Classic's *Hollywood Shootout*, Brosnan said that, as of that date, there was no script for the next Bond feature because the producers didn't know the direction to go. In Brosnan's opinion, *Die Another Day* had been EON's attempt to respond to the competition of other big-action films like 2002's XXX. He thought Michael Wilson and Barbara Broccoli hadn't decided whether or not to continue with this trend or go with a more character-driven Bond entry in a more classic Bond style.

Later that month, before Brosnan announced his surprise retirement from the 007 role, *Die Another Day* screenwriters Robert Wade and Neal Purvis revealed a script was indeed under way. At the Orange Screenwriters Seminar at the British Library in London, Wade noted that it is a challenge coming up with a fresh angle on the franchise: "I don't think there's a more difficult task. It's all been done. The 20th film was harder than the 19th. It's very difficult to think of new ways to blow things up! But character is the thing; it's finding new ways to explore the character" ("Robert" 2004).

With such questions about the future of the most successful and longest-running franchise in the spy genre, what then of other projects in fiction and film without the preexisting market for fans of the most famous logo in entertainment? Indeed, in a genre that had taken seemingly every turn possible, twisted every contrivance scriptwriters could imagine, and seemingly exhausted all fresh ideas, could there be any future for fictional espionage in the twenty-first century? With the cold war now unremembered history for a new generation of DVD buyers and younger fans more interested in games than books, what could be left for new explorations into the covert world? And, to add a tragic dimension to these questions, what would espionage be in the public consciousness after 9/11?

There is one thing you Americans have never quite grasped is how very deep anti-Americanism grows. In this post–Cold War era, many people around the world feel that they live under the American economic occupation. You speak of "globalization" and they hear "Americanization." You Americans see televised images of anti-American demonstrations . . . and you think these are aberrant events. On the contrary, these are harbingers of a storm, the first few spittle-like drops you feel before a cloudburst.

Robert Ludlum, *The Jansen Directive*

Every day that we're not in the news is a day that we have won.
CIA agent Matt Callan in the CBS television series *The Agency*

From the fall morning when four planes changed the world, one matter seemed clear: Fact had caught up with fiction. Many quickly noted just how contemporary events mirrored formerly fantastic stories of the imagination. For example, on November 15, 2001, deejays on the number one talk radio show in Chicago—the "Roe and Garry Show" on WLS-AM—discussed the day's summit between George Bush and Russia's Vladimir Putin. They noted that no one could have predicted the post–cold war era of cooperation and the coming together of old enemies to fight evil. Garry said "It's like *The Man from U.N.C.L.E.*!" Roe agreed, and said the James Bond movies were also prophetic: "Do you suppose Osama sits in his cave, stroking a cat?" Writer Jim Leach also saw parallels between Osama bin Laden and James Bond's old nemesis, Ernst Stavro Blofeld. In Leach's view, fact was now seen in terms of special effects. Our adversaries had used fantasy against the fantasy makers (Linder 2003, 250). No wonder a number of October 2001 magazine articles suggested that Hollywood scriptwriters and intelligence officers should meet and collaborate. After all, Hollywood had been imagining scenarios, and solving them, for years (Britton 2004, 311).

More important questions, perhaps, were just what was to be done with the new breed of evil. In the February 22, 2004, issue of the *New York Times Book Review*, Ethan Brauner reviewed eight separate books in one week exploring the impact of the "Patriot Act" on civil rights, the "muffling of the media," the expanded place of surveillance in the workplace, and increased access into American private records, from gym memberships to health care. Americans had become more likely to be monitored, photographed, and tracked to the point where "facial structure and retinal patterns are recorded" in the name of public safety (2004, 10). Before 9/11, Brauner observed, few Americans would voluntarily allow themselves to live under "the gaze of a network of bio-metric surveillance cameras peering at them in government buildings, shopping malls, subways and stadiums" (2004, 10). The volume of words devoted to such worries and the thoughtfulness of those speaking from all angles of these issues suggest "there is a great deal to think through for a society that needs to protect itself from a new kind of enemy, a stateless terrorist consortium while keeping in check an old one, a zealous government with an enormous amount of power at its disposal" (2004, 11).

The intelligence agencies of "this zealous government" were, as usual, not faring well in public consciousness. Before 9/11, CNN intelligence reporter David Ensor noted that the CIA was cooperating with the producers of a new spy show, *The Agency*, in an attempt to rebuild the CIA's public image and help stimulate recruitment because new agents were harder to come by after the end of the cold war (Britton 2004, 315). But the show debuted after both 9/11 and news reports of anthrax mailings. Suddenly, criticism of the CIA was hotter than ever before. For a time, defenders of the intelligence community were angrily vocal. In the view of many, the key problem with intelligence failures was that past worries had resulted in too many hands being tied to be effective. On a September 2001 Fox News interview, former secretary of state James Baker claimed that the United States had too long carried over the sentiments and suspicions of the 1970s. He believed Americans feared dipping their hands too deeply in the "messy business of spying." Author Tom Clancy also appeared on CNN, angrily stating that America needed to upgrade and update its intelligence assets in the CIA, saying "you can't find out what's in a person's mind without talking to him." America, he said, does not love its intelligence community.[2]

On the other side of the discussion, criticism about the obvious series of intelligence failures continued and were compounded when President Bush claimed that CIA intelligence about weapons of mass destruction (WMDs) was the principal reason America should go to war with Iraq. After a year of fighting and no WMDs were found, someone's head had to roll. In this case, seven-year CIA head George Tenet fell on his sword in June 2004, accepting responsibility for the bad "intel." To make matters murkier, the administration was suspected of leaking the name of an undercover CIA operative, Valerie Plame, as revenge for her husband, Joseph Wilson's opposition to the war policy. On the same day that Tenet resigned, the president hired an attorney to represent him in the investigation of the leaks. To make espionage news even muddier, reports began to circulate about Iraqi leader Ahmed Chalabi who, on one hand, was said to be the principal source for the WMD intel and, on the other, was a provider of secret information to Iran. In an election year, intelligence was an important issue and Americans were divided on what they expected and wanted. Then, within two weeks of George W. Bush's second win, discussions brewed when a series of high-level CIA officials resigned after new director Porter Goss began implementing policies that were seen by some as needed reform, by others as a clear partisan attempt to politicize the spy community. This uncertainty also affected what viewers wanted in popular media.

Every morning, the president receives a report that updates the most active threats against the United States. This report is called the "Threat Matrix." The Department of Homeland Security hand picks teams of agents from the CIA, the FBI, and the NSA who analyze and respond to the "Threat Matrix" report. Now, their job is to keep us safe. . . . We are making progress.

Preamble to *Threat Matrix*

Perhaps a few offerings from network and cable television indicate different angles of new public perception. For example, in fall 2001, three new spy outings debuted—ABC's *Alias*, Fox's *24*, and CBS's *The Agency*. Of these, *The Agency* was the only series promoted as an attempt at mirroring the actual lives of CIA agents. The show's producers happily touted CIA support for the drama by allowing them to film sequences at CIA headquarters. But despite cast changes, a shift in creative direction, and a move to a less competitive time slot, *The Agency* disappeared. Realism lost to the fantasy of *Alias* and the tense innovations that distinguished *24*.

In fall 2003, ABC's Thursday night *Threat Matrix* was another attempt to bring post–9/11 realities into prime time entertainment. *Threat Matrix* featured a highly specialized, elite task force trained and equipped to counter any threat to America. Created by the Homeland Security Agency, the head of this secret team was ex-FBI special agent John Kilmer (James Denton), who reported directly to the president by way of special liaison Col. Roger Atkins (Will Lyman). Kilmer had authority to call upon the technical skills, firepower, and specialist agents of the FBI, CIA, NSA, and presumably any other needed resource.

With obvious nods to *Mission: Impossible*, Kilmer's team was based in the "Vault" hidden in Fort Meade and included Mo (Anthony Azizi), an Egyptian American former CIA operative stationed in the Middle East. Lia "Lark" Larkin (Melora Walters) was a former FBI forensics specialist. Tim Vargas (Kurt Caceres) came from the DEA (Drug Enforcement Agency), and Jelani (Mahershalalhashbaz Ali) was the African American computer genius intercepting phone, fax, and radio signals from around the world. She supported the team with

225

the latest NSA technology. But despite the quality of the scripts and the depth of the character development, *Threat Matrix* lasted a mere sixteen episodes. Americans were eating up so-called reality shows built on forensic detectives and courtroom duels between law enforcement in the multiple *Crime Scene Investigations* and *Law and Order* series. But fighting terrorists in a war that couldn't be won in hour-long scripts didn't spark much viewer interest. "We are making progress," the motto for *Threat Matrix*, wasn't enough, apparently, in prime-time hours following evening news broadcasts that sent a different message.

Still, in July 2004, TNT launched its heavily promoted six-hour series, *The Grid*, starring Julianna Margulies and Dylan McDermott. Realism and topicality were clearly the point as National Security Council (NSC) director Margolis, as sexy as a governmental administrator should be, attempted to fight terrorists by cutting through bureaucracies, get around turf wars, make connections with both American and British agencies, and face failures in her decisions. Clearly, oil was now the ultimate McGuffin in spy fiction. All secrets, all cultural battles now revolved around control of the globe's most important resource. Ironically, the complex series debuted the very day a report was issued suggesting a new cabinet-level administrator should be created to accomplish the very same tasks, having one person responsible for the now fourteen intelligence agencies in the United States. But even in this new war, reminders of the old were evident. In one scene in the final hour, one character, very reminiscent of the duels between George Smiley and Carla, discovered she was becoming too much like her Islamic adversary. To create "cells to battle cells," new agents were fearful they'd become no better than the terrorists at war with the West.

If they think they're Bond, they're about to get burned.
Promo for *Spy Master*

Fascination with actual spycraft had its moments on the small screen, although most successes were comparatively small themselves in terms of audience size. In March 2004, the Learning Channel began its answer to *Survivor*, the reality-based *Spymaster*. The premise was to take six men and six women and put them through three weeks of training by actual agents of the FBI, CIA, and special forces. In each episode, the recruits were narrowed down until one would be declared "Spymaster." In each episode, the recruits were trained in fast car driving, physical combat, and shooting on target ranges. Real-world experts supervised each competition and made the final evaluations. Espionage buffs not only saw glimpses into the tough training agents go through, but saw the decision-making process of the trainers. For example, in the first hour, we saw a recruit having difficulty literally shedding her outside identity—all recruits had to strip in a parking lot—to mold herself into the new way of thinking as a spy.

Students were rated not so much for their performance but their ability to take orders and demonstrate grace under pressure and stress. That week, the two discharged recruits were chosen—one was too cocky to be a team player and the other too tentative in her actions—not the types, they were told, that a spy would want as a backup in the real world. Among the tasks required of the recruits were demands that they build "legends" (fake identities) before being sent into bars to get information from strangers. Eight contestants learned how to free-fall with parachutes, fight through an urban gang, and find a "safe house" in the woods before being captured, interrogated, and endure hours of sensory deprivation. In the last episode, four spies—two men and two women—competed in undercover operations behind "enemy lines" in Mexico. The final four tried to conduct surveillance, take photographs, and seek to find a kidnapped scientist in a warehouse. Jennifer Garner would have been proud—the men were eliminated early, leaving two females to battle it out in the last moments.

Spy Master, however, wasn't on a major network and was deliberately short-lived. There was no million dollar prize for the win—merely bragging rights as a new television "Spymaster." Still, the series indicated that becoming a secret agent continues to meet one aspect of popular wish fulfillment. Without question, this desire is now being fed not only by traditional media, but also by a new range of products for new generations. While realism remained an important thread in literature, the fantasies popularized by 007 had a stronger place in popular culture.

REACHING TO THE FUTURE

With the advent of the Internet and the popularity of electronic games, several new dimensions in popular culture included new ways to play with espionage. Even before the World Wide Web became internationally accessible, the vogue of "fanzines" had sprouted in the 1980s. Lovers of nostalgia and the characters of their youth had pumped out a wide variety of privately published newsletters and magazines. They featured news items on favorite actors, along with new stories based on characters from shows like *The Wild Wild West* and *Get Smart*. A fondness for childhood heroes, and heartthrobs, was one motivation. But on a deeper level, fans loved to contribute something to the mythology and ephemera of a genre seemingly relegated to hard-to-find videos and later DVD releases. The Internet allowed for an explosion of Web sites devoted to favorite characters, with new "fanzines" both attempting to keep the flavor of old friends alive as well as sites that gave their inspirations more sexual freedom than they'd enjoyed on network television. Presently, such sites devoted to *Scarecrow and Mrs. King* and *The Man from U.N.C.L.E.*, among others, are not hard to find. Old spies, it seems, will never die.[3]

Alias never pretends to be reality as it joyously celebrates the genre that brought us James Bond, Honey West, and, yes, Austin Powers. It's a comic-book explosion of global fashion, cloned villains, kick-boxing babes, and fierce emotionality.

Matthew Gilbert

At the same time, the new vogue for electronic games, not surprisingly, included famous film, television, and original secret agents. Jennifer Garner's *Alias*, Pierce Brosnan's 007 (*Everything or Nothing*), and various Tom Clancy franchises (*Rainbow Six, Splintered Cells*) became Console computer games alongside adventures for X-Box and Game Cube. Players could be either spies or terrorists and enjoy theme music written especially for the games.

However, publishers of old-fashioned print books also looked for new ways to attract a new generation into espionage fiction. With the success of ABC television's *Alias*, Bantam Books turned to the old use of tie-in paperbacks to promote the series. This time, they deliberately targeted young readers, primarily adolescent girls. Commissioned authors included Lynn Mason, Laura Peyton Roberts, Elizabeth Skurnick, and Emma Harrison. All created prequels to the show, as well as books based both on Sydney Bristo and Michael Vaughn. Such projects prompted the CIA to take note. They realized Jennifer Garner was just the sort of star who might interest a new generation to consider spying as a career. In fall 2003, they hired Garner (at no cost) to film a brief introduction for a six- to-seven-minute video to be shown at job fairs and college campuses ("Garner" 2003, 22). According to CIA entertainment liaison Chase Brandon, "Jennifer's character—in fact, Jennifer herself—has the qualities of dedication, patriotism, intelligence and creativity that we look for in people we recruit" ("Garner" 2003, 22).[4]

Garner's Sydney Bristow wasn't alone in projects geared for younger readers. In March 2004, the same month when worries about directions for the film and literary Bond were being discussed, Ian Fleming Publications Ltd. announced that in March 2005, Charlie Higson would introduce a new James Bond series set in the 1930s, when Bond was a teenager ("News" 2004). Aimed primarily at the nine- to twelve-year-old market, the stories have Bond, thirteen years old, about to begin at Eton having been educated at home by his Aunt Charmian since the death of his parents. Also in Britain, Anthony Horowitz issued a popular series of original spy novels also designed for teenagers. They featured Alex Rider, a fourteen-year-old boy brought up by his uncle after his parents died. The uncle is killed and Alex begins poking around to find out that his uncle worked for British intelligence and that he was quietly grooming Alex to be a spy. While Alex is reluctant, he is blackmailed by his uncle's former boss, who is in control of the money held in trust for Alex. By the publication of *Scorpia* (2003), the series was topping Amazon's list for children's literature. Even nonspy projects used wish fulfillment in their plots. Lindsay Camp's 1996 *The Midnight Feast* (later filmed as *A Feast at Midnight*) was about a boy in an English boarding school. At one point, he sneaks away from school to go into the nearby town where he pretends he's 007, as he escapes detection by hitching a ride away from school.

Hollywood also has the youngest demographic in mind when selling new spies. In summer 2001, the widely praised children's film, *Spy Kids*, became the number one box office draw, showcasing the adventures of pubescent spies working to free their parents. Something of our romantic ideals came through in one scene, where a young boy exclaims, "Our parents can't be spies! They're not cool." In July, the animated *Cats and Dogs* took the spy genre several steps lower, making dogs the hottest secret agents of the summer. *Spy Kids* returned with *Spy Kids 2: The Island of Lost Dreams* (2002), and one more time with the old 1950s gimmick of 3-D in, naturally, *Spy Kids 3: Game Over* (2003). In the same year, we got *Agent Cody Banks*. In 2005, the small screen also had its share of family-oriented spies. Fox aired two thirty-minute tries, including *The Inside* starring Rachel Nichols as a twenty-two-year-old federal agent working undercover as a high school student. On Sundays, *American Dad* was an animated series about a family man who is a CIA agent always on the alert for terrorist activity. More such light fare appeared on the Cartoon Network, which offered *Code Name: Kids Next Door* and *Totally Spies*. Clearly, the vogue for agents too young for driver's licenses but able to outfox governments and criminal organizations alike is here to stay. For one more example, in 2004, *Catch That Kid*, in the *Spy Kids* mold, had yet three more precocious adolescents able to rob banks under the noses of the best security experts Hollywood could script.

Of course, family entertainment doesn't always involve smart-aleck youngsters. A television movie, *My Mother the Spy* (2000), had book editor Jane Brook discovering that Mom (Dyan Cannon) worked for the CIA, and so had Dad and Grandma. Perhaps no format is better at reaching a multigenerational audience than films merging live action with cartoon characters, blending nostalgia with laughs for family viewings. The 2000 *The Adventures of Rocky and Bullwinkle* pitted the dimwitted moose and his friend, the sometimes flying squirrel, against their perennial adversaries, Boris (Jason Alexander), Natasha (Rene Russo), and Fearless Leader (Robert De Niro). These animated Cold Warriors, brought to life via Hollywood and transdimensional magic, plotted to take over the United States with RBTV (Really Bad Television) broadcasting twenty-four-hour spy adventures turning viewers into zombies. To yet another revised version of the "Secret Agent Man" theme, RBTV included "Three wacky spies and their horse who will also be a spy!" Likewise, *Looney Toons: Back in Action* (2003) brought back Bugs Bunny and Daffy Duck, who set out to rescue Timothy Dalton. The former Bond played a superspy using the cover as an actor playing superspies. Bugs, Daffy, and company looked for the supernatural "Blue Monkey," which they learn, by way of Peter Graves doing one of his many *Mission: Impossible* takeoffs, was a device that the evil Acme products can use to turn humans into monkeys to make products and be turned back into humans to buy the products. In short, America's love affair with fantastic spies was far from over. While quasi-realism had moved off center stage, adventure stories remained as popular as ever. So the final question is clearly: What is the future of espionage in popular culture?

I didn't let myself try to figure it out. One thing you learn early in the business is not to waste cerebral energy trying to solve the problems for which answers are already available at the back of the book.

Donald Hamilton, *The Silencers*

One government official in Robert Ludlum's original *The Bourne Supremacy* put his finger on two key reasons spies are still so interesting to modern readers and viewers: "These people do things the rest of us only dream about or fantasize or watch on a screen, disbelieving every moment because it's so outrageously implausible. We wouldn't have such dreams or fantasize or stay mesmerized by invention if the fundamentals weren't in the human experience" (1987, 642). Beneath the gunfire and spectacle, there are indeed fundamentals that go deeper than 5.1 Surround Sound digitally enhanced stunt fights. On one hand, diverting entertainment takes average people out of the commonplace world and provides wish fulfillment for some, hope for others, and escapism from real danger for most. Perhaps one of these fundamentals is the drive for justice or vengeance often denied within legal constraints. In the covert world, heroes and antiheroes alike do what many of us can only fantasize about or, at least, hope some group can perform on our behalf. One continuing motif in spy fiction has been the aggrieved loner out to get the villains who did them personal harm. The most dominant type of character in these stories remains the amateur who steps out of normal life, either willingly or by force, to solve problems even professionals can't address. Such stories are age old and likely to be retold in many forms in centuries to come.

Within the shadow world of spies and quasi-spies, avengers can fight evil with a license to do so or, at least, have cover to hide it.

A handful of other observers have sought the underlining reasons that stimulate such fundamentals. According to John Cawilti and Bruce Rosenberg, we now live in a climate of "clandestinity," in which bureaucracy and corporate structures make outsiders of us all in the business world. In 2000, Timothy Melley developed this idea in his *Empire of Conspiracy*. Using various literary models, he stressed that many workers deal in occupations speaking in codes understood only by insiders. Bureaucracies are apparently controlled by mysterious, shadow powers that seem motivated by the health and wealth of an institution at the expense of both employees and client/customers. In such discussions, we respond to modern spies because we work in disconnected, compartmentalized cubicles resulting in alienation, moral ambiguities, and uncertainties about organizations and culture. Like spies, we work under the eyes of security cameras, while supervisors claim the right to oversee what electronic correspondence comes and goes from our computers. In this climate, we use fictional characters like secret agents to project our frustrations with corporate superiors, bureaucratic regulations, and professional conventions (Cawilti and Rosenberg 1987, xi–xii, 43).

Of course, new concerns beyond workplace ethics will have much to do with new directions. For example, in June 2004, CNN reported that a new surveillance drone, the UAB, was flying over southern American borders, as worries about new terrorism were connected to that year's high-profile election events. In the same month, coastal ports were put on a high state of alert. The old issue of illegal immigration was thus intertwined with the ability of terrorists to have easy access to American cities. In the new millennium, espionage was now a concern with racial, ethnic, and religious overtones that widened the canvas of old-fashioned paranoia.

Still, to look to the future, we need to understand the past. At the beginning of the twentieth century, of course, racial divides were part of the first spy fiction. But imperial attitudes were somewhat different than what would become acceptable after the movement for "political correctness." During the "Clubland" era, literary espionage was populated by independent, patriotic adventurers who saw spying as "a great game" and "a capital sport!" Most such gentlemen amateurs had shared one characteristic—they were British Islanders seeking to protect their homeland from outside invaders. In America, such gentlemen were no gentlemen at all. In peacetime, espionage was distasteful until the rise of Adolf Hitler and Communism. From 1941 until the 1960s, the enemies of Western values seemed apparent and worthy of any action to stop unmistakable evil.

Then, the cold war became more complex. Not only were methods and morals questionable, but just where evil dwelled was no longer certain. In both America and Britain, many saw "shadow governments" as being as worrisome as their opposition. Espionage was more than national defense; it had become meddling in the affairs of other nations in cold war proxy battles, as well as undercover actions to protect commercial interests. Even before the Reagan era, the world of espionage was seen as a realm that matched the fears expressed by isolationists from the first half of the century when the CIA and FBI found themselves involved in civil dissent against government policies. Then came the 1980s, when the cold war was reignited just before its unexpected and sudden demise. Overnight, it seemed, the role of espionage was a confusing matter in fact and fiction. Once, insiders like "Wild Bill" Donovan and William Casey worked to make espionage part of our cultural mythos. Now, unlike previous eras, the twenty-first century began with all aspects of spying now an integral part of our evening news, entertainment, and our history. From the ridiculous to the terrifying, espionage had become intertwined with nearly every aspect of our lives.

Perhaps the place that best emblemizes our collective fascination with all things espionage is the International Spy Museum in Washington, D.C. I well remember my first visit in fall 2002, when I stood in a line on a blustery day as a range of visitors, from the very young to senior citizens, waited their turn to wander through the new museum's two floors of exhibits of past spies. Inside the front doors, we were invited to choose a "legend," a false identity to play for the day. Throughout the museum, in between crawling through heating ducts and listening to videos describing various eras in espionage, crowds of young would-be agents gathered around computer terminals to learn how well they could play at being their legend. Exhibits included artifacts from biblical times to the twenty-first century, such as a 1774 letter from George Washington establishing a spy network in

New York, a KGB lipstick gun, and radio transmitters hidden in shoe heels and tree stumps.

I was among the first one hundred thousand visitors that August 2002; by January 2004, one million visitors had toured the site of the International Spy Museum at 800 F Street in its first eighteen months.[5] Seeking to educate the public about the motivations, conceptions, and misconceptions of spycraft in both global and apolitical terms, this successful tourist attraction represents the importance of espionage in history and in a culture that wants to be both informed and entertained by it. Clearly, the International Spy Museum does not merely capture a time frozen in the past as do similar memorials to particular wars and eras. Writers and spies regularly appear to discuss the present and future of espionage. New spy products like jackets with hidden pockets, CDs of spy music, and new collectors' items spice up the gift shop on a regular basis. Our interest in all this will continue, just as espionage itself must remain part of our security and preparation in current events. As W. Somerset Maugham put it back in 1928:

But there will always be espionage and there will always be counter-espionage. Their conditions may have altered, their difficulties may be greater when war is raging. There will always be secrets which one side jealously guards and which the other will use every means to discover. There will always be men, who for malice or for money, will betray their kith and kin and there will always be men who, from love of adventure or a sense of duty, will risk a shameful death to secure information vital to their country. (Maugham 1941, iv)

Notes

CHAPTER ONE

1. The Montgomery/Lupino version of *The 39 Steps* is on the CD collection *AMC Movie Classics Presents the Lux Radio Theatre, 1930s* (CBS Enterprises, 2001). The *Lux Radio Theatre* version was not the only radio dramatization of Buchan's novel. In 1937, Orson Welles proudly touted his *Mercury Theatre* version as being truer to the original novel, not adding the additional characters in the Hitchcock projects. Later, other producers tried the story for movie theaters, as in Kenneth Moore's 1959 version and again in 1978 starring Robert Powell.

2. Ken Mogg discussed another possible influence by Buchan on Hitchcock in his review of *"The 39 Steps": A British Film Guide* (Mogg 2004). Mogg believes the cross-country chase scenes in Hitchcock's *Marnie* (1964) could have come from Buchan's 1922 historical thriller, *Midwinter*.

3. More details about the definitions of "cloak and dagger" can be found at: http://www.takeourword.com and http://www.users.tinyonline.co.uk/gswithenbank/sayingsc.htm#Cloak-and-dagger.

CHAPTER TWO

1. *The Book of Spies: An Anthology of Literary Espionage*, edited by Alan Furst, appeared in 2003 and included one chapter of *Ashenden*. In the main, the book contains chapters from spy novels and not stories designed to be short pieces. In the opinion of one reviewer, the book shows that the best espionage fiction seems to be in full-length novels and that there are apparently few classic spy short stories (Miller 2004, 39). The collection is indeed puzzling for what it includes and what it omits, including short tales by the likes of Dornford Yates, Ian Fleming, and Ted Allbuery, among others. Still, it does seem apparent that the

best espionage literature depends on developed and intertwining plot lines, complex characters, and situations requiring elements beyond what can be found in genres like detective or science-fiction stories.

2. The degree of Ambler's realism influenced at least one Bond novel. In 1957, Ian Fleming acknowledged Ambler's contributions to the Istanbul sequences in his *From Russia With Love* by having Bond reading *The Mask of Dimitrious*, the novel Fleming had used as a tour guide during his first trip to the city (Lycett 1995, 272).

3. The Saint, often considered more a "Robin Hood" crook than spy, had much to do with fictional espionage from 1928 through the 1990s in literature, on radio, television, and film. For a full discussion on Simon Templar in espionage, see chapter 7 in my *Spy Television* (2004).

4. While Graham Greene's purpose was unquestionably satiric and not intended as a window into spycraft, the Office of Strategic Services (OSS) took coal deliveries quite seriously during World War II. Among the artifacts on display at the International Spy Museum is a piece of camouflaged, hollow coal used to hide explosives. When heated, German industry had problems.

5. According to one Dorothy L. Sayers fan, Sayers's detective, Lord Peter Wimsey, was a sometime spy. In various stories, he was referred to as doing dangerous overseas work on behalf of the Foreign Office, including "The Abominable History of the Man with the Copper Fingers" and "The Bibulous Business of a Matter of Taste." During the war years, the *London Spectator* ran a series of articles by Sayers in the form of correspondence among members of the Wimsey family discussing Lord Peter's intelligence work.

CHAPTER THREE

1. A similar group of both professionals and worried civil servants gathered around Winston Churchill during his "Wilderness Years," when the future prime minister was exiled from power. Like the opponents to isolationism in the United States, Churchill's secret informants worried about their government's appeasement policy with Hitler (Lycett 1995, 78, 90).

2. Hoover's penchant continued for decades, as when the American Broadcasting Company (ABC) worked on a documentary series called *The FBI: The Untold Story*. The FBI had complete veto power over the content. When the producers wanted to cover the story of an agent who'd killed an informer he'd impregnated, the press office blocked the story (Kessler 2002, 304). Some later connections would be less controversial, such as the role of William Baker, who worked at both the CIA and as an assistant director for the FBI before leaving to become senior vice president of the Motion Picture Association of America and then president of its Motion Picture Association, which represents Hollywood overseas (Kessler 2002, 264).

3. One present-day connection between films of the 1930s and the FBI can be found in "Hogan's Alley" in Quantaco, the mock-up town where trainees practice their arms skills. The town has a replica of the Biograph Theatre that continually shows the gangster hit *Manhattan Melodrama* (1934) starring Clark Gable and Myrna Loy. This was the film John Dillinger saw just before being gunned down by FBI agents in Chicago on July 22, 1934. Ironically, the film's last minutes showed a convicted gangster walking to the executioner's electric chair. In 2004, another "Hogan's Alley" appeared on the Learning Channel's reality series *Spymaster*, where would-be spies competed to show their potential as secret agents.

4. The climactic shoot-out in *The Man Who Knew Too Much* was inspired by a 1911 battle in the East End of London, an incident reworked in Robert Baker's low-budget 1960 *The Siege of Sidney Street* (Porton 1999, 23).

5. In 1944, Hitchcock contributed to the war effort by working on two short twenty-five-minute propaganda films for the British Ministry of Information. The first of these "four-reelers," *Bon Voyage* (1944), featured a Royal Air Force (RAF) pilot who learns he's been traveling with a Polish Gestapo double agent. Designed to aid the French Resistance, the cast and crew consisted of exiles from France. But disagreements among the Free French leaders led to both films being shelved and never used (Truffaut and Scott 1967, 116).

6. According to Dan Ford, the Communist government of Vietnam didn't like the 1958 movie version of Graham Greene's *The Quiet American*, which eliminated the novel's anti-Americanism. But the dictators approved the script for the 2002 version that Philip Noyce directed for Miramax. Producer Bill Horberg was allowed to shut down Ho Chi Minh Square for nearly a week, dressing Hanoi's busiest intersection to look as it had in 1952, filling it with hundreds of extras, and blowing up a few cars. Other reviews noted the timeliness of the movie, which pointed to themes about American involvement overseas as U.S. troops were again in harm's way in Iraq and Afghanistan. See http://www.danford.net/quietam.htm.

7. Possibly due to Higham's revelations, Timothy Dalton's character, Neville Sinclair, in the Disney movie *The Rocketeer* (1991) was based on Flynn and was the villain of the story.

CHAPTER FOUR

1. I must thank Matt Cvetic, Jr., for our telephone conversations in spring 2004 about his memories of his father. I was glad to hear his insights; his personal observations were quite different from major print publications he hadn't read.

2. An interesting Lee Harvey Oswald/Herbert Philbric connection was discussed in a "Daily Rant" for a July 2003 online *Behind the Barricades*. According to Kenneth Kahn, Oswald may have been a double agent for the U.S. govern-

ment infiltrating pro-Castro Communist groups. Kahn lists the various possibilities supporting conspiracy advocates who think this had something to do with the Kennedy assassination. On the other hand, Kahn notes that Herbert Philbric had other ideas that he included in a 1974 edition of *I Led Three Lives*. Philbric felt that the Paine family hadn't done their American duty by not reporting Oswald to the FBI when he made his support of Communism clear in Dallas.

3. Since I cover the television spy genre in great detail in *Spy Television* (2004), my notes here are but quick mentions of what is discussed in that book. Comments throughout this book are either very short uses of information needed to flesh out the contexts of the time or are new points not covered in *Spy Television*.

CHAPTER FIVE

1. Ironically, both Pearson's and Amis's books were somewhat disinherited from the Bond canon. In 2004, novelist Raymond Benson revealed that he'd been told he could disregard the events in these novels in terms of his own 007 adventures. EON Productions planned to call their bad guy "Colonel Sun" for the 2002 *Die Another Day*, but dropped the idea when the Fleming estate insisted on royalties for the name.

2. The discussion here about sci-fi shows and comic books relies heavily on information from Bill Koenig and Thomas Rucki.

3. Much of this information comes from my research for a review of the "Stainless Steel Rat" series for *Magill's Guide to Science Fiction and Fantasy* (Pasadena, CA: Salem Press, 1995).

CHAPTER SIX

1. In England, the "Cambridge Spy Ring" seemed of endless fascination for films, novels, stage plays, and television movies. Playwright Alan Bennett's 1984 BBC teleplay, *The Englishman Abroad*, looked at Guy Burgess in exile. His 1992 *A Question of Attribution* explored the motives of Anthony Blount (Britton 2004, 214). John Banville's 1997 novel, *The Untouchable* was also a loose depiction of Blount (Hitz 2004, 19).

CHAPTER SEVEN

1. Lee Pfeiffer's notes came from e-mail correspondence with this author on June 18, 2004.

2. Comments on Trevanian and the text of the cited footnote came from Tim Naumann in a private e-mail on July 1, 2004.

CHAPTER EIGHT

1. In 1971, Tony Mendez had approached mask designer John Chambers (*Planet of the Apes*) to help create disguises for intelligence officers. Chambers's first contribution was to design two latex masks for spies in Laos. In 1979, he was flown to Washington in an aborted plan to help create a false shah of Iran to fake the ailing leader leaving the United States in order to help lessen tensions in the first days of the Iranian hostage crisis.

President Carter opted not to be pressured by Iranian demonstrators into any such action. In 1980, however, Chambers helped in the mission described in this chapter. According to the 2001 AMC television special, "Into the Shadows: The CIA in Hollywood," Chambers contacted producer Bob Siddell, who established fake identities for the Americans as a movie crew seeking locations in the desert. For fifteen years, Chambers worked for both movie studios and the CIA, and by the time his story was declassified in 2001, his Oscar sat beside his other most prized possession, his Medal of Honor for special services.

2. From a private e-mail to this author from Bob Short, March 12, 2004.

3. For considerable information about the world of Tom Clancy, see http://www.clancyfaq.com and http://www.tcic.org.

CHAPTER NINE

1. As I describe in *Spy Television*, James Bond and his creator appeared in projects other than the Pierce Brosnan films and Raymond Benson books. Two syndicated television movies purported to tell the story of Ian Fleming during World War II. In 1989, Charles Dance played Fleming in the low-key *GoldenEye: A Story of James Bond*. In 1990, Jason Connery, son of Sean, played a more fanciful version in *Spy Maker: The Secret Life of Ian Fleming*. In 1992, the syndicated cartoon, *James Bond, Jr.*, came to television and comic books. For more details, see *Spy Television*, page 222.

2. Spy humor still occasionally pops up in literature. In 2000, Tom Robbins issued the comic best seller *Fierce Invalids Home from Hot Climates*. In this witty swipe at espionage and other aspects of modern life, CIA agent Switers gets a shaman's curse, which will mean death if his feet touch the ground, so he completes his next mission from a wheelchair. Along the way, Switers comments on the two types of spies, "Cowboys and Angels." Angels are "smart, educated,

young, self-reliant, healthy, unencumbered" and like sex, drugs, and rock 'n' roll. "Cowboys" are the flag-waving, Bible-thumping, "trigger-happy patriots . . . who create the international incidents and are always embarrassing the CIA and the United States and getting innocent people killed" (Robbins 2000, 33). They earn promotions because they're cut from the same mold as "the dour faced, stiff-minded suck butt, kick butt, buzz-cut, macho dickheads who oversee the company." They get in the way and cause nothing but misery for all (2000, 33). For Switers, international globe-trotting has its advantages. Agents don't have to suffer storm window salesman, Jehovah's Witnesses pushing *The Watchtower*, and condo association meetings.

CONCLUSION

1. Taken from "Don DeLillo: An Annotated Bibliography" at: http://www. perival.com/delillo/ddbiblio.html#anchor94532.

2. Broadcast October 1, 2001, on CNN *Saturday Morning*.

3. Beyond fan bases, the most obvious presence of old spies occurred in the use of theme music and comic nods in films and commercials. In December 2003, Peter Graves traded on his *Mission: Impossible* background to play a mysterious figure promoting new AOL security programs. For ostensibly the same older demographic, the *Get Smart* theme was used to sell security for American Express in February 2003. In January 2004, the 1966 theme "Secret Agent Man," was reworked into "The Rollback Man" for Wal-Mart commercials, and the *Mission: Impossible* theme was trotted out yet again for the animated *Shrek II*, when the unlikely heroes try to rescue an imprisoned princess. The opening narration for *The Six Million Dollar Man* has been used for at least three separate products, including Dodge trucks.

4. For those wishing to see the Garner recruitment video, go to: http://www. odci.gov/employment/garner/index.html.

5. Beyond my own observations, Amanda Abrell from the Public Relations Office at the International Spy Museum provided me with attendance figures and a comprehensive press kit cited here.

Works Cited

BOOKS

Allbeury, Ted. *The Lantern Network*. New York: Mysterious Press, 1978.

Allen, Thomas. *International Spy Museum Souvenir Book*. Springfield, VA: Goetz Printing, 2002.

Ambler, Eric. *The Light of Day*. New York: Knopf, 1962.

Amis, Kingsley. *The James Bond Dossier*. New York: New American Library, 1965.

Bamford, James. *Body of Secrets: Anatomy of the Ultra-Secret National Security Agency from the Cold War to the Dawn of a New Century*. New York: Doubleday, 2001.

Barnouw, Eric. *Tube of Plenty: The Evolution of American Television*. 2nd rev. ed. New York: Oxford University Press, 1990.

Barson, Michael, and Steven Heller. *Red Scared: The Commie Menace in Propaganda and Popular Culture*. San Francisco: Chronicle Books, 2001.

Baxter, John. *Science Fiction in the Cinema: A Complete Critical Review of SF Films from A Trip to the Moon (1902) to 2001: A Space Odyssey*. New York: Paperback Library, 1970.

Belton, John. *American Cinema/American Culture*. New York: McGraw-Hill, 1994.

Benson, Raymond. *Never Dream of Dying*. New York: Putnam, 2001.

Black, Jeremy. *The Politics of James Bond: From Fleming's Novels to the Big Screen*. Westport, CT: Praeger, 2001.

Bloom, Harold. *John Le Carré*. New York: Chelsea, 1987.

Bold, Alan Norman. *The Quest for Le Carré*. New York: St. Martin's, 1988.

Britton, Wesley. *Spy Television*. Westport, CT: Praeger, 2004.

Brooks, Tim, and Earle Marsh. *The Complete Directory to Prime Network and Cable TV Shows: 1946–Present*. 7th ed. New York: Ballantine Books, 1999.

Buchan, John. *The Four Adventures of Richard Hannay*: The 39 Steps, Green Mantle, Mr. Standfast, The Three Hostages. Introduction by Robin W. Winks. Boston: D. R. Godine, 1988.

Buckley, William F., Jr. *Tucker's Last Stand*. New York: Random House, 1990.

Cawilti, John G., and Bruce A. Rosenberg. *The Spy Story*. Chicago, IL: University of Chicago Press, 1987.

Chesterson, G. K. *The Man Who Was Thursday*. Miami: Books on the Road, 1985. Audio book.

Connors, Martin, and Jim Craddock. *Video Hounds Golden Movie Retriever*. Detroit: Visible Ink Press, 1999.

Conrad, Joseph. *The Secret Agent*. New York: Knopf, 1992.

Cooper, James Fenimore. *The Spy: A Tale of the Neutral Ground*. Edited with an Introduction by James H. Pickering. East Lansing, MI: Michigan State University; College and University Press Services Inc., 1971.

Cvetic, Matt. *The Big Decision*. (Self-published by author.) 1959.

Davenport, Robert. *The Encyclopedia of War Movies: The Authoritative Guide to Movies About Wars of the 20th Century*. New York: Facts on File Publications, 2004.

Deighton, Len. *The Billion Dollar Brain*. New York: G. P. Putnam's Sons, 1966.

———. *Horse Under Water*. New York: G. P. Putnam's Sons, 1968.

Dunning, John. *On the Air: The Encyclopedia of Old Time Radio*. New York: Oxford University Press, 1998.

East, Andy. *The Cold War File*. Metuchen, NJ: Scarecrow Press, 1983.

Fleming, Ian. *Casino Royale*. New York: Penguin Books, 2002.

———. *From Russia with Love*. New York: New American Library, 1996.

———. *The Man with the Golden Gun*. New York: New American Library, 1965.

———. *Moonraker*. New York: Charter Publications, 1955.

Follett, Kenneth. *Night Over Water*. New York: Simon and Schuster, 1991.

Forsythe, Frederick. *The Avenger*. Los Angeles: Audio Renaissance, 2003.

Gardner, Gerald. *Censorship Papers: Movie Censorship Letters from the Hays Office, 1934 to 1968*. New York: Dobbs, Mead and Company, 1987.

Gardner, John. *No Deals, Mister Bond*. New York: Simon and Schuster Audioworks, 1987.

Gerrold, David. *The World of Star Trek*. New York: Ballantine Books, 1973.

Gorman, Ed, Lee Serber, and Martin H. Greenburg, eds. *The Big Book of Noir*. New York: Carroll and Graf Publications, 1998.

Grady, James. *Thunder*. New York: Warner Books, 1994.

Green, Joey. *The Get Smart Handbook*. Toronto: Collier Books of Canada, 1993.

Greene, Graham. *The Confidential Agent*. London: W. Heinemann, 1939.

———. *The Pleasure-Dome: Collected Film Criticism 1935–1940*. Ed. John Russell Taylor. Oxford: Oxford University Press, 1980.

————. *The Quiet American*. New York: Random House, 1992.

————. *The Third Man and the Fallen Idol*. New York: Penguin, 1977.

Hall, Adam. *Quiller: Salamander*. New York: Otto Penzler Books, 1994.

Hamilton, Donald. *Murderer's Row*. Greenwich, CT: Fawcett Editions, 1962.

————. *The Silencers*. Greenwich, CT: Fawcett Gold Medal Books, 1962.

Hayes, John Earl, and Harvey Klehr. *Vevona: Decoding Soviet Espionage in America*. New Haven, CT: Yale University Press, 1999.

Higham, Charles. *Errol Flynn: The Untold Story*. New York: Doubleday, 1980.

Higham, Charles, and Joel Greenberg. *Hollywood in the Forties*. New York: Paperback Library, 1968.

Hitz, Frederick. *The Great Game: The Myth and Reality of Espionage*. New York: Knopf, 2004.

Hoffman, Todd. *John Le Carré's Landscape*. Montreal: McGill's Queens University Press, 2001.

Katz, Ephriam. *The Film Encyclopedia*. 3rd ed. New York: HarperCollins, 1998.

Kessler, Ronald. *The Bureau: The Secret History of the FBI*. New York: St. Martin's, 2002.

Leab, Daniel G. *I Was a Communist for the FBI: The Unhappy Life of Matt Cvetic*. University Park: Pennsylvania University Press, 2000.

Lindner, Christoph. *The James Bond Phenomenon: A Critical Reader*. Manchester: Manchester University Press, 2003.

Ludlum, Robert. *The Bourne Supremacy*. New York: Bantam Books, 1987.

————. *The Holcroft Covenant*. New York: Random House Audiobooks, 1989.

————. *The Jansen Directive*. New York: St. Martin's, 2002.

————. *The Matarese Circle*. New York: Bantam Audiobooks, 1987.

Lycett, Andrew. *Ian Fleming: The Man Behind James Bond*. Atlanta: Turner Publications Inc., 1995.

MacDonald, J. Fred. *Television and the Red Menace: The Video Road to Vietnam*. New York: Praeger, 1985.

Mailer, Norman. *Harlot's Ghost*. New York: Random House, 1991.

Maltin, Leonard. *Leonard Maltin's Movie Encyclopedia*. New York: Penguin Books, 1994.

Marrs, Ken. *Crossfire: The Plot to Kill Kennedy*. New York: Carroll and Graf, 1989.

Maugham, W. Somerset. *Ashenden: Or the British Agent*. New York: Doubleday, 1941.

McCarry, Charles. *The Last Supper*. New York: E. P. Dutton, 1983.

McCormick, Donald. *Who's Who in Spy Fiction*. New York: Taplinger, 1977.

Melley, Timothy. *Empire of Conspiracy: The Culture of Paranoia in Postwar America*. Ithaca, NY, and London: Cornell University Press, 2000.

Miller, Ron. *Mystery! A Celebration. Stalking Public Television's Greatest Sleuths*. San Francisco: Bay Books, 1996.

WORKS CITED

The Movie Guide: The Most Comprehensive Film Reference of Its Kind. Compiled by the editors of *Cinemabooks*. New York: Perigee Books 1998.

Osbourne, Richard. *Clubland Heroes*. London: Constable and Co., 1953.

Pearson, John. *The Life of Ian Fleming*. New York: McGraw-Hill, 1966.

Persico, Joseph. *Casey: From the OSS to the CIA*. New York: Viking, 1990.

————. *Roosevelt's Secret War: FDR and World War II Espionage*. New York: Random House, 2001.

Porton, Richard. *Film and the Anarchist Imagination*. London/New York: Verso Books, 1999.

Richelson, Jeffrey T. *A Century of Spies: Intelligence in the Twentieth Century*. New York: Oxford, 1995.

Robbins, Tom. *Fierce Invalids Home from Hot Climates*. New York: Bantam Books, 2000.

Safire, William. *Sleeper Spy*. New York: St. Martin's, 1995.

Sauerberg, Lars. *Secret Agents in Fiction: Ian Fleming, John Le Carré, and Len Deighton*. New York: St. Martin's, 1984.

Schatz, Thomas. *Hollywood Genres: Formulas, Filmmaking, and the Studio System*. New York: Random House, 1981.

Shaw, Tony. *British Cinema and the Cold War: The State, Propaganda, and Consensus*. New York: St. Martin's, 2001.

Silva, Daniel. *The Kill Artist*. New York: Random House Audiobooks, 2000.

Spoto, Donald. *The Dark Side of Genius: The Life of Alfred Hitchcock*. New York: Ballentine Books, 1983.

Srodes, James. *Allen Dulles: Master of Spies*. Lanhan, MD: Regency Publications, 1999.

Stafford, Gene. *Secret Agent K-7* (adapted from the Radio Scripps). Akron, OH: Saalfield Publications, 1940.

Strada, Michael, and Harold Troper. *Friend or Foe: Russians in American Film and Foreign Policy (1933–1991)*. Lanhan, MD: Scarecrow Press, 1997.

Trevanian. *Shibumi*. New York: Crown Publications, 1979.

Truffaut, Francois, with the collaboration of Helen G. Scott. *Hitchcock*. New York: Simon and Schuster, 1967.

Weinstein, Allen, and Alexander Vassiliev. *The Haunted Wood. Soviet Espionage in America: The Stalin Era*. New York: Random House, 1999.

Winks, Robin. *Modus Operandi: An Excursion into Detective Fiction*. Boston: David R. Godine Publications, 1982.

Wise, David. *Mole Hunt: The Secret Search for Traitors that Shattered the CIA*. New York: Random House, 1992.

————. *Spy: The Inside Story of How the FBI's Robert Hanssen Betrayed America*. New York: Random House, 2002.

Wolfe, Peter. *Alarms and Epitaphs: The Art of Eric Ambler*. Bowling Green, KY: Bowling Green University Press, 1993.

Wood, Robin. *Hitchcock's Films Revisited*. New York: Columbia University Press, 1989.

ARTICLES

"*Alias* Star Shoots Video for the CIA." *Chicago Sun-Times*. August 29, 2003, F56.

Allen, Brook. Review of *Somerset Maugham—A Life*, by Jefferey Myers. *New York Times Book Review*. March 14, 2004, late and final editions, sec. 7, col. 1, 9.

Anderson, Patrick. "Tom Clancy's Fraternal Order." *Washington Post*. September 8, 2003, final edition, C4.

Barthel, Joan. "An Enigma Comes to American TV." *TV Guide*. May 25, 1968, 13.

Brauner, Ethan. "Collateral Damage: The Effects of the War on Terrorism on American Freedom and Privacy Are Not Easy to Assess." *New York Times Book Review*. February 22, 2004, late edition, sec. 7, col. 1, 10–11.

Broeske, Pat E. "Will History Sink 'Red October'?" *Los Angeles Times*. March 1, 1990, home edition, 1.

"Charles McCarry." *Contemporary Authors Online*, Gale, 2002. http://www .flicklives.com/search/search.html (accessed June 3, 2004).

Cox, John. "The Raymond Benson CBN Interview." CommanderBond Network.org. http://www.commanderBond.net/Public/Stories/2306-1 .shtml (accessed March 23–24, 2004).

"Don DeLillo: The Word, The Image, and the Gun." Dir. Kim Evans. BBC 1. September 27, 1991. http://www.perival.com/delillo/ddbbc.html (accessed June 6, 2004).

"Eric Ambler." *Books and Writers*. 2000. http://www.kirjasto.sci.fi/greene.htm (accessed June 6, 2004).

Galbraith, Jane. "Paramount to Reshoot *Patriot Games* Ending." *Los Angeles Times*. April 30, 1992, home edition, 2.

Gardner, Curt, and Phil Nel. "Don Delillo: An Annotated Bibliography." March 18, 2003. http://perival.com/delillo/ddbiblio.html#anchor94532 (accessed June 6, 2004).

"Garner's New Alias: Recruiter." *People*. September 15, 2003, 22.

Gergely, Hubai. "The Spy Who Loved Mysteries: The True story of TSWLM!" Absolutely James Bond—The Definitive Unofficial James Bond 007 Community. June 3, 2004. http://www.ajb007.co.uk/articles/007/tswlm/ (accessed June 8, 2004).

Gerston, Jill. "You Look . . . Different, Jack." *New York Times*. May 12, 2002, late edition, sec. 2a, col. 4, 37.

Grace, Roger M. "Channel 11 Loads Its Schedule with Syndicated Shows." *Metropolitan News-Enterprise*, reminiscing column, January 22, 2003, 22.

WORKS CITED

"Graham Greene." *Books and Writers.* 2000. http://www.kirjasto.sci.fi/greene.htm (accessed June 6, 2004).

Grant, Hank. "Reviews of New TV Shows: *The Girl from U.N.C.L.E.*" *Hollywood Reporter.* September 14, 1966, 10.

Greenberg, David. "One Pledge, Hold the 'Under God.'" *Christian Science Monitor.* March 25, 2004, ALL edition, 9.

Grost, Michael E. "The Films of Alfred Hitchcock." *Classic Film and Television.* September 17, 2003. http://www.members.aol.com/MG4273/hitch.htm (accessed June 6, 2004).

Hitchens, Christopher. "Great Scot: Between Kipling and Fleming Stands John Buchan, Father of the Modern Spy Thriller." Review of *John Buchan: The Presbyterian Cavalier,* by Andrew Lownie. *Atlantic Monthly.* March 2004, vol. 293, no. 2, 104–107.

"The Jackal and the Day of the Jackal." *The DVD Journal.* 1998. http://www.dvdjournal.com/reviews/j/jackal.d.feature.shtml (accessed June 6, 2004).

"John Le Carré (1931–)." *Books and Writers.* 2003. http://www.kirjasto.sci.fi/lecarre.htm (accessed June 6, 2004).

Kahn, Kenneth R. "Will the Real Ruth and Michael Paine Please Stand Up?" *Behind the Barricades.* Daily Rant for July 25, 2003. http://www.home.earthlink.net/~ringo01/dailyrant5-15-03.html (accessed June 6, 2004).

Krebbs, Joseph. "Review: *Pickup On South Street.*" *Sound and Vision Magazine.* May 2004, 97.

Leab, Dan. "I Was a Communist for the FBI." *History Today Magazine.* December 1, 1996, 42–47.

Lehman, John. "Bookshelf: Jack Ryan's New Gizmos Save Another Day." *Wall Street Journal.* September 2, 1994, A7.

Markstein, Don. "Toonopedia: Secret Agent X-9." 2001. http://www.toonopedia.com.x-9.htm (accessed June 6, 2004).

McKee, Marty. "Adventures in B-Festing." January 26, 2003. http://www.mhvf.net/special.shtml-7k (accessed April 3, 2004).

Miller, Laura. "The Last Word: Smiley's People." *New York Times Book Review.* June 6, 2004, late edition, sec. 7, col. 1, 39.

Mogg, Ken. Review of *"The 39 Steps": A British Film Guide* by Mark Glancy. May 4, 2004. http://www.latrobe.edu.au/screeningthepast/reviews/rev_16/KMbr16a.html (accessed June 6, 2004).

"News: The Wait Is Over." *Ian Fleming Publications Ltd.* April 12, 2004. http://www.ianflemingcentre.com/index.cfm?page=news (accessed May 4, 2004).

Ornstein, Bill. " 'U.N.C.L.E. Is Thrill-a-Minute." *Hollywood Reporter.* September 23, 1964, 3.

Persico, Joseph E. Review of *Intelligence in War: Knowledge of the Enemy from Napoleon to Al Qaeda* by John Keagan. *New York Times Book Review*. November 9, 2003, late edition, sec. 7, col. 1, 10.

"Peter O'Donnell on Modesty Blaise." *Crime Time*. http://www.crimetime.co.uk/features/modestyblaise.html (accessed June 6, 2004).

Pringle, Kenneth. "J. Edgar Hoover No Fan of U.N.C.L.E.: FBI File Shows Director Irked by TV Show." Associated Press News Report, August 24, 2000. http://www.apbnews.com/media/gfiles/uncle/uncle0824_01.html (accessed November 18, 2002).

"The Quiller Memorandum." *The Harold Pinter Homepage*. http://www.haroldpinter.org (accessed June 3, 2004).

"Robert Wade and Neil Purvis Speak, Part 1." *MI6*. March 14, 2004. http://www.mi6.co.uk/sections/articles/literature_penguin_modern_classics04.ph (accessed March 15, 2004).

Simmels, Steve. "Review: *Bad Company*." *Sound and Vision Magazine*. February/March 2003, 98.

Skinner, Robert. "Donald Hamilton." Wikipedia-Donald Hamilton-Matt Helm-The Unofficial/Home Page. http://www.members.aol.com/macdorden/intro.html (accessed March 14, 2004).

Steyn, Mark. "The Imperfect Spy: Michael Strait 1916–2004." *Atlantic Monthly*. March 2004, vol. 293, no. 2, 46.

Struckel, Katie. "The WD interview: A Conversation with Tom Clancy." *Writers Digest*. January 2001, 20–21.

"Ted Allbeury." *St. James Guide to Crime and Mystery Writers*. 4th ed. Farmington Hills, MI: St. James Press, 1996.

"Theodore Edward le Bouthillier Allbeury." *Contemporary Authors Online*, Gale, 2003. http://www.flicklives.com/search/search.html (accessed July 13, 2004).

Towers, Robert. "From the Grassy Knoll." *The New York Review of Books*. August 18, 1988, vol. XXXV, no. 13, 6–7.

"Unofficial Jack Higgins Homepage." http://www.esintilla.utwente.nl/users/gert/higgins/html/main.etmail (accessed March 21, 2004).

Index

True Lies (film), 200–201
Truman, Harry, 62, 69
Tucker's Last Stand (William Buckley
    novel), 154

U-Boat 29 (film), 57
Undercover (TV series), 185
Underground (film), 60
Under Siege (film series), 179
Underworld (DeLillo novel), 188
Untouchable, The (Banville novel), 238
Uris, Leon, 142
USS Cole, 217
U.S. Spy Ship Liberty, 124–25
U.S. Spy Ship Pueblo, 125
Ustinov, Peter, 28

Vaughn, Robert, 115, 170, 186
Veidt, Conrad, 57, 59
Venetian Affair, The (MacInnes novel,
    film), 115
Video games, 228
Vietnam War in films and literature,
    31–32, 118, 140, 210, 237
View to a Kill, A (film), 183
Voices of the Violin (film), 45
Vonnegut, Kurt, Jr., 144
Voyage to the Bottom of the Sea (TV
    series), 118–19
VR5 (TV series), 205

Wade, Robert, 221–22
Wager, Walter, 171
Walk a Crooked Mile (film), 76
Walker, John, 125, 175
Wallace, Edgar, 9–10
Wallach, Eli, 182
Washington, Denzel, 139
Washington, George, 3, 4
Water on the Brain (Mackenzie
    novel), 34–35

Wayne, John 67, 84
Welles, Orson, 27, 56, 57–58, 170, 235
Wheatley, Dennis, 35, 212
Wheel Spins, The (White novel), 52
Whelan, Tim, 57
Where Eagles Dare (MacLean novel,
    film), 143
Where the Spies Are (film), 107
Whip Hand, The (film), 54
Whitaker, Rodney, 163–64
White, Ethel, 52
Whitemore, Hugh, 212
Whitfield, Raoul, 46
Who's on First (William Buckley
    novel), 154
Widmark, Richard, 84–85, 143
Wild Wild West: film, 203; TV series,
    90, 108, 116, 185
Willis, Bruce, 158
Wilson Chance (film), 203
Wilson, Joseph, 224
Wilson, Michael, 198, 221
Wilson, Peta, 212
Winchell, Walter, 43
Windsor Protocol, The (film), 166
WindTalkers (film), 212
Without Remorse (Clancy novel), 191
Woman on Pier 13, The (film), 84
Women, roles of: before and during
    World War II, 3, 17, 48–52, 54–56;
    in 1950s, 78, 88, 92; in 1960s, 120,
    127; in 1970s, 169, 170; after
    1990, 227; in Bond films, 101–4,
    150, 199. *See also* Sexuality
Wonder Woman (comic book, TV se-
    ries), 68, 172
Woods, Christopher, 149, 183
Woods, William, 64
Woodward, Edward, 71, 144, 185
World Is Not Enough, The (film), 200,
    220

About the Author

WESLEY BRITTON is the author of *Spy Television* (Praeger, 2004), the first book-length study of espionage television series. He is also the author of several articles for journals, encyclopedias, and periodicals, as well as book reviews and poetry.